Victim Of Circumstances

A True Story

By: **Shirley Hamilton**

Dedicated to those that have helped and inspired me in writing my memoirs.

Victim of Circumstances is a true story of how one woman coped with unfortunate circumstances in her early years. She had five children and survived three husbands, a vengeful cheat, a murderer, and a pedophile.

With the help of letters dating back over time and stories my Grandmother told me, I have pieced together the first few chapters of my book.

In writing my memoirs, it was never my intention to discredit anyone other than the perpetrators therefore, I would like to apologise to those who may be offended. Upsetting the innocent was never my intention; my only purpose is to write about the trauma that I and my children have endured as I uncover truthful events from the past.

I have been judged in the past for everything that has happened but no one should pass judgement without being in possession of all the facts. Everything I have written, to the best of my knowledge, is true. I was legally advised to change names and places.

Table of Contents

Chapter One

My Grandparents

Virginia left school at 13 and began working in a factory making fine gold chains for ladies evening bags, it was here that she met Quinton whose Father owned the factory, Virginia and Quinton dated briefly before marrying in 1916, they set up home in Islington and had four children, William was born January 1917, Katherine arrived June 1918, Elizabeth came along in December 1920 and last to make an appearance was Joan in October 1921.

Quinton was 6ft tall and good looking he had dark hair and wore glasses. Most evenings he'd call into the public house for a drink on his way home where he loved to entertain punters with Al Johnson impersonation. Quinton was a generous man when socializing but was different at home with his family, although he was earning good money a man that drinks is always broke.

At nights, he could be seen weaving his way thought the streets clutching his key in one hand and cigarette in the other, Virginia would glance at the clock knowing he would stagger through the door any moment looking for an argument, Quinton was a hard man to please and frequently lost his temper and disturb his children sleeping in the adjoining room, when funds ran dry he used to demand the rent money from his wife, when she refused he'd search their home looking for her purse. I remember Nan saying that getting money out of him was difficult at the best of times she wasn't giving it back so he could drink it away but Quinton was demanding and frequently lost his temper and could be heavy handed if he didn't get his own way, the children used to hide under the bed covers to block out the rows and their Mother's cries.

Another of Nan's stories was when she marched into the pub one Friday to get housekeeping, she knew most of his wages would be gone before he got home if she didn't. Quinton did not take kindly to being humiliated in public and fumbled through his wage packet mumbling under his breath, some mornings she pleaded for money before he left for work, he'd begrudgingly throw loose change on the table before slamming the door...she looked at the pittance wondering how she could stretch the coppers that lay before her, she often cooked boiled rice for the children and went without herself which resulted in Katherine being born with rickets.

Joan was about 4 when Virginia found a letter propped against the clock on the mantelpiece, the handwriting was unfamiliar and the envelope was unsealed so she read the letter...My darling Quinton...the letter was from another woman, betrayed and angry she paced the floor waiting for him to return home.

The row that followed that night resulted in Quinton leaving to stay with his sister Grace. Virginia was left sobbing with four children and no money, how was she going to survive, thankfully Grace came to the rescue, she got money out of him which she took to Virginia.

It could have been weeks or even months before Grace persuaded him to return home that Virginia gave him a second chance, they left Islington and rented a three-bedroom house in Essex.

Virginia was thrilled to have a house with a garden she didn't have much in the way of furniture but she had the essentials. The girls shared the back bedroom and William had the box room at the front but it wasn't long before their father began drinking, Sunday afternoons he would demand peace and quiet - no one dared to breathe as he slept in the fireside chair, this continued even after the Doctor warned *you do realise that if you don't stop drinking it is going to kill you* Quinton shrugged the sensible advice off and continued to drink and smoke.

As the children grew William would intervene when his Father became abusive, one night William grabbed his Father by the scruff of the neck and wrestled him to the floor, it took all three girls to drag their brother off - Quinton never attacked his wife again.

Interested in woodwork William left school and started work in a piano factory, he became a skilled carpenter and made friends with a colleague who was to become his father in law.

Katherine took up midwifery, cycling in all weathers delivering babies did not deter her in the least in fact she welcomed the challenge of bringing new life into the world.

Elizabeth had a job in a factory not far from home.

Joan joined the ATS and made some long-time friends with whom she stayed loyal until they each passed away.

Quinton passed away in May 1940 from pulmonary tuberculosis, he was 44 years of age and his family went onto live a quiet and peaceful life.

Chapter Two

Elizabeth and Allister

Elizabeth and Allister had been married for 17 months before I came into their lives, but it all began in 1937 when Elizabeth and a couple of colleagues arranged to meet and go to the aerodrome in Hornchurch; the girls had worked for the same company since leaving school and became friends almost immediately.

It had been a gruelling week in the cold factory but the girls were looking forward to the dance that evening - they talked of nothing else.

Elizabeth hurried home and chatted excitedly over dinner before rushing upstairs to change; she curled her hair with heating tongs then rushed to meet Camilla and Imogine who were anxiously waiting as the bus turned the corner.

When they arrived there were a lot of people hovering at the entrance leaving little room for them to enter, eager to get out of the cold they squeezed past as a gust of wind followed them, each time the door opened men turned, the girls eased their way through the crowds looking for seating, Elizabeth - aware she was being watched turned to see a young man in uniform watching with a cigarette between his lips, she shyly smiled then hurried to catch up with her friends, within minutes he was beside her - smiling he extended his hand *hello my name is Allister may I join you* he said to Elizabeth politely nodding towards her friends *no two guesses what I do* he laughed pointing to his uniform as he stubbed his cigarette in the ashtray, Allister told Elizabeth he was knew to this part of the Country, they chatted briefly then he asked if she would care to dance, without waiting for a reply he took her hand and guided her onto the floor, when the music stopped he walked her back to her friends and made himself comfortable by her side which is where he stayed the rest of the night. They spent the evening talking although most of his conversation was directed at Elizabeth much to the annoyance of her friends.

Although Camilla and Imogine danced with young men, they did not take their eyes off Allister; when they weren't trying to attract his attention, they were scowling at Elizabeth; she was confused by their behaviour and dismissed their frosty glares and concentrated on the young man who had swept her off her feet.

With the evening drawing to a close, the band announced the last waltz; Elizabeth waited with bated breath, hoping he would ask to see her again - before the dance was over, he asked if she was free the following evening, smiling she gave him directions to her home which he scribbled down then slipped the paper into his breast pocket - this did not go unnoticed, clasping her hand he escorted her back to the table and said he would see her on Saturday, he bid farewell to her friends - kissed her fingers and disappeared.

The journey home disturbed Elizabeth. Her friends were whispering and sniggering in the seat behind but she was not going to let them dampen her spirits - everything would be fine by Monday, she thought.

It didn't take her long to forget the girls once she arrived home, where she spent the next hour talking about Allister. Virginia had never seen her daughter so excited and eager to meet the young man responsible; it was gone midnight when Elizabeth snuggled under her eiderdown, she slept peacefully until morning.

Elizabeth spent most of Saturday singing and fussing over her appearance until it was time for him to arrive; their first date was spent in front of the fire with her family. Allister felt comfortable in their company and talked about his life in service - Elizabeth drank in every word when he spoke of world events and future ambitions, she was glowing.

I will never know whether it was love at first sight and can only quote what my Father said that he was captivated by her smile and winning personality - *she was a breath of fresh air,* he once said.

They dated as often as possible; when they were short of money which was most of the time, they brought chips to share whilst out strolling, sometimes they stayed home and listened to the radio; they did not mind where they were as long as they were together.

Allister was fastidious and took pride in his appearance; he had a great sense of humour and could see the funny side of most situations. He was always playing tricks and teased Elizabeth who laughed at his silly jokes but she was full of mischief so they were well suited; it was no surprise to the family when they talked about a future together.

It was a few months before Allister noticed a change in Elizabeth…she struggled to laugh at his jokes but was reluctant to talk about her troubles; after much persuasion, she told him how Imogine and Camilla had distanced themselves and were making her life miserable if either of them passed by they'd knock into her then make faces when she looked there way, upset by their behavior she fought tears, Allister was shocked when she showed him a note that had left on her bench (we will get him in the end, you wait and see) another note threatened to stick a knife in her back. Allister's reassurance did little to help the daily taunting then one night, she collapsed in the arms of her Mother. Allister watched the woman he loved suffer a breakdown and did everything possible to comfort her. I am unsure why legal action was never taken against these individuals or why management was not informed but perhaps things were different then.

They had spoken of marriage but no plans had been made until the episode of my Mother's breakdown.

Father was soon to be transferred and suggested they marry so he could take his bride with him *Oh, that's a wonderful idea, Allister* said to her Mother *that's just what she needs.*

The couple were married in October 1938, the reception was held in Edison Avenue, pictures were taken in the back garden by the archway where the tea roses had started to fade; Allister remembers little about the reception as he passed out on the front lawn - when Elizabeth tried to wake him he whispered *Shush don't tell my wife I'm out here I think I may have had too much to drink.*

They spent the early part of their married life in a cottage near where Allister was stationed, away from the stress. Elizabeth was eating well and gaining weight; their cosy evenings were spent in front of the fire as Allister studied with his wife beside him.

One afternoon, she returned from posting a letter to her mother - she took off her wet coat and placed it over the kitchen chair to dry. She filled the kettle to make tea; when she opened the tea caddy, she found a ten-shilling note; assuming her husband had put it there for safety thought nothing more until she reached for the matches and saw another note propped against the clock...*Okay, Allister I know you're here somewhere* she said, laughing; she turned to see her husband's face beaming through the half-open pantry door; throwing herself into him, they collapsed with laughter but were interrupted by the whistling kettle. What a wonderful surprise to have him home earlier than expected.

There was another time when she walked into the lounge and saw her husband engrossed in the newspaper; she watched in admiration then reached for the fruit dish – picked up an orange and hurled it at his paper which he dropped in surprise; she ran from the room squealing with delight with Allister close behind, they were so much in love and enjoyed all that married life had to offer.

Jumping ahead…I was 12 years old when I entered the dining room and saw my Father reading the paper. I stood for a moment, wondering how he could spend so much time reading the same paper over again. I took an orange from the fruit dish and threw it at the paper - he jumped out of his skin. I waited for the scolding but his startled expression changed to one of amusement, smiling as he invited me to sit with him. I sighed with relief and walked into his open arms and climbed on his knee; his smile turned to laughter *my darling Olivia - did I ever tell you the time when your Mother and I were first married?* I stirred some treasured moments of their brief time together which he shared with me that afternoon - memories of my Mother who I am convinced inspired me to throw the orange.

Allister loved life in the Forces; his ambition was to do well so he could give his wife the life she deserved; they talked of owning their own home 'aim high' was his motto which he instilled in me as a child, study hard, learn all you can - education is valuable it can open many doors, people will admire you for your knowledge and you will be able to mix with anyone and discuss world events so pay attention it is very important.

In 1939, England declared war with Germany; it was also confirmed that Elizabeth was pregnant so she returned to Essex and rented a bungalow a few houses from where they celebrated their wedding less than a year ago. Allister was relieved knowing his wife would be close to her family, Katherine was now a qualified midwife and would be available with sensible advice during the pregnancy.

Elizabeth missed her husband but she was pleased to be home and enjoyed spending nights with the family, at nights her Mother would be knitting in front of the fire while Elizabeth embroidered baby clothes, pillow cases, table cloths and anything she could find; she brought Allister a silk scarf and embroidered his initials on the corner.

One Saturday, Elizabeth and her Mother where out shopping when they bumped into Margo from where she once worked. She had not seen Margo since her wedding so it was nice catching up. She was surprised to hear Camilla and Imogine were planning a trip to where Allister was stationed; Elizabeth was alarmed her husband did not write often but she consoled herself it was due to the war and letters were getting lost. At nights with only her fears to keep her company, her imagination played cruel tricks, her nightmares returned and she'd wake sobbing; if only she could see Allister, she needed his reassuring arms; unable to escape from her nightmares, she sent a telegram to say she would arrive at the weekend, he replied by return to say he would be on the platform waiting. Elizabeth informed her Mother who recognised her daughter was beginning to struggle and accepted her decision.

Elizabeth was a million miles away. As she took her overnight bag from the wardrobe, she sifted through draws looking for something to wear. The weather had been kind but had now turned cold and she was coming down with a chill.

Elizabeth chose her warmest clothes even though there was little choice as nothing seemed to fit. She took her Mother's advice and had a check-up before leaving. Her Doctor advised against making the journey but she assured him she would be fine; once her mind was set and no-one was going to change it, besides spending time with her husband was the only tonic she needed then her fears would vanish.

Friday morning, she was up before the sun; she made her bed whilst waiting for the kettle then lit the gas oven so she could dress in the warm kitchen; she absently glanced in the mirror and realised she was smiling.

Elizabeth hurried through the barrier for the train to London where she would catch another taking her to her final destination. She slept on and off throughout the journey, waking with a jolt each time the train stopped; she woke for the umpteenth time when the porter shouted her station. Clutching her overnight case and handbag - ticket between gloved fingers, she made her way to the door which was open with passengers making their way off and struggling past those waiting to start their journey; she stood for a moment then noticed him standing on the bench waving, she rushed over dropped her case and fell into his arms, as he expressed words of love she looked into his smiling face and knew she'd made the right decision, he reached for her case and made their way to the barrier.

They were allowed time together which was important to them both; over dinner, she brought him up to date with the news of their unborn child who was due in February. He listened with interest and asked how everyone was back home; he was surprised to hear Camilla and Imogene were planning a visit *there is no need for concern*. He begun *no one can possibly come between us* he assured *besides, they have made no attempt to contact me so please don't worry, my love*. She studied his face for any tell-tale signs. If they had been in touch, he wouldn't have given anything away; they talked until her reservations faded then she slept peacefully in his arms. This was the first of many trips even though her husband advised against travelling in her condition, it was also dangerous with a raging war when the sirens sounded, people scattered to the nearest shelter which made travelling hazardous.

She returned home one Sunday aching from head to toe. She crawled into bed with a hot water bottle and slept restlessly; when the Doctor made a house call the following morning, he told Virginia that her daughter was suffering from a severe bout of influenza that could turn to pneumonia if she was not careful, he advised complete bed rest and suggested against making any more trips until after the baby arrives.

Elizabeth hated being away from her husband, never knowing if he would return; when her pregnancy had been confirmed, she was as happy as the day of her wedding but now she was full of doubt and misery…damn those vicious cows that were determined to destroy her marriage and blast the war that was keeping her from her husband, she felt retched and insecure.

Chapter Three

Birth of a Victim

February 4th, 1940, at 11.15 pm, Elizabeth gave birth to a baby girl, I was named Olivia Virginia Rosa; Virginia and Rosa were the names of my two Grandparents.

My parents enjoyed precious moments studying their new arrival until my Father returned to base. It took a-while before Mother found a routine that suited us with Father away. She did not feel so lonely now she had this little person who was taking up most of her time. She observed every move so she could inform Allister in her next letter.

I'd lay in my wicker crib in front of the fire and smile whenever she looked my way; she could never resist coming over to gently touch me and remind me how special I was. I loved listening to her stories about all the wonderful things we were going to do once the war was over - but the cough she'd had since before I was born was getting worse and keeping her awake.

It was late 1940 when my Father was due leave. He studied his wife and noticed she'd lost weight; her eyes were sunken and the dimples had gone from her cheeks. Maybe that's what happens when women have babies, he thought but tonight was no time for sadness; there was a dance for the servicemen and their wives at the aerodrome. It would be wonderful returning to where they met three years ago. Now they were man and wife and where taking me along.

I was 10 months old and standing alone - they couldn't wait to show me off.

Elizabeth applied colour to her cheeks and teased a few stray curls that fell over her brow. She was humming to music on the radio while Father kept me amused in front of the fire. She dreamt of this moment for so long - having her husband and baby to herself, she prayed their night would not be disturbed by sirens.

The first thing Elizabeth noticed when they entered was the bar had been moved to the far side of the hall. She turned to her husband and commented on how relaxed everyone appeared. *You wouldn't believe there was a war, would you darling.* She said, trying to compete with the music and laughter; *look how happy everyone is,* she gestured, glancing around. Allister was searching for seats then noticed someone heading towards him. *Allister, how good to see you.* W*hen did you get back* said Paddy, vigorously shaking the hand of my Father who turned towards Mother. *You remember Elizabeth, don't you, Paddy,* said Father *and this is our daughter Olivia.* I buried my face in his neck which made them laugh; eager to show me off, he stood me down then someone knocked into me and I landed with a thud. I grizzled briefly until Mother scooped me up and soothed me with gentle words then I was wriggling to get down again.

They enjoyed their evening in the place where their love story first began but it was getting late so mother decided they would have one more dance before taking me home to my cot. As the band played 'String of Pearls' my parents waltzed with me in their arms for what would be our first and last dance together.

Chapter Four

The Cruel Hand of Fate

Grandmother noticed Mother was losing weight. *It's nothing really, Mum* said Elizabeth, *do stop worrying; I will look and feel much better once the war is over and Allister and I can settle down to a normal life with Olivia* but eventually, Elizabeth realised her health could be ignored no longer and failed to mention she was coughing blood, she reluctantly agreed to visit the Doctor who - once aware of the blood sent her to hospital *Its probably nothing but better safe than sorry* said the Doctor reassuringly but his concern did not go unnoticed.

After blood tests and X-rays, they were asked to sit in the waiting area; it was ages before the nurse took them back to the consulting room where the Dr was studying his notes; *the news I have. Mrs. Hawkins is not good,* he looked at both women then chose his words carefully. *You have shadowing on the lungs.* Turning to the screen, he pointed *you see here and here; I am sorry to say you have tuberculosis* he waited for the news to penetrate then added softly *we will need to admit you right away – you will be put in isolation where you will have complete bed rest* he paused for a moment *only your husband and mother will be allowed to visit, they will be given protective clothing and masks, I must ask that no contact be made like kissing during these visits* he looked my way *no children will be allowed at the moment but let us take one step at a time.*

Nan fumbled for her handkerchief while Mum looked on helplessly. She gently squeezed my hands and whispered *Nanny is going to take care of you for a while my darling, just until Mummy is better.* I held up my arms and began to cry...something was dreadfully wrong.

The tearful women were allowed a little time before Elizabeth was taken to the ward; she gave her mother a list of essentials she would need then it was time to say goodbye, *take care of Olivia for me Mum, kiss her every day and don't forget to tell her I love her, she is very precious and tell Allister not to worry I will write and explain everything, take care my darlings.*

Dad was allowed compassionate leave to visit his wife who was a mere shadow. Her eyes were sunken as were her cheeks, how he ached to hold her.

It was months before Mum responded to treatment. She had put on weight, she was eating well and her condition was stable; her consultant agreed she was ready to receive another visitor on condition there would be no kissing.

There was plenty of excitement the day Elizabeth discussed my visit with the staff; she had dreamt of this moment for so long. *Calm yourself* said the nurse. *If your blood pressure rises, the Doctor will change his mind so stay calm.*

But how can I stay calm she said excitedly reaching for the picture of me on her bedside table. *I haven't seen Olivia for so long. I bet she's changed. Do you think she will remember me...oh goodness, suppose she doesn't remember me?* Her expression changed from excitement to concern. The nurse laughed *of course she will remember you wait and see.*

Her eyes glued to the door, she could hardly contain herself then gasped as I walked in. Grandmother sat me at the bottom of the bed - I tried to wriggle free but she held me firmly. Tears filled my Mother's eyes as I called her name. She reached to touch my fingers and spoke in the gentle voice I remembered so well. I held out my arms and began to cry so our visit was cut short.

I had been holding my head to the side since before Mother went into hospital which was getting worse. Nan took me to the Doctor who was equally baffled so he advised a visit to the hospital. If he had any idea what was causing the problem, he wasn't giving anything away.

The following morning, Nan guided my pushchair down the same corridor she had walked with my Mother not so long ago. After X-rays and blood tests, we were taken to where the doctor was waiting. *I'm afraid I have bad news, Mrs. Daniels, your Granddaughter has a fractured spine, you can see here,* he said, pointing at the screen - he waited before adding *but that is not all we are dealing with. Olivia has tuberculosis in her spine too, I know her Mother is recovering from TB so it is possible she was born with the condition* he allowed Nan to gather herself before continuing; *we are unable to treat her fracture at this hospital, she will need to go to Black Notley in Chelmsford, I will arrange for her to see Mr Wilkinson who is an excellent bone specialist, he will do all he can for your granddaughter, I will inform Mr Wilkinson who will expect you first thing tomorrow, try not to worry my dear Olivia will be in good hands. If you have any questions, Mr Wilkinson will be able to answer them for you,* tearfully she asked *Olivia will be alright, won't she, doctor?* He gave her a comforting smile. *I'm sure she will be just fine but Mr. Wilkinson will be the one to advise you from here.*

The following morning, we made our way to Chelmsford. Grandmother was as sad as anyone could be; she cradled me on her lap and whispered repeatedly that I was a good girl. I paid little attention to the kisses she planted on my curls.

We were shown to a room where Mr. Wilkinson was waiting. He shook Grandmother's hand and asked her to take a seat; he gave me some toys and watched me play. There was silence as he examined the film then he called a nurse to bring tea. She searched his face, looking for hope eventually, he spoke.

My dear woman, I am very concerned with your granddaughter - we are dealing with more than one problem here so I must warn you if Olivia recovers from spinal tuberculosis, it could leave her crippled; as for the fracture, I would advise against surgery an operation of this kind would be too intricate with the risk of paralyses but try not to be alarmed my dear we will do everything we can. I think our best and safest option would be to put Olivia in plaster right away. It is imperative she remain perfectly still. I don't know when the fracture occurred but she has been remarkably lucky not to have done further damage. I will have a mirror fitted above her bed so she can look about her so please don't be alarmed, remember everything we do will be for Olivia; he observed me turning pages in a torn book while Nan sobbed quietly into her handkerchief - *visiting* he continued *will be every afternoon between 2 and 4 - I know you don't live local so I hope this will not be a problem, I am here most days but if you need to speak to me you can contact my assistant Mrs Blake or my secretary Miss Stephenson they are very accommodating - and now we must get Olivia settled, you can stay until we have made her comfortable, I know you will want to say goodnight, she is going to be upset so we will give her something to make her drowsy, does her Mother know the situation?*

I was cased in plaster from my head to my bottom then taken to the ward. I can't imagine how Grandmother felt seeing me strapped to the bed like a joint of beef. I had weights around my feet so I could not lift them and my head secured to prevent me from turning. All that was visible were my chubby cheeks - then it was time for her to leave. She kissed me goodnight and said she would see me soon. Poor love, I don't know how she coped listening to my screams. I am unsure how they would treat a child with these injuries today but in 1941, this seemed the only solution.

Virginia wondered how she was going to keep the news from her daughter the following afternoon. She arrived early so she could speak to the Doctor. *Elizabeth has made remarkable progress;* he said *I would hate to see her go downhill;* he remained silent as he pondered, trying to consider the best option for his patient. *I think it would be wise to keep the news from Elizabeth for as long as possible, I know it is going to be difficult but if she should find out I will have a nurse waiting with a sedative should it be necessary and don't forget my dear I will be here should either of you need me, I wish there was something I could say or do to ease your pain and make your burden lighter - good luck my dear* he eased her out of the chair where she appeared rooted, she felt numb as he led her out of his office to where Elizabeth was waiting.

Virginia glanced through the porthole to see her daughter patiently doing her embroidery; she hovered before entering, *Hello my dear, sorry I'm late; you're doing well with your embroidery; the tablecloth is beautiful.* Elizabeth placed her sewing on the bed and observed her visitor. *Is everything okay, Mum?* She asked. *Yes, of course,* said Virginia. *I am a little tired, that's all; I missed the bus and had to wait ages for another - Alf next door gave me some apples and kept me talking;* she examined the table cloth wondering what she could say next.

Are you sure there is nothing wrong, Mum? You're not hiding anything, are you - is Olivia alright she said, ignoring chit-chat about apples and busses; she leaned forward to look closer into the face of her Mother. *How is Allister? Have you heard from him...you will tell me if anything is wrong, won't you?*

Nan began to fidget; this was going to be a long visit, she thought, glancing at the clock...she couldn't wait to leave.

The following day it was bitterly cold as she made her way to catch her bus which was delayed due to fog but she was grateful for her late arrival and walked slowly to the ward. Elizabeth stared at her Mother as she entered and watched as she fell clumsily into the empty chair. *Okay,* said Elizabeth, patting the bedcovers; *there is something very wrong and you are not leaving here until you have told me everything; it's not Olivia, is it?* She lowered her head so she could study her Mother's face. Virginia sat twisting the bed round her fingers and her lips quivered; *oh my God...it is Olivia... Mum, what is wrong...please tell me...is Olivia alright? Please tell me* Virginia began to cry as she relayed the story, Elizabeth rocked back and forth and cried hysterically, she tore at her clothes; *my baby – my baby* is all she could say - a nurse gave her a light sedative but it was sometime before she became quiet, she drifted in and out of a restless sleep releasing little sobs as she whispered Olivia over and over, Nan sat close, stoking her Daughter's hand - wiping away silent tears that rolled down her own cheeks, she was given extended visitation so she could be near her Daughter who would need her when she woke with more questions to which she had no answers.

It was late when she left the hospital but she was grateful for the darkness that surrounded her as she made her way to an empty house; the dimly lit Streets masked her tear-stained face along with the noisy traffic that concealed her sobs.

Visiting became difficult; Elizabeth sank into depression and fired questions upon questions to her Mother who could bring little comfort. Elizabeth prayed for a miracle – if only she could visit her baby but it was out of the question; she slipped into depression, speaking only to ask of her daughter's welfare then Father had a breakdown and was admitted to hospital, his wife and daughter in separated hospitals both with life-threatening illnesses were the cause, he was released after a week on medication so he could visit them.

I don't know how long it was before Mother's health improved when her Doctor agreed that she was well enough to visit me; she could hardly contain her excitement as she waited for the ambulance to take her to Chelmsford. Katherine was on duty that morning and poked her head around the door and found Elizabeth sitting on the edge of the bed holding her chest. *Are you alright, Elizabeth? You don't look good – you're not in pain, are you?* Elizabeth replied in barely a whisper. *I feel as though I have had too much oxygen pumped into me. I feel as though I am about to burst.* Katherine saw the colour drain from the face of her sister and rushed to get the doctor but it was too late – Elizabeth fell back on the bed as both lungs collapsed.

My Mother passed away 16th January, nineteen days after her 21st birthday and nineteen days before my 2nd birthday. She was laid to rest on 24th January 1942. Nan cried, having lost a precious Daughter and she cried for the Granddaughter that would never know her Mother. She despised the two women responsible for her daughter's sorrow during her short marriage; they were the reason Elizabeth travelled in freezing conditions to be with her husband to gain peace of mind. They did not destroy the marriage but they succeeded in destroying a beautiful woman with their threats. Elizabeth's four years of marriage should have been her happiest but

Camilla and Imogine set out to destroy what time they had together. They were responsible for her sadness and insecurity.

It was three months after my Mother's funeral when Nan received a telegram to say I was in a critical state with meningitis then Dad was re-admitted with another breakdown. His world was falling apart, having lost his wife to TB and his daughter suffering the same and now with meningitis but he was released with medication so he could be by my side.

Nan and Dad along with Mr. Wilkinson surrounded me as the registrar read something from the Bible...as the story goes... I ignored those surrounding me then I opened my eyes and spoke to the empty space at the foot of my bed...the fever had broken and I was out of danger Mr. Wilkinson suggested I may have seen the spirit of my dead Mother if so I would love to know what she said to me that day, probably that it was not my time to join her because I had some important stuff to do here.

Every Sunday, Grandmother would run to my bedside and smother me with beautiful kisses. She used to sing (you are my sunshine) and now I was greeting her with that same ballad. It never failed to make her cry. When visiting was over, I never let her go without a fight; she had to prize my fingers from her coat. I never made it easy for her - the poor darling was just as upset to leave me as I was to see her go.

It was about 18 months after losing Mother that Dad began dating again; 18 months doesn't seem long to grieve but with the war raging, people grabbed whatever happiness they could.

Vera owned a farm not far from the hospital so she was able to visit me every day. She used to bring fresh eggs which she left in the hospital kitchen but eggs were rationed so I don't know how many I ate, if any. I loved the stories she told me about the animals on the farm and how the chickens waddled after her for food. She read me stories from my favourite book about Briar Rabbit and the fox. Nan told me Dad and Vera were going to get married when I leave hospital then I could live on the farm too.

Nan began coaching me every Sunday; she taught me the alphabet - how to count and how to speak correctly which pleased my Father whose diction was perfect. With nothing else to occupy me, I probably enjoyed my weekly tuition.

I was admitted to the hospital in 1941 and discharged in 1945 when the war ended 4 years seems a long time but medical science was not advanced in the early 40s and there is no one to fill me in with the correct details. I did ask Auntie Joan in her later years who told me I was in hospital for 5 years.

I was a teenager when Nan showed me a picture of when I was in plaster strapped to my bed but I found it distressing and refused to look but wish I had taken more notice now.

After what seemed a lifetime, my plaster and weights were removed, unable to move my legs or sit. I slumped like a rag doll so physiotherapy was on my daily agenda. I probably enjoyed my therapy because it was one step closer to going home.

Chapter Five

The Wedding

When Dad had holiday owing, he often spent it with Nan. She enjoyed his company and made sure time was set aside for my visits but today, she noticed he looked edgy - she did not have to wait long to find out why. He lit another cigarette and told her he was getting married in three weeks-time. She clasped her hands in glee. *Oh, that is wonderful, Allister. I am so pleased for you both but Olivia will be disappointed; you told her you were going to wait until she leaves the hospital; she's looking forward to the wedding, you know.* He pondered for a moment and chose his words carefully then dropped a bombshell *actually Mum I am not marrying Vera I have met someone else...her name is Janice* he watched her expression change *so what about Vera she must have been devastated poor girl, more to the point what about Olivia - where does she fit in with this...what's her name.*

Janice Mum...it's Janice. I would like to bring her round to meet you. She's looking forward to meeting Olivia, too. There was silence as Dad was about to drop another bombshell.

I would like to ask a favour of you, Mum. Vera doesn't know yet - I wonder if you could break the news to me. My train leaves early tomorrow so I will not have time to see her. Nan's lips were tight as she turned to glare *so you want me to do your dirty work for you? My God, you're a coward and now you want me to break the girl's heart.* She stormed into the kitchen with her mind racing...was there

23

another reason for this wedding to take place at speed...surely not well, time would tell, she thought; banging the kettle on the stove – she took two cups from the dresser and slammed them in their saucers Father would have heard the disapproving sounds through the open door which would have added to the tension that afternoon.

She waited until the following day before writing to Vera. It would give her time to decide how she was going to break the news - and her heart at the same time.

She always enjoyed the company of this delightful lady but dreaded their next meeting; she wondered whether Vera would continue to visit me – if she chose against visiting then Olivia would also bear the impact of Allister's change of heart.

Vera arrived looking radiant; she brought flowers and fresh eggs but knew something was wrong as she entered. That afternoon, both women cried in each other's arms. The friendship they thought would last a lifetime came to an end; Vera left with a tear-stained face as she walked down the footpath and out of our lives.

Their wedding took place in September 1943. Dad was in uniform and Janice wore white; two of Dad's sisters were among the guests and Nan attended on my behalf.

Janice gave birth to Claudia in December. Two children later, they divorced when he discovered she was cheating on him.

Chapter Six

Leaving Hospital

Mr. Wilkinson guided Nan into his office for what she hoped would be the last time; he shook her hand and gestured her to sit opposite. *You must realize, Mrs. Daniels that Olivia will never lead a normal life - she may spend her days in a wheelchair.* He waited for her to absorb everything he was about to say; *she will always be frail and need constant care. I must advise that you keep her limbs warm during the winter months. Hand-knitted vests and stockings would be advisable.* He looked into her eager face and could not remember having seen her this happy; in fact, she rarely smiled so it was rewarding to give good news to a parent. He was aware she was now my guardian…he continued to speak to the enthusiastic woman sitting before him. *You must protect Olivia's neck from the sun's rays which can be harmful. You must keep it covered at all times and avoid sudden jolts. Her spine will always be weak. I would hate to see our work undone; she has been a lucky little girl.*

The nurses in physio had watched me struggle to get out of my wheelchair when I thought no one was looking; only God could possibly know why because I would have collapsed like a deck of cards. They informed my consultant who was inspired by my determination. *I think Olivia could benefit from wearing a brace,* he smiled. *It will support her back and help her to sit straight. I would like her to be measured before you leave today. He* paused once again, waiting for any questions she may have then he continued…*Olivia has been isolated for a long time and will catch all sorts of germs when she leaves so I would like her to eat liver as it contains iron. Make sure she drinks plenty of full cream milk; it has calcium and is good for her bones. I want her to have cod liver oil and malt every day. I will arrange for a book of tokens to be sent to you so you can collect these items from your nearest clinic - now my dear, do not let her have late nights. She will need all the sleep she can get but you are a sensible woman and I know you will do what is right for your Granddaughter. I will need to see her again in 12 months. A letter will be sent as a reminder and I will arrange transport. If you have any problems, you know where you can reach me and now we must get Olivia measured.*

I don't recall leaving the hospital, but Nan told me I was captivated watching women walking with babies in prams—people shopping and noisy traffic—and I had never seen a shop window. We joined a long queue, then a man in uniform helped Nan climb aboard the green bus with my pushchair. Nan said he was a conductor; the conductor had a machine around his neck that rang a bell when he punched holes in tickets… I remained silent until we reached our destination.

As soon as we arrived home, Nan lit a fire then prepared our evening meal. That night, she read me a story in front of the fire before taking me to my bed. I snuggled down in my cot and listened to her pottering downstairs, happy to have me home after what must have seemed a lifetime.

I remember sitting by the window one morning, watching children with their mothers. Nan said they were going to school, but the sound I loved most was the milk cart and the horse's hooves clip-clopping along the road. The milkman made a lot of noise delivering milk from door to door—clanging the empty bottles as he loaded them into the crate.

I spent hours gazing out the window; there was always something interesting to see, even if it was a stray dog. I loved the sound of the rain beating on the window, too. Sometimes, the windows rattled if it was windy, which was comforting as I moved closer to the fire. But the best part of being home was when my guardian sat me on her lap in front of the fire at night and read me stories from my favourite book. I didn't mind going to bed because we slept in the same room. If it was cold, Nan used to light a fire in the bedroom. I'd snuggle under the covers and listen to the fire spit and crackle and watch the flames dance across the ceiling until I drifted off to sleep. Every day brought a new sound or something different to see.

Each night before bed, Nan sat me on the kitchen table and massaged my legs with some white stuff from a bottle. I don't know what it was, but it was icy cold and had a strange smell. I cannot imagine how I could benefit from the white stuff, but I was not wise like the Grandmother.

The day arrived when Nan received a letter to say my brace was ready. We made our way to the hospital and were shown to a room where my trusted consultant was waiting with the nurse. She opened the box and took out its contents. I stared in horror at the scary contraption but was assured all would be well. Then Nan watched the nurse strap me inside the creature. The brace was metal and covered in leather. It started at the back of my head to the base of my spine. Once inside, there was no escape. The corset was made of leather and laced at the front. There were two metal arms that wrapped snugly around my bust; that too was covered in leather. The back of the brace was crooked but fitted me perfectly. At the back of the brace, there was what looked like a hand for my head to rest in. There was also another attachment that looked like a saucer under my chin, which clipped at the back of the brace. It was to keep my head from falling forward. I still have the scars behind my ears where the buckles used to dig into me. The saucer was to stop me from leaning forward, but it also prevented me from looking up, down, left, or right. The brace was heavy and ugly, and I hated being trapped inside. Then I realised I was standing on my own. With the nurse beside me, I shuffled forward, barely lifting my feet off the ground—one step at a time, little by little, until I reached Nan. Then I fell into her arms, laughing. Nan was crying, and Mr. Wilkinson clapped his hands in glee. We bid the miracle man farewell and made our way home, taking more valuable advice. Nan guided my pushchair into the busy street. People stared, but I didn't care; children don't seem to worry about these things like grown-ups.

Weeks of physiotherapy and with the help of my brace, I began walking unaided. Nan scolded me once for attempting the stairs—nothing I did went unnoticed. I was a daring little devil (her words, not mine).

Chapter Seven

Starting School

I skipped through school and came out the other end with low grades. I was the eldest in the class but the youngest academically, so I struggled, which did little to build my confidence. I was picked on and bullied, so I'd look for somewhere to hide, but there was always someone to hunt me down and ask about the contraption I was wearing. Then they'd run away laughing. Nan was always marching into school, complaining about the girls tormenting me. She said there was not enough supervision and pleaded with them to let me stay inside during break, but I was never allowed that privilege.

I was about six years old when Aunt Katherine took me to London for the day, we went to the Tower of London and joined a queue to see the crown jewels when the beefeater noticed me he came and spoke to my Aunt then he picked me up and shouted like the town crier *make way for Olivia - she wants to see the crown jewels - make way for Olivia* he held me high so I towered above everyone people turned and kindly stood back to allow me through, that must have been the only benefit from wearing my brace in public, after the Tower we had lunch then went to the ballet to see swan lake.

When my brace became a thing of the past, I was making the journey to school on my own. It gave me the independence I desired but I was still unable to take part in sports or anything that required physical exertion.

When Dad was on leave, he met me from school; I'd ask him to wear his uniform which did not take much persuasion. I looked forward to seeing him at the gates whistling with a rolled-up newspaper in his hand, patiently banging it against his leg; the girls used to crowd around and ask him silly questions - fighting to be heard over one another then smiling, I'd take his hand so we could walk home, I was so proud and loved sharing him.

Chapter Eight

Family History

Uncle William was still working at the same factory from when he left school. Arthur was one of the co-workers who introduced the young assistant to his daughter, Eileen. I will never know if it was love at first sight; I can only repeat what Nan told me, that Uncle William did not like girls because they were silly creatures that giggled a lot. Perhaps that comes from having been brought up with three sisters, although I am not sure there was much giggling going on when they were children. Within a year, William and Eileen were planning their wedding. People lived sparsely years ago, and the tradition was to pass things down. Nan was thrilled when William asked if Eileen could borrow the headdress and veil my mother had worn at her wedding. I remember the sun beaming through the bay window of our front room the day she brought the dusty box from the attic. I watched intently as she unwrapped its contents. I was in awe of the headdress and veil she carefully took from the black tissue paper that had protected it over the years but still looked immaculate. I examined the box of treasures then spotted my mother's silver sandals. I tried to claim them, but they were taken from me. She knew I would have been tempted to wear them when alone, and she wasn't about to let me do anything where I could end up back in hospital. "Hospital," "spine," "fracture," and "neck" were words I was used to hearing whenever I did anything she thought was dangerous.

For the first part of married life, Eileen and William lived with her parents in Crescent Way. Within two years, Eileen gave birth to Ryan; Ian followed 18 months later.

Eileen's sister and husband also lived in Crescent Way with their daughter, Crystal. She was two years younger than me. Nan worked from home as an outdoor machinist so she could care for me. The company delivered her work every week—she also took private orders, working well into the night. She made a lot of my clothes from leftover material and lace, bias binding, and bric-a-brac, so I was never hard up for something nice to wear. If she wasn't on her machine, she was knitting me cardigans, sweaters, and bonnets. She could make anything on her Singer machine, having had plenty of practice when her children were young, by cutting up clothes that had been given to her.

Shortly after my parents' wedding, Auntie Joan married Dad's brother Howard, so now we had two Hawkins in the family. Desperate to have children, they adopted Scott, a handsome 10-month-old. A couple of years later, Joan gave birth to Danny. Mathew followed in 1955, then in 1960, they had the little girl they'd always wanted.

Joan made many friends while serving in the ATS—Melvin being one of them, whom she introduced to her sister Katherine. I was a bridesmaid when they married in 1949.

For the first part of married life, Katherine and Melvin lived upstairs to us in Edison Avenue. The newlyweds helped Nan move furniture about and turned the dining room into our bedroom. I loved sleeping downstairs. It was comforting to know Nan was in the next room.

Our converted bedroom held many memories but I only remember a few - it was wear Auntie Katherine celebrated her wedding, I am not sure about Auntie Joan. The dining room was where my parents did their courting and celebrated their wedding; the dining room was where I threw the orange at my father and now it was our bedroom.

Nan often cooked chips during the evening. She always made extra for any unexpected guests without fail. The stairs used to creek and the door slowly opened as two heads peeked in. *Are you cooking chips, Mum? Couldn't spare a few, could you?* Nan had set a plate aside for the young couple, knowing they could never resist the smell that wafted upstairs. Katherine and Melvin became parents to Haley in 1950 and in 1952, they immigrated to Canada.

I must have been about 9 when Dad took me to the London Zoo. Days out with my Father were rare. I hung onto his arm and never let him out of my sight until I saw a white parrot chained to a post with jesses for the public to fuss. I fell in love with this beautiful creature. Each time I walked away, it squawked; unable to resist, I went back time and again to fuss and stroke until Dad had to drag me away…I began to plead and never gave him a moment of piece. *Please can I have a parrot of my own, Daddy - I promise I will never ask for anything in my whole life if you buy me a parrot - please, Daddy can I have a parrot for my birthday or Christmas, I will be very good really I will*…he looked at me and smiled *Daddy promises to buy you a parrot all of your very own when you are a big girl* trying to pin him down I persisted *how old will I be daddy can you tell me please* I said running sideways to look into his face, he threw his head back laughing *my darling daughter, on your 21st birthday Daddy promised he will have a big party for you then I will buy you a parrot all of your very own.*

I was 13 when I decided it was time to have a bicycle – that is until Nan intervened and said that a bicycle would be a waste of money because I did not know how to ride; springing to my defence I replied excitedly. *Oh yes, I can - Angela taught me to ride hers.* Angela was a neighbour of Auntie Joan's who taught me to ride her mother's old bike. I turned from the look of horror on Nan's face and continued to plead. I could see he was beginning to soften with his gentle smile then he pulled me down to where he was sitting and told me if I wanted a bike, I was going to have to earn it, not with money but by studying hard and taking notice of my teacher, he wanted me to concentrate on my arithmetic - spellings and my handwriting which he said looked like chicken scratch, he needed to see a vast improvement before his next leave then…and only then he promised that next time he came home, I could take my pick of any bike in the shop.

Monday morning, I hurried into class, relieved to see the teacher at her desk. I asked if she could give me some work to take home; she was not only pleased but impressed by my enthusiasm. Once everyone had left that afternoon, I waited while she prepared something for me. Friday afternoon, I stayed behind and watched as she planted ticks on each page then I raced home so Nan could post them in her next letter. I continued sending Dad my homework and waited patiently for him to reply.

I was eating breakfast when I heard the letterbox clatter. I raced to collect the mail and squealed with delight when I saw the writing. I watched as Nan tore the envelope then she handed me the pages with my name across the top. I glanced at page one then skipped to page two and there it was. *My darling daughter, Daddy is very pleased to see how you have progressed. I can see you have studied hard; I knew you had it in you so keep up the good work and now a promise is a promise. I will be coming home next Friday then I will take you to Romford on Saturday morning to buy your bicycle.*

The night he was due, I could not sleep - each time Nan left the sitting room, I held my breath but she went into the kitchen to make a drink…a while later, she was on the move again but went upstairs to the bathroom…I fought sleep, wondering if he would ever arrive then I heard the street door click and whispering in the hall…*Daddy*…I shouted…the bedroom door slowly opened and he poked his head around to kiss me goodnight, reminding me we had a date the following morning…not that I was likely to forget, foolish man.

Saturday morning, we entered the shop where the eager salesman came rushing over at a possible sale. I left the men talking and wandered off to look for my bicycle then I spotted the most beautiful blood red metallic bike with shinny wheels, it was really heavy because it had every imaginable gadget on, the salesman told Dad I had chosen the most expensive cycle in the shop my Father raised his head to the heavens laughing *that's my daughter for you she has expensive taste* with the legal stuff out of the way we left the shop and I rode my bike home. I kept that bike like new and refused to take it out in the rain but if I got caught in an unexpected shower, I'd stand the bike in a shop doorway or under a tree and leave myself exposed to the elements then cycle home quickly to wipe the chrome till it shone like new, I never let anyone ride my bike after seeing how they discarded theirs at the drop of a hat when the ice cream man appeared or when playing stupid games by crashing into one another, I wasn't about to let anyone damage my pride and joy.

Chapter Nine

A Face From The Past

I remember the Saturday Nan took me to Romford to buy a winter coat. Nan made all my clothes so buying from the store was a treat, we tried every shop in town and the market but could find nothing suitable, our last stop was a little shop inside the arcade called Shirley's, as we entered the assistant came rushing over and greeted Nan like an old friend but could not take her eyes off me - *this is Allister's daughter Olivia* Nan said to the assistant, eager to try on the maroon coat I paid little interest in their conversation, Nan decided the coat was a sensible buy so brought it with a little discount from this woman who - as we left called out *remember me to Allister won't you Mrs. Daniels* we allowed the door to close without looking back, on our way home Nan told me the woman had been a friend of my Mothers before I was born, that evening she wrote to my Father and passed on greetings from 'Camilla'.

The following week, Dad arrived with their usual fish supper, which they ate in front of the fire. I could hardly wait for Saturday morning; it was a ritual for Dad and I to catch the bus into Romford and wander through the market, call into Lyons tea house for our morning coffee, then buy something nice for our tea. I was mortified when, on this occasion, he left me behind. I sulked until he returned, looking rather pleased with himself, having visited Camilla at her place of work. They exchanged addresses and were going to keep in touch.

A week after Dad returned to base, Camilla invited Nan and I for tea at her prefab. She introduced us to her two children, Alice and Duncan, who were both younger than me. The following week, Nan returned the invitation. Our Sunday teas became regular, which I did not relish. Camilla's home was nothing like ours—not that we had anything special—but I felt uncomfortable.

In Dad's next letter, he said the forces were sending him to Aden for two years but would tell us more when he came home, I couldn't wait to see him but devastated to think of him going so far away, I counted the days leading up to his arrival and threw myself into him as he walked through the door but my excitement quickly faded when he spoke of his coming trip, it depressed me hearing him talk of Aden although he seemed thrilled with the idea he tried to cheer me and said two years would soon pass and I would be a working woman when he returned, he had already made enquiries about me flying out for a holiday but my trip would be during the school holidays so it would not interfere with my valuable education *there is no need to fret* he assured me *you will fly with the red cross, I'll be there to meet you as you get off the plane and you will stay in my quarters, the Forces are allowing me holiday so we can spend time together then I can show you around, it is very hot in Aden so you will not need your winter clothes but I will write to Nana when I know more* I had reservations about leaving Nan and wished she was coming too, I never wanted to be away from her for one minute I loved her and felt safe when she was around, when I was little I used to cry because I did not want her to die – not that she was ill but I could not imagine life without her.

Then, the day arrived for him to leave. The atmosphere was strained and I hurt like crazy but shed no tears. I found it impossible to laugh at his silly jokes while he made light of his going away then he pulled me into his arms and his expression changed. He did not speak of his departure, only of his return…

When I come home my darling daughter you will be a grown woman, I may not even recognise you after two years he stretched out his arm and pointed into the distant *I can see me standing in the airport lounge patiently waiting for my daughter* he cupped my chin with his remaining hand and looked into my face *my eyes will be scanning the airport lounge as I search for my little girl then I see this beautiful young lady heading towards me with the biggest smile - I say to myself 'who is that beautiful young woman' then you come rushing over and throw your arms around me and I realise it is my darling Olivia* laughing he took my hands and kissed them then his expression changed and spoke seriously *now remember what daddy tells you my darling, don't forget to clean your teeth after every meal and before bed, take great care of your hands and nails, always look people in the eye when talking and pay attention to what people say and please, please don't put all that paint on your face you don't need that rubbish you have a lovely complexion just like your Mother. Now my dear, when I return, it will be a day to remember. I want you and Nanna to meet me at the airport with a bottle of champagne. I will be so happy to step onto English soil that I will get down on both knees and kiss the ground.* He laughed at his ridiculous comment, then he continued *don't forget my darling - I want you to study as hard as you can these next few years are very important - your Mothers dream was for you to make something of yourself - it is my dream too, I know you don't like writing but please write every week I will be waiting for your letters and try harder with your spellings above all pay attention to your teachers now - I want you to remember my darling - Daddy loves you very much so don't listen to the lies that your uncle says about me it doesn't bother me just as long as I don't hear them, his lies are jealousy and nothing else...remember - the truth will surface in the end.*

The following morning, he was up early and ready to leave. I had never felt so sad and empty in my whole life. Clinging to him, I wanted to beg him not to leave but knew it would be a waste of time. I was going to miss him terribly.

Nan and I went with him to the station. We had never seen the platform so crowded. All we could hear were carriage doors slamming amidst the hub of voices from the many wives, mothers, and children that were being left behind, as God knows how many servicemen were shouting farewell... Then the whistle blew, and steam screeched from the funnel. I was rooted to the spot as his train pulled slowly away from the platform. Dad was leaning out of the window along with the other servicemen, but I could see him through the thick steam as a sea of arms waved from carriage windows. The train gathered speed, but not wanting to lose sight, I concentrated on his face and watched as he blew endless kisses, then mouthed the words "DON'T FORGET TO WRITE" and waved his finger in mid-air as if writing on imaginary paper. As the train turned a bend, the sound grew fainter. I was rooted to the spot and refused to move. I craned my ears until there was nothing left to hear.

"Come on, Miss, it's time to go," said Nan. I tucked my handkerchief in my pocket—I had used it to wave him off. I could not believe I would not see him for two years. I wanted to cry. How was I going to cope without him?

Chapter Ten

Flight Sargent Hawkins

Dad made further enquiries about my trip and confirmed I would fly with the Red Cross. He said the Forces would contact Nan with instructions on how to obtain my passport and what vaccinations I would need. His letters were all about my holiday and what clothes I would need. He said he'd brought me something flimsy to wear… assuming he meant underwear, I felt embarrassed. Nan had only ever bought my undergarments.

Each time we saw Camilla, she talked about Dad and nothing else. She said Alice and Duncan wrote every Sunday and that she mailed him the weekly newspapers. She even sent him a cake that she'd baked. I hated writing, so he never got many letters from me, but that didn't mean I loved him any less because I adored him. Nan was always reminding me to "drop a few lines." Little did I realise, by not writing, I was playing into Camilla's hands. But no amount of letters from me would have made the slightest difference to what my future held.

In Dad's next letter, he said he'd bought me an 18-carat gold watch that was dust-proof, anti-magnetic, shock-proof, waterproof, and hopefully smell-proof because he was going to send it in a pair of old socks, which made me laugh. He'd also bought me a glass-domed clock, but I would have to wait until he came home. He had something for Nan too but would not tell me what it was because he could not trust me to keep a secret—he knew me so well.

I treasured every card and letter and carried them around to show my school friends. His letters always started the same: "My dearest darling daughter" or "My darling daughter Olivia."

Sometimes, he wrote "darling daughter" right across the page, ending with: "Remember, your Daddy loves you very much and always will, and don't forget to pay attention to your teachers." Trust him to mention education. His cards and letters were grubby and creased from being handled and kissed. One picture was so creased where I kissed it every night. The girls at school wanted to know when he would return; they missed him, too.

It amused me to hear he had a servant. The thought of someone making my bed and cleaning my shoes rather appealed to me. Dad was fastidious about clean shoes and said the arch was just as important as the tops. When he was on leave, I used to polish the brass buttons on his jacket and the buckle on his belt. He had a brass plate that slid underneath the buttons to avoid getting polished on his uniform. One day, he told me to use elbow grease; puzzled, I asked Nan where we could buy some elbow grease. He laughed till tears rolled down his cheeks. Those were happy times perhaps I remember with such detail because they were so few – like when he showed me the sleeve of his uniform jacket baring three stripes - wings and crest, his achievement he said was due to the perseverance and dedication of his wife as much as his own *I couldn't have done it without your Mother* he said *I am where I am because of her* he was a proud man.

Unable to work in the sweltering heat, everyone rested from 11 am to 3 pm and continued with their duties when the weather cooled. Dad decided that a hobby would while away the time; he had always been interested in photography so he brought a decent camera and took pictures of wildlife then he developed the film and sent it to

Camilla. Unfortunately, she was reluctant to part with any and held her hand out for me to return them.

I don't know why he sent everything to her; perhaps it was because they wrote frequently, where I only put pen to paper when Nan nagged me.

HRH Queen Elizabeth and Prince Philip were on a six-month tour of the Commonwealth. It was announced that the Royal couple would stop off in Aden for the Queen to visit the sick. Dad's photography skills had not gone unnoticed, and he was granted permission to enter the hospital to take pictures of our Sovereign. In one of the many pictures, the Queen was just feet away and smiling into the lens. He developed the film with care and placed them in a wedding album, starting with their arrival and ending with the Queen and the Prince waving on the steps of the plane. Dad sent the album to Camilla with a letter to say I could borrow the album to show the family and my teachers. He sent the negatives to Buckingham Palace and was thrilled when they offered him a job as a Royal photographer when he retired from the forces. The letter and envelope bearing the Royal crest were placed in the front of the album, where it remains to this day.

Jumping ahead—it was many years later when I phoned Dad and asked if I could borrow the album to show my children. Camilla refused and said Alice had it for safekeeping. Unbeknown to me, my father was ill and unable to speak for himself, which she took great advantage of. Christ, I wasn't planning on stealing it; I only wanted to show my family. Camilla has shown to be untrustworthy— clearly, she was judging me by her own standards. The album is worth a lot of money and, over time, will increase in value. What a pity he never developed a set of prints for me before sending the negatives to the Palace.

Back to the present—my holiday was never mentioned again. Nan suspected Camilla had something to do with that, but I didn't care. In fact, I was relieved. I left school at 15 and got a job in London as a typist/filing clerk and started earning £4.10 a week. I counted the months for Dad's return but was concerned he had not told us of the actual date. The only information we had was sometime in June…then it arrived. I excitedly tore the envelope: *Dear Olivia, I would like you and Nanna* (very formal*) I would like you and Nanna to go to Camilla's on Friday evening at 6 o'clock. Camilla is going to prepare a lovely tea for us. I will look forward to seeing you; love Dad.*

What in the hell… when did he arrive, and what happened to 'Daddy'? And why in God's name had she met him? And what about the bottle of champagne we were going to crack open? Nan was furious, but I was hurting beyond belief. In fact, my heart was in pieces. I had waited for this moment for two years; now, the thrill and excitement of greeting him had been stolen from me.

I put on my brave face as we made our way to their house. I dreaded seeing Camilla and her kids but could not wait to see Dad. One thing for sure: I would not be throwing myself into him as I had in the past—something I'd been looking forward to from the moment he left.

Camilla opened the door looking very smug. She led us into the dining room, where Dad was sitting with Duncan, Alice, and Camilla's mother. He got up from the chair to greet me, then shook Nan's hand and kissed her on the cheek—formal once again. He said how wonderful it was to be back home. Then he clasped my hand and talked excitedly of his time abroad. Then he handed me a gift that I opened with care. My eyes fell on a pretty round compact with a plastic top the size of 10pence. Underneath the plastic top was a pretty hand-embroidered flower. Then Alice whisked her compact out of the air, which was superior to mine. Her compact was square, and the entire top was plastic, with a bunch of embroidered flowers underneath.

Perhaps he gave her first choice, so I can't blame her for taking the prettiest and biggest. Then Camilla shoved her arm in my face to show me her gold watch. She said it was dust-proof, waterproof, and all the other proofs but left out smell-proof… that must have been the one that never arrived in a pair of socks. Then she pointed to her new glass-domed clock on the mantelpiece with the spinning pendulum… which also brought back memories. She was glowing like a Cheshire cat. I can't imagine what was going through Dad's mind; he must have wished the ground would swallow him. Goodness knows what happened to the gift he brought for Nan; perhaps Camilla's mother was the lucky recipient there, too. I smiled and hoped they never saw I was close to tears, but I listened with interest to the stories he told.

Once we had eaten, Dad took me into the garden. I think he wanted me to himself for a while but Duncan and Alice followed and stood on either side of him. Alice locked her arm in Dad's and glared at me. Perhaps I looked like a demon because my presents seemed to be upsetting. I can't imagine why my Father allowed this behaviour but he was outnumbered. It's ironic how I was more than happy to share my Father with them and now they were treating me like an intruder...I couldn't wait to leave; thank goodness I had Nan. I could not imagine what I would have done without her; she was the most wonderful, loyal and protective Nan anyone could wish for. Dad never stayed with us again.

On Dad's next leave, he took Camilla and her kids to London Zoo; my cousin Scott and I were invited along. It was arranged that we'd meet at Liverpool Street station, but Camilla made it obvious we were in the way every time Scott and I stopped to look at something. They disappeared. Camilla hung onto his arm, giggling like a silly teenager. Then he took her kids into a shop and left me outside with Camilla. She took the opportunity to tell me she'd been to a fortune teller who said she would marry again to a man in uniform. I couldn't wait to leave.

We made our way to the station. Duncan and Alice were skipping ahead, whispering and sniggering, occasionally turning to grin. I was not surprised when they left Scott and me to catch the slow train. They could have travelled with us, but they headed for the fast train that was due to leave. Our last sighting was of them waving vigorously as their train pulled away.

As I walked through the door, Nan knew something was wrong. Once she wormed it out of me, she decided she was going to write him a stiff letter (stiff being one of her favourite words). I made her promise not to say anything for fear of making things worse than they already were. Besides, I did not want them to know I was hurting.

I was about 15 when I became aware of the protruding bone in my neck. I could rest my chin on my chest with no difficulty. This only came to light when the collar of my new lemon turtleneck sweater curled over. No amount of encouragement from me seemed to make the slightest difference, so I stripped to my underwear, clipped my hair up, and reached for the hand mirror to view myself from behind... and was I shocked... I knew about my time in hospital but was unaware of the deformity it had left behind. Heading to the kitchen, I asked Nan why corrective surgery had not been performed. She told me surgery would have been too dangerous, with the risk of paralysis. I was mortified to think I had to live with this deformity for the rest of my days, so I began studying my profile from every angle, trying to disguise the problem.

Chapter Eleven

True Colours

The progress Camilla made with my Father in a short space of time was alarming; my relationship with Alice and Duncan had also become strained. Alice liked showing off; she'd tilt her head to the side and swivel from side to side with a smirk. *Uncle Allister said he is going to buy me this. Uncle Allister said he's going to take me there.* I was seeing another side to her that wasn't flattering but in all honesty, there never was anything flattering about her in the first place.

Dad's birthday was 5 days after mine - I arrived at the house with his card and pullover neatly wrapped. He placed the unopened gift and card on the table and went into the kitchen, returning seconds later with a five-pound note and handed it to me with no card. I was upset he'd forgotten the anniversary of my birth. Alice was beaming and showed me the typewriter "Uncle Allister" had brought her then we were interrupted by Duncan who told me Uncle Allister was going to teach him the art of photography and development. I tried to look interested but found it difficult. Dad looked uneasy too perhaps he remembered his letters telling me how he was going to teach me photography. My visit that afternoon was brief.

I received his letter about three days after he returned to base. I was always pleased to hear from him and ripped the envelope in excitement; he said he'd got some wonderful news to share on his next visit.

He arrived Saturday lunchtime; it was a joy having him to myself for a change – just like old times. I sat close, waiting for him to speak then he dropped a bombshell *Camilla and I are getting married in June; what do you think of that? He* said with a broad grin *now you will have a Brother and Sister. Isn't that wonderful news, my dear* he continued without waiting for a response…*I want you and Nana to come to my wedding and I want Uncle Howard to be my best man. This is just what your Dad needs - now we can be one big happy family. I am going to buy myself out of the forces so I can be a proper family man with a wife and be father to Duncan and Alice;* my name was not mentioned, I wanted to tell him the whole idea sucks but I smiled and wished him luck…luck was something I thought he was going to need.

I do not remember the service at the registry office, only the reception at her squatty prefab with her friends and family in a fog of cigarette smoke, plenty of drink and laughter as she celebrated all she had achieved. It had taken 18 years but her patients had paid off…well done Camilla, my Mother must be turning in her grave.

Someone took a picture of Dad and myself which conveniently disappeared along with all the others of me, I don't recall him taking pictures of Camilla's children but I was never around much. Alice was younger than me by about two years she had hard features with thin lines representing lips that she smeared with cerise lipstick, she had no dress sense and spoke like a fish wife and those were her good points but they did not prevent her from showing off which was embarrassing because she had nothing to show off with, I must sound like a bitch but I only speak the truth…well isn't that what Dad always told me?

It was shortly after the wedding when Dad and I went to the park (I can't imagine she allowed us out without Alice and Duncan). In the park was a huge rose bed. Dad singled out one particular rose and asked me to kneel down and cup the blossom - lift my head slightly, close my eyes and sniff the delicate fragrance. It was a real pose. Once developed, my proud Father pinned the picture on the door of his locker. He eventually sent it to Camilla and asked her to give it to me, it must have been a nice picture because I never saw it. I can't imagine why he sent everything to her but he trusted the woman and was oblivious to her jealousy. He was a trusting man who saw good in everyone…a trait I inherited which was to be my downfall.

True to his word, Dad brought himself out of the forces; due to his rank and number of years in service, he came away with a decent pension.

When Camilla contacted the council, informing them of her marriage, they were moved from the squatty prefab into a three-bedroom house. She didn't waste time spending his money either but in all fairness, there were things needed like curtains and carpets, dining table and chairs, then there was her new wardrobe and a fur coat, not to mention Alice and Duncan with their wants and needs, now she had free will of his revenue there was no stopping her.

I must apologise as I repeatedly refer to prefabs as being 'squatty' because I have nothing against them - Nan and I would have been delighted to live in one. I only refer to Camilla's as squatty because of how cold and unattractive it was…much like the tenants.

Until Dad became a full-time civilian, he came home every weekend. It was lovely seeing him on Sunday but I always left feeling miserable; whenever I had his attention, the wife would throw herself onto his lap - pull his face from me and smother him with kisses then she was tickling him. I understood she was happy but I was no threat to them or their future. I was not the other woman, for Christ's sake I was his daughter; unsure where to put my face, I'd leave the room but it was always the same, she would either call him to do something or send Alice into the rescue she would climb on his lap and scowl at me, I found her behaviour childish and embarrassing as I am sure my Father did but he never said anything, he should have addressed the situation but I think he feared the consequences. I did not begrudge them their life, neither was I jealous of their new surroundings; in fact, I loved having him around, knowing he did not have to return to base where he would be gone for weeks or months so I was confused by their animosity towards me…then realised, I had served my purpose and now I was in the way.

Nan kept Aunt Katherine informed of my situation in regular letters; Katherine had not forgotten the heartache Camilla put her sister through. Her solution was for Nan and I to join her. *Canada is a wonderful country Mum, it would be a crying shame for Olivia to miss out on the wonderful opportunities we have. She could have a new life with a marvellous future. Think about it, Mum, to deprive her of a future here would be a crying shame.*

After much persuasion, Nan decided to take the plunge; leaving the country seemed the perfect solution but first, I would need a letter from Dad and a release form from Mr. Wilkinson who she hoped would confirm I had a clean bill of health.

Dad was shocked and reluctant to give his consent. *I will have to think about that and let you know* he said with a frown. I was also disturbed to be leaving him but Canada seemed to be the only answer. He must have discussed it with the wife because much our delight, he wrote a letter for us to take to Canada's house - it would have been Camilla who persuaded him. She had proved how manipulating she could be and this was her chance to get me out of his life.

I felt grand climbing into a limousine for my yearly check-up with the specialist I had got to know well; Nan came with me for what we hoped would me my last visit...the visit that would give me a clean bill of health to start a new life in a new Country.

After my examination, Mr Wilkinson turned to Nan. *I am very pleased with this young lady* he said with a smile; *you have done a marvellous job, Mrs. Daniels, I think a new life in Canada would be a wonderful experience but I must warn you – their weather is not like ours, our climate is warm and damp but theirs is hot and dry, their sun is stronger so I am warning you not to expose her neck to the sun* he looked at me and smiled *do you understand Olivia,* 'stupid man' I thought, 'I would never expose my neck to the sun or to anyone, in fact, I go to great lengths to hide my ugly shape' he gave us further advice - more as a friend than the professional man that he was, he opened my folder and began to write, we watched as he signed the papers for us to take to Canada House and a letter for me to hand to my new GP. Mr Wilkinson was specific that they understood my condition now that he was signing me off his register. He hugged us both then wished us a safe journey and a lifetime of happiness. We walked out of his office for the last time. I felt sad knowing we would never meet again. He had been a part of my life for as long as I could remember, I had so much to thank him for.

Uncle Melvin worked for the airline so he arranged our flights. Nan had a matter of weeks in which to sell her home. I was very upset to be moving so far away from Dad but since his wedding, he had become distant. I had to accept he was gone from me and my life.

My last visit with my Father was not pleasant. The weatherman promised rain but so far had remained dry in-spite of the dark skies that loomed but to be on the safe side, I took my new umbrella. Dad greeted me then was given some chores and disappeared. I was left in the sitting room with Alice and Duncan who were whispering and sniggering, so I chose to leave earlier than planned. I put on my coat and picked up my brolly from the hall stand and saw two spokes had been snapped, I pretended not to notice. I walked down the foot path and turned to wave to Dad and Camilla at the door then I saw Duncan and Alice at the lounge window poking their tongues out - with thumbs in their ears, they waved their remaining fingers in the air…such class, I had done nothing to warrant such resentment, Christ - they had my Father and his money what more did they want, we could have been a family but that is not what they wanted, Aunt Katherine was right, Canada was the best place for me.

It was around this time Nan told me about the relationship between Camilla and my Mother. I could hardly believe my ears. My goodness, what was my Father thinking getting mixed up with the likes of this woman…now I know why I felt uncomfortable in her presence and why she used to watch me. I knew something wasn't right but I was too young to identify what I was feeling. The smile she wore in our presents was not who she was - underneath her exterior was a devious woman full of hate. The apprehension I had was not my childish imagination after all. Her true colours had surfaced.

I dread to think how many times my Mother must have turned in her grave seeing me in the company of the same woman who tried to destroy her; aware of the grief lurking in the shadows, my Mother watched this woman slowly weave her web of deceit in snaring my Father. Camilla had been unsuccessful in taking him from my Mother but had succeeded in taking him from his only daughter.

As our departure date grew close, Nan wished the rest of her family were joining us. We visited Joan and Howard every week but did not see much of William because of the distance but frequent letters were exchanged. Very few people had house phones but in an emergency, there was always a kind neighbour - failing that, it was the phone box or telegram.

We had just finished breakfast when a telegram arrived from William *will be flying in two days. See you in Canada,* she read the cable once more and wept tears of joy.

William chose to keep their plans a secret in case anything should go wrong, Nan was thrilled and wished Joan were joining us too.

March 12[th,] Howard and Joan drove us to the airport. Dad was pacing the floor because we were running late; he could not disguise his sadness at seeing me leave unlike Camilla who could not hide her joy.

We hardly had time for goodbyes when our flight was called. Dad hugged me and whispered *don't forget to write and please send me a telegram as soon as you reach New York.* New York was our two-hour stop for refuelling then loud speakers announced our flight for the last time and we were ushered to where our plane was waiting. I turned to look at my Father. I had never seen him so sad I wanted to run to him - throw my arms about him but the devil woman was watching. Nan gave me a gentle nudge and they disappeared from sight.

Chapter Twelve

Canada 1975

Our flight to Winnipeg took two days; when we arrived, Uncle Melvin was allowed the extended break to drive us home to Katherine who rushed outside to greet us as we pulled onto the drive. Eileen was in the kitchen making tea then cooked us a hearty breakfast. My first breakfast in Winnipeg was one I will never forget. It tasted so different but amazing; after our meal and with Katherine's permission, I crept into her bedroom to get my 7-month-old cousin who had been woken by the commotion. Oliver stared in confusion at this stranger who had the audacity to take him from his cot, I carried him to the kitchen where he reached out to his Mom…he turned to me and frowned as if to say…and don't do that again.

I couldn't wait to see Haley and we had yet to meet her young brother Timothy who was at school along with my English cousins Ryan and Ian. Uncle William started work within days of arriving, I can't imagine how Aunt Katherine got everyone settled so quickly; she did the same with Nan and me; within three days, Winnipeg's leading newspaper hired me as a junior to work in the office. Nan was hired as a machinist in a factory. Katherine also worked 3 nights a week. She was sister in charge at the maternity hospital so it was a busy house juggling the family around everyone's jobs.

Like any first day at work, I was nervous - even more so being in a strange Country but everyone was friendly and made me welcome. One girl became my mentor and showed me the ropes. Connie asked many questions about British history but I hated the subject so I was unable to feed her lust; she said *you know honey, if I had been in your shoes, I would have examined every inch of London before I could walk – I would have eaten it for breakfast* she added with a smile the only thing we had in common was music except her choice was superior to mine, I was into pop and Connie loved the classics.

Once I became familiar with my surroundings, I was taking short cuts through the printing department, one evening I saw this handsome guy standing by the entrance; each night, I took the same route hoping to see him again but he was never around then a couple of weeks later there he was…encouraged by his smile I walked over but before we could speak another guy from the building joined us, he introduced himself as Phillipe he said *this is my kid brother Jean Pierre but we call him Johnny* Phillipe worked in the printing section at the press I was delighted when he offered me a lift, on the journey he asked about my home Country then he nudged his brother *aren't you going to ask Olivia for her number then* Johnny quickly responded *Oh sure, what's your number.*

I couldn't wait to tell Connie the following morning *that's nice, sweetie. Just be careful, okay? You've only just met this Johnny guy.* That was just the response I expected, considering my friend was younger than me she was really smart.

I waited weeks for Johnny to call but had since given up when he phoned and invited me to a picnic on the lake with a couple of friends. Hank and Karen were in the car when he picked me up - when they weren't snogging, they spoke quietly amongst themselves so I didn't get a lot of encouragement in the conversation department. I was unsure what to make of them until I mentioned music then Karen sprang into life and said she loved to party and could jive all night. Jiving was something I had never done but had never had the opportunity to do. Her favourite pop stars were Bill Haley, Fats Domino, Gene Vincent and Elvis but her absolute favourite was Little Richard.

Opposite to Karen was Connie who hated parties and shuddered if you mentioned the hit parade. She loathed country and western but adored the classics; it was from here that Connie began to educate me in what she called the finer music. She spoke of the composers and the hardships they encountered in their homeland. She said every piece of music holds a beautiful story full of passion or sadness that could reduce a person to tears. I loved spending evenings at her home listening to the fiery Gypsy music, Slavonic dances and many others but my favourite was Tchaikovsky. It brought back memories of the ballet when I was six.

Thanks to my new friend, I valued the finer music as well as the hit parade.

After months of living in an overcrowded house, Nan found an apartment; it was very quiet without the hustle and bustle of my cousins but I missed my Aunt's cooking and looked forward to invites at the weekend. Canadian food is a lot richer and far tastier than what we'd been used to.

It was early December and Christmas was fast approaching; a group of us girls was sitting in the booth during coffee break. I was listening to everyone debating what alcohol to bring to the office party. Lenore turned and asked if I was going to bring a Micky *Who's Micky?* I asked in all innocence – they nearly fell out of the booth laughing. I wondered what I had said that was so funny then Connie explained that Micky was half a bottle of liquor and a full bottle they refer to as '26'.

Karen only lived 20 minutes from our apartment since our picnic on the lake. We kept in touch. She called round one evening and invited me for coffee at the Inn - a four-minute walk from our apartment. Nan intervened and said she'd brought fresh coffee and suggested we stay home *but Nan* I said pleadingly...*the coffee bar has a jukebox and sells burgers and hot cakes with syrup and cream; it is theee place to beee* – I proceeded to explain how sitting in a booth while feeding dimes and quarters in the duke box was an amazing experience I was crazy for this life and couldn't get enough, we were about to leave when she called *don't you be late miss you'll knock yourself up* Karen turned to me and glared, I rolled my eyes *these old timers could be so square* I said as we made our way downstairs, it was months later when Karen told me 'to knock yourself up' was to get pregnant so understandably she was shocked.

It was summer when Johnny took me to my very first drive-in movie with Karen and Hank. Drive-ins can only be shown at night. They start with trailers, then the news which is followed by adds and a brief intermission then the main movie begins. Once the film ends, it takes ages to leave the park/field with cars nose to tail so you don't get home till the early hours; not wanting to disturb Nan, I crept in. I*s that you, Miss,* she whispered; *well who else would it be?* I muttered under my breath. I knew a lecture was on the cards in the morning.

Another night, I came home late from visiting Karen. Nan was waiting with a stern face *what time do you call this then?* I told her it was 11.30 so she gave me hell for answering back. *Don't you come to that lark with me, my girl*...what on earth was she talking about - what did she think I'd been up to? For heaven's sake, I had no intention of doing anything dishonourable; she must have told the family because they decided I was up to no good which crushed me.

I had done nothing wrong. I was a teenager doing what all teenagers do. Surely having fun did not make me a bad person.

One Sunday, Johnny took me to a midnight movie. I don't know what the rules would be today, but in the '50s, it was unacceptable to open a movie house on the Sabbath. Hence, doors did not open until one minute past midnight. Well, it doesn't take much to figure that if doors don't open until midnight, you're not getting out much before 2:30. Nan obviously told the family, who were convinced I was up to mischief. They said my behaviour was disgraceful. It was upsetting to think they thought so little of me. Aunt Katherine was quick to voice her opinion, but Uncle William — a man of few words — never passed judgment, but the look was enough. Eventually, I stopped visiting. What was the point? I was rarely included in conversation, so I stayed silent, but my silence made me look guilty.

Being the eldest grandchild, my family had never had any interaction with teenagers, but someone needed to give them a few tips real soon because Haley was not far behind and showing great interest in girly stuff and anything that did not include a school uniform. She was never far away when I opened my make-up bag and watched with interest when I set my hair. The rest of my cousins, being boys, would have more freedom and be given tips and advice from Fathers about the dating game. Maybe the family thought I was up to mischief because they were still living with the old-fashioned ways and ideas they brought from England when the deadline for arriving home (in the '40s) would have been roughly 10 o'clock. This did not make them bad people, of course, but they were not understanding or sympathetic towards this teenager who was made to feel guilty for no reason.

England was years behind Canada. My family spent their teenage years in the UK and had never experienced sitting in coffee shops for hours, playing the jukebox while eating burgers and fries or hot cakes — normal teenage stuff — because they were adults with families when they set foot in Canada, by which time they had outgrown the teenage stuff. But I repeat, this did not make them bad people. They were not understanding where I was concerned.

I had never dated in England and didn't have a clue about the dating game, but each day in this beautiful country came with a new experience. However, I did know right from wrong and good from bad, much to my father's delight and approval. Nan brought me up to be a decent young lady, so it hurt knowing they had a low opinion of me. It only takes one to voice an opinion, and the ripples travel far.

Due to my protruding bone in my neck, I did my best to hide the problem with baggy clothes. I grew my hair long and never passed a mirror without checking my reflection. Then, I was accused of being vain and told to stop admiring myself. I said nothing — to have answered back would have been impertinent, and I would have been reprimanded. Besides, I did not want them to know how miserable I felt with the condition that was controlling my life. I never said anything to Nan because I did not want her discussing the problem with the family, who I assume had forgotten about my time in hospital and the defect it had left behind.

I could not understand why the family got angry with Nan because of the attention she lavished on me. Was it jealousy, I wondered? I bet they weren't jealous when I was in hospital strapped to my bed, and what about being orphaned at an early age with a mother lying in her grave... the mother that had been snatched from me before I got to know her? Then there was my father, who I rarely saw, who had also been taken from me. I bet they weren't jealous of me then. My family did not realise just how lucky they were not to have had a child with my medical condition because my needs took up a lot of Nan's time and money, but she never complained. What she did for me, she did with love. She raised, nurtured, and protected me, for which I will be forever grateful. I dread to think where I would have ended up if she had not stepped in and rescued me from the clutches of being shoved in a home where — without her love, care, and dedication — goodness knows where I would have ended up. But this beautiful woman persevered and encouraged me to walk so I could face the life that was in front of me. God bless her.

My family had healthy children. My cousins were lucky to have both parents to sit with them and discuss daily events with mothers to tuck them in at night. I would have given anything for my dad to sit with me each night, and I dearly missed not having a mother. Not that I would have traded Nan for all the tea in China, but until you have been brought up without a mother, you cannot imagine how it feels not being able to walk through the door and call "Mum."

I woke up one morning miserable and depressed. I dreamt that I woke from my sleep and I was surrounded by a cold, damp mist. There was no colour to be seen. The sky was grey so were the buildings; it looked menacing. I was depressed and couldn't wait to get to work in the busy office to shake off my nightmare - *Snap out of it, kiddo* said Connie, *it's only a bad dream* but the foreboding stayed with me the entire day. A few years later, I realised it was not a bad dream but an omen.

Chapter Thirteen

Farewell Nan-Safe Journey

I was in my robe listening to my music - brooding over Johnny who I had not seen in weeks, when Connie arrived. *Now you listen to me, kiddo. Best you snap out of this thing you have for this Johnny guy. Nothing is gained by crying over spilled milk; you've gotta start looking after number one. You hear what I'm saying? First of all, you can stop playing those damn love songs. Secondly, you want to get out there and start living again – socialize, mingle, shit; there's a load of guys out there just waiting for you to surface, damn it – why don't you come out with Ivan and me...who knows you might even enjoy yourself* her tone changed and she spoke softly *come on sweetie, smarten up before it's too late and you wake up one morning to find some old maid staring back at you in the mirror* only Connie could lecture with kindness, I knew she was right of course but I felt sorry for myself and hurting more than I thought possible.

Karen never changed...*Cripes, you're not still drooling over him, are you...never did like the guy much anyway, why don't you turn that crap off and play some Little Richard or Gene Vincent...hey this dreamy guy in our block is throwing a party at the weekend, Mom is going off to Grans so you can stay over...come on ole' girl put your glad rags on and paint your face and party with me we'll have a ball* that was typical of Karen but I stayed home and continued to brood.

As if things couldn't get any worse, I was fired from my job because of my extended lunch breaks, but luck was just around the corner. I was listening to the radio when the announcer said there was a vacancy for a record librarian at the station and anyone interested should call at 9 a.m., but only if you could type and knew a little about music. Well, I ticked both boxes, anxious to find employment. I was on the phone before 9 and put through to Herbie, who asked me to go for an interview immediately. Wow — working for my favourite station, CKY, was my ultimate dream.

The first thing Herbie asked was if I could type. He handed me a sheet of paper and pointed to the machine on the opposite desk. Then he gave me the hit parade list to copy. I could have typed that with my eyes closed. I tapped away at the keyboard whilst looking at the vast collection of records surrounding me. Then Herbie told me to stop typing and asked if I could start the following morning. I could hardly believe my luck. I had just clinched the job every teenager would give their right arm for — unless your name was Connie, who never listened to CKY.

Once I got to know the announcers and the type of music they played, they often asked me to choose their music when they were away. But I could only choose what was acceptable for the time of day. I was thrilled when Mike asked me to select his show. I naturally chose my favorites. When the ratings came in, Mike told me his had climbed on the weeks I chose his music. This did not go down well with Herbie, who buried his head in the papers but knew he was listening by his flushed cheeks. But it was understandable — until I came along, choosing music had been his job.

It was a few weeks before Christmas when the music director asked me to record a Christmas story with him for our child listeners.

He gave me the script, which we read together (me being the little girl). The story was aired on Christmas Eve... great success.

Another highlight was when celebrities visited the station to discuss upcoming interviews or plug their latest records. Unable to talk in the busy office, they'd congregate in the library with the delegated announcer. I loved hearing them talk about everyday life, such as walking the dog, their latest tour, recipes, and even health issues. I couldn't wait to tell Karen where's Connie said, *"That's nice, sweetie,"* down to earth and blasé — but that was Connie.

We were shocked when Nan said she was homesick and would be returning to the UK. Also, Joan had written to say she was pregnant. Unfortunately, before Nan could book her passage home, she was involved in an accident when some jerk pulled out in front of the bus she was traveling on. The bus driver slammed his brakes to avoid a collision, causing Nan to fall on the metal coin dispenser, badly gashing her forehead and narrowly missing her eye. The poor darling was in so much pain and was not given pain relief. The upper part of her face was various shades of black and blue for weeks... that was the final straw. She couldn't get away quick enough.

It was a sad day for everyone the morning she left. The family huddled around, saying their final goodbyes, taking in turns to kiss her one last time — wishing her good luck, safe journey, write soon. Then the porter blew his whistle — our cue to leave the train. We looked up to where she was seated by the window. I had never seen her so sad. Her eyes were red from crying. Doors slammed, and the porter checked each carriage as steam screeched from the funnel. Then, the train pulled slowly away... our last sighting was of her beautiful face pressed against the glass as the train eased its way around the bend. I saw her lift a hanky to wipe her tears... I waited until the train faded into the distance before leaving, just as I had with my father as a child. I wondered if we would ever meet again. She had been everything to me, and now she was gone. Her journey to Montreal took two days. Then she boarded the 'Cunard Liner' for a 7-day voyage to England.

Chapter Fourteen

A Lecture From Connie

It was early 1960 when Connie said she was getting married to Ivan, who was French and came from Quebec. Ivan and Connie met in Ontario when they worked for the same company. Connie worked in the office, and Ivan worked down the mines. I was thrilled when Connie asked me to be a bridesmaid at their wedding. Ivan was Catholic, but Connie was adamant about having a Ukrainian wedding, which is steeped in history, mystery, and rituals where guests and the community celebrate well into the night, which can last for days.

A month after the wedding, Connie arranged for us to have our fortune told by a sand reader who had been recommended by a colleague from work. My friend was a little sceptical and stood back, allowing me to enter. I walked into the room and took my seat. In the centre of the table was a large wooden tray with some fine sand. The lady asked me to make a mark. Then she amazed me with her knowledge.

You're from the old Country, aren't you – I cannot see your Father clearly because he is still over there, I do not see your mother but someone stands in her place – did you know your Father does not receive your letters, they are being kept from him - the letters he writes to you do not reach the mail box – he is going to regret not having known you. Unfortunately, this won't be until he is much older when he has time to think but he will realize when it is too late.

Within a year, you will be in hospital with your stomach, but don't worry, it is nothing serious. She said more but could not remember if only it had been written down.

It was Christmas 1960 — my first Christmas without Nan, who I missed terribly. Johnny and I had been invited to a party at his friend's home. I had not seen him since the wedding and was looking forward to the celebrations. I have no idea what time we left, but Johnny suggested going back to his for coffee. I knew he was dying to show me his apartment, which I had yet to see. I didn't realise how much I'd drunk until I stepped outside and fell into his car, giggling.

What I remember about his apartment is very little, but everything would have been neat and tidy, unlike mine, which I had left in turmoil. I left him making coffee while I flicked through his records, looking for something dreamy to play. I recall wrapping my arms around him and swaying to the music I had chosen — we danced and we kissed. I was aware things were getting out of hand, but I didn't care and did nothing to stop what was happening.

I disturbed him when I turned to look at the clock. I was grateful when he got up to make coffee, so I seized the opportunity to quickly dress. I don't know which one of us was more embarrassed as he drove me home. Thank goodness Nan was in the UK, otherwise how would I explain my night out? I felt embarrassed, but I consoled myself that every kid I knew was sleeping around, and most were younger than me. So, I brushed the guilt away and wished I could remember our night together.

It was late afternoon when Connie phoned to see how I enjoyed the party. She was mortified when I told her I stayed out. *"You did what?"* She screamed down the receiver. I looked at my reflection in the mirror and pulled a face. Maybe I shouldn't have said anything. Connie told me to get a cab and get the hell over there right away. "Shit," why did I have to open my mouth? I didn't need a grandmother to chastise me — not when I had Connie.

Ivan opened the door, looking angry as hell then he pointed to the lounge where his wife was waiting. Christ you'd have thought I had committed murder the way the pair of them looked at me. *Okay, kiddo, now tell me exactly what happened; he didn't rape you, did he?* She looked relieved when I told her he hadn't, *so what in the hell happened? Did he go all the way?*

If you mean, did he make love to me, yes?

Oh, for Christ's sake...what did he use?

She could see I didn't have a clue what she was talking about, *Ivan. Will you get me a beer? I need a drink; you better get something for Olivia too.* She turned to face me. *Did he wear something – did he take precautions? U*nable to reply, I remained silent.

For Christ's sake, Olivia, how could you allow this creep to take something from you that was so precious? What the hell where you thinking? Do you realize what you have done - you were different from all the other kids? You were pure and innocent, that is so rare and then you let this creep take advantage of you. If you carry on like that, you'll be the same as all the other bitches out there - Olivia, you are a crazy fool. Oh my God, Ivan, say something please she said, throwing her hair over her shoulders but before he could open his mouth, she spoke *My God, do you think so little of yourself, cripes? What do you think your Nana would say, Jesus - I still can't believe it, you stupid - stupid - stupid.*

The lecture went on for ages, with Ivan adding little comments when he could get a word in. Connie paced the floor and gazed absently through the window, then she came, sat beside me and spoke a little calmer. *I have always been so proud of you, my little English friend. You are special to us both;* she paused to light another cigarette - inhaled deeply and turned to face me. *I'm sorry if you think we're being hard on you, sweetie but it's because we love you. Do you understand, I am angry, angry mad that you allowed this bastard to take advantage of you or perhaps he took advantage of the situation because you had been drinking...Yes, that's it,* she said, raising her voice again *the fucking bastard took advantage of you...the creep.*

I remained silent, waiting for her to become calmer; eventually her anger subsided so decided it was safe to speak, by which time my friend was at the window gazing at the falling snow. *Okay, guys, I'm sorry...so what? I made a mistake, no good bitching about it now. The worst that can happen is I could be pregnant,* I said, trying to break the ice with my casual comment. Connie came to where I was sitting - leaned over until her face was inches away; *never spit in the well, my sweet; you may end up drinking the water.*

The lecture from Connie made me regret what I had done. I stayed with my friends for the rest of the day. We ate pot roast, played cards and smoked but nothing else was said about my night with Johnny. Every time I looked at my friend, she was frowning then she'd glance at me and shake her head in disbelief.

We always enjoyed our card games. Each time Ivan lost, we laughed because he took the game seriously. Then he accused us of cheating, which we never did, but Ivan always lost and got angry, which made us laugh. The more we laughed, the madder he got. Then he'd throw his cards on the table and storm into the kitchen, swearing in his beautiful French accent... but not this time. Connie spent all afternoon shaking her head and muttering *"fucking*

bastard" or *"stupid – stupid – stupid."* My night with Johnny had
sunk in, but there was nothing I could do now. Connie's lecture was
worse than what I would have gotten from Nan.

With the New Year behind us, it was back to work. I jumped
out of bed, flicked the kettle on, and made my way to the bathroom.
I hated being late. Herbie never said anything but would watch me
hurry to my desk, then lift his head and stare up at the clock. He
couldn't have made it more obvious if he tried. I don't know why he
didn't say something and get it over with.

I dropped the bread in the toaster, popped a tea bag in a mug,
and opened the curtains. It was snowing again, but that's all it ever
seems to do. I poured water into my mug, then screwed my nose at
the aroma that wafted up. I tipped it away and made coffee.

It was days later when I had my usual tummy pains. When
nothing happened, I assumed my visitor would arrive during the
night, but that didn't happen either. By the end of the week, they had
fizzled out altogether. I had just eaten lunch when I lit a cigarette. I
screwed my face in disgust—it was vile. First, the tea, now the
cigarette. *What in the hell...* It was time to talk to Connie. I invited
my friends for a Chinese takeout and some much-needed advice.

*So, kiddo, what do you plan to do now...Olivia, talk to me,
please and turn that crap off the stereo. We will help you in anyway
we can if you choose to have an abortion. We can ask around or you
can put the baby up for adoption, then you can continue to live your
life and no one will be any the wiser.* She saw the look of horror on
my face but continued with sensible advice: *Well sweetie, you can't
look after a baby. How will you support it on your own? What sort
of life could you offer a child or are you hoping the grease ball is
going to jump in like a knight in shining armour and marry you?
Come on, sweetie wake up, for Christ's sake.*

I knew what my friend was saying made perfect sense, but I never let sensible advice get in the way of my heart. Ever since I can remember, I had dreamt of having babies, so abortion was out of the question, and I had absolutely no intention of giving my baby to total strangers. But my only problem was the family. I was a coward not to talk to them, but I feared the outcome. Then there was Nan. I wondered how to break the news that I knew would break her heart.

My next letter to Nan was the hardest I had ever written. I visualised her joy at seeing the envelope on the doormat but reading my news. I was aware her pleasure would quickly fade.

Her telegram arrived by return: "Come home, all is well. Letter on the way, tickets to follow." I was jumping for joy—relieved she had forgiven me and I would be going back to England. I just hoped it would be before my condition became visible for all to see. I admired my posture in the mirror and wondered how long it would be before my little treasure made his/her presence visible. I had crossed the first hurdle, and my second would be announcing my baby's presence was going to be permanent. This baby needed me as much as I needed her/him. No one could or would love and understand my baby as me. My responsibility from now on would be to protect this little one at all times.

Nan sent a parcel for my 21st birthday containing sensible gifts that only grandmothers think of. She enclosed a picture of her five-month-old granddaughter Charlotte, who came into the world in September. She was the apple of everyone's eye—a pretty little thing with fair curly hair. I could see cousins and aunties from the Hawkins side of the family in her little face.

I also received a card from my father, but it was something you would send to someone you barely knew. I wouldn't have had the nerve to buy it unless I wanted to insult the recipient, assuming the stepmother had brought it and searched for the smallest. Any fool could see the card was for a boy—the blue bow on the front was a giveaway. But this was another attempt to stick the knife in deeper. She wasn't satisfied knowing I was miles away; she was still turning the blade. The pitiful card was signed *"From Dad."* It made me feel worthless. Personally, I would have been too embarrassed to purchase the thing, and it certainly wasn't worth the price of a stamp. I still have the card as a reminder in case I should ever doubt my judgment of her. I wondered if my father remembered his promise to me when I was a child: a party and a parrot for my 21st.

Chapter Fifteen

Farewell My Friends

In Nan's next letter, she enclosed the tickets for my voyage with instructions on what to do, how I wished she were with me now, it scared me to hell knowing I would be travelling hundreds of miles across the ocean without her, Connie said *you must do whatever you have to do in order to survive and don't look back* – my friend was so wise.

I called Johnny to say I would be returning to England. He fell silent, then said he'd be in touch. I didn't hold my breath, but the following week, he took me to a restaurant on the other side of town. The restaurant had a cabaret on the first floor, with speakers in the restaurant so you could listen to the entertainment while eating. We had almost finished our meal when the entertainer announced a request to a young lady who was due to sail to England. She mentioned my name and said the request was from Johnny. Silence fell as she sang, *"Now is the Hour."* In one verse, she sang, *"Soon you'll be sailing far across the sea, while I'm away, please remember me."* Then Johnny offered me a ring… Was this his attempt at asking me to marry him, I wondered. I did not respond but have often wondered how my life with our child would have turned out had I accepted that ring and stayed in Canada, which I could not have done without disappointing Nan, who paid for my ticket.

The day of my departure, Johnny drove me to the station in silence. I wished with all my heart I wasn't leaving him and my friends behind and the way of life I had become accustomed to in a country I had grown to love. Johnny had the radio tuned into CKY. Mike was on the air, playing some of my favorites and dedicating everyone to me. Johnny reached to turn up the volume as Mike said, *"And now I have a selection of music for our little English librarian who is on her way back to her home country. If you're listening, Olivia, I would like to thank you for your help. It has been a pleasure knowing you—you will be greatly missed. I wish you a safe journey, bon voyage."* And now, here are some of your favorites. In the background, I heard Frank Chacksfield playing *'It Ain't Necessarily So'* from *Porgy and Bess*, followed by *'Summertime'*. Then he played *"P.S. I Love You"*—it's almost tomorrow—and more of my favourites. Just as we reached the station, Mike played Gracie Fields' *'Now is The Hour.'*

It was a sad journey and one that made me realise I had more friends than I realised, assuming having left the station, I would soon be forgotten—out of sight, out of mind, sort of thing. But on the contrary, how thoughtful of Mike and Johnny, who contacted the station with the date and time of my departure.

We barely spoke on the short journey, but what could we say in what little time we had left? I did not want to leave everyone behind, least of all the father of my unborn child. My heart ached. Johnny and I were compatible. He was quiet and shy, much like myself, so a future together may have worked, but neither of us attempted to break the ice that morning.

There were a few family members on the platform waiting, along with Connie and Ivan and Dorothy from the radio station. Connie rushed to take my hand. *"Hi, honey. Why are you so late?*

We were beginning to wonder what happened to you. Your train is due to leave right away… oh well, never mind, you're here now." Before I realised it, I was being bustled on board. No time for reminiscing—just a few hugs and kisses, then the whistle blew as Connie shoved a parcel through the open window.

"Here you are, sweetie. Take good care of yourself and send me a card from the ship. I want to know everything you do. Have a wonderful life and a safe journey home and say hi to your Nana." As the train pulled away, I watched their faces until they became distant specs… Reality sunk in. Was it too late to change my mind? I could catch the next train back, assuming there was a train heading back to Winnipeg, but I couldn't let Nan down. She would be disappointed if I failed to arrive. Besides, she would have made preparations for my homecoming. I should have thought this through. Then I remembered the reason for my hasty retreat. I was ashamed and scared of what the family would say—leaving was the only alternative.

I waited for the station to disappear, then opened the parcel Connie had put together. There was a card with an air balloon on the front with the words *'bon voyage'*. Inside, she had written, *"Take care, my little English friend and write soon."* She packed an apple, sandwiches, and some boiled sweets. There was also a brown leather folder with a writing pad and envelopes—her way of encouraging me to write. How like Connie to have thought of sending me on my long journey with amenities. She had always been there for me. I will never find another friend quite like her. I was going to miss her friendship and her loving lectures. I was about to take a seven-day journey across the ocean, returning to a country where I had only known hostility from Stepmother Gruella. There were so many thoughts to keep me occupied on my long voyage. My journey took two days; we were unable to board our ship until the following morning, but reservations had been made at the Queen's Hotel.

I will never forget the morning we were due to sail. I was in bed, gazing around my hotel room, when I felt my baby move for the first time. It was the most wonderful feeling, but there was no one to share my joy with—perhaps my little one was also anxious about our journey across the ocean.

Chapter Sixteen

English Soil

Once on board, I was shown to my cabin. Regrettably, I had to share with two other women—guess who had the top bunk? I was bored out of my mind and pining to be with my friends. I did not mix with those who shared my cabin and imagined everyone talking about me. I spent hours walking the deck alone, but I should have realized no one was bothered about me; they were too excited, going about their business.

I woke up one morning and realized the engines had stopped. I jumped from my bunk, threw on my clothes, and rushed on deck, then I stopped... Everything was grey. I felt the damp mist, so I pulled my coat in tighter. I glanced about and saw the grey buildings in the distance. Depression flooded in as I recognized what I thought was a 'dream' was, in fact, an omen. I pushed my thoughts away—somewhere out there, my Nan was waiting.

I got through customs then spotted her face among the crowd, waving frantically with my uncle by her side. It was so good to see this woman again. I saw her eyes drift swiftly over my body, but there was nothing to see. We caught up with my luggage and headed for the train to London, where Uncle Howard had left his car. We stopped for a brief lunch before continuing into Essex. As of yet, there was no mention of my pregnancy. I suspected that would be a subject for when we were alone.

Joan was at the gate, beaming with Charlotte in her arms. The smell of roast chicken greeted us as we entered the kitchen. We were starving. Nan and Howard were glad to be back home, but I felt lost. The omen from my dream was still with me—pulling me down.

It was late when Uncle Howard drove us to the home I would share with Nan and my baby, although parting with my infant was going to be a surprise to one and all. Everyone assumed my baby was going to be adopted, and I needed the guts to tell them otherwise.

Our flat was the upstairs of a chalet bungalow. The bedroom was at the front, and our sitting room was at the rear, with French doors leading onto a large veranda that overlooked a lovely garden with a greenhouse and flowerbeds with spring bulbs ready to bloom. We had a tiny bathroom and a galley kitchen. The flat was very small, but it was cosy. The owners were an elderly couple who lived downstairs.

Every Wednesday, Howard and his assistant, George, picked me up so I could eat lunch and spend the afternoon with my Aunt. We always found plenty to talk about but had not yet mentioned my baby—that is until we were out shopping when I stopped to look in the window of a baby linen shop. I pointed to some matinee jackets and casually said I would like to buy some for my baby. Joan sighed and said she was pleased I had decided to keep the baby. She wondered how I could possibly walk away from a child I had carried for 9 months. I swung around and told her that adoption had never entered my head, so goodness knows where *'decided'* came from. On the way home, we talked openly about my baby that was due in approximately 4 months—now all I had to do was break the news to Nan, and I did not have long to wait before the situation presented itself either.

We were in Woolworths when Nan had just made a purchase. Whilst waiting for her change, I wandered over to the baby counter. As she approached, I held up a pair of rubber pants with tiny polka dots. *"Look at these, Nan, aren't they cute?"* She ignored me and walked to the entrance. I resisted the temptation to look in her direction and fumbled in my purse. With my purchase safely clasped in my hand, I walked to where she was waiting...

"So you're keeping it then?" she said sternly. *"If you mean the baby, yes, of course,"* I said, walking briskly past into the busy street. We travelled home in silence, and the subject was never mentioned again.

Monday evening, she arrived from work carrying a bag of white baby wool. Out came the needles and baby patterns. I rested my hand on my protruding tummy and whispered, *"That went rather well, didn't it, my little one?"* I sighed with relief—my decision had been accepted, and my baby was here to stay. Now I could look forward to his/her arrival.

I often used to rest my hand on my bump reassuringly and whisper, *"No one will ever take you away from me, my little one. I promise to keep you safe."* To have a child out of wedlock in 1961 was unacceptable. Unmarried mothers were often sent away to have their babies, where they were put up for adoption. Mothers had no say in the matter, but my unborn was very precious to me and would always be so. 50 years on, no one bats an eyelid.

Nan made me some maternity smocks, and with her help, I made a nightgown for my baby. Then, I embroidered little birds and flowers around the yoke. I embroidered Nan's pillowcases and Charlotte's dresses, too. Was my mother watching, I wondered? I was doing for my baby as she had done for me 21 years ago.

One afternoon, I peeked at my Auntie's air-mail letter. I wasn't being nosey; I was interested in any news from the country that I missed. I was not surprised to see my name.

"Olivia has behaved disgracefully. She's destroyed her reputation, and she's a worry to Nan, but she's to blame for spoiling her in the first place. She allowed Olivia far too much freedom. Thank goodness Elizabeth was not alive to see what she is up to." Hurt, I replaced the letter in the envelope. But it serves me right for reading it in the first place. Then, my precious bump gave me an encouraging kick, reminding me to hold my head high.

Thursday afternoon, Howard and Joan drove to Romford on business. I had nothing to do, so I went along for the ride. We passed the shop where Nan had bought my coat some years ago. Camilla was still the manageress. Now that Father had retired, she got him a job in the office upstairs. Perhaps she wanted to keep an eye on him in case some woman did the same to her that she had done to my mother.

Howard asked if I would like to see Dad. At first, I said no, but then changed my mind. He was about to become a grandfather, so we might as well get it over with. I asked Joan and Howard to walk in ahead. Camilla came to greet them, then noticed me and stopped. Her face dropped, but she passed it off as being surprised. She greeted me with a smile, but her eyes were cold and sharp. She barely touched my cheek with her deadly kiss, then quickly pulled away. *"I'll go and get Allister. I won't be a minute,"* she said hastily, she couldn't get away quick enough. She must have been livid, having convinced my father to get rid of me, and now I was back home and pregnant. I would love to know how many swear words she muttered on her way up those stairs. She looked like she'd seen a ghost, but in a way, I suppose she had. The last time she saw me,

I was 17, and now I was a woman of 21 who looked a lot like my mother—the resemblance was striking, *'so I've been told'*.

Camilla needed to compose herself, I made her promise not to tell Dad about my homecoming then hid behind a rack of clothes.

I heard his footsteps getting close and listened as he greeted his brother and sister-in-law with handshakes. I slowly moved the clothes to one side and stepped out. He half-turned, then did a double take. How he never had a heart attack, I will never know. *"Bless my soul, good lord above,"* was all he could manage as he held me close. He kissed me repeatedly, then pulled away and hugged me again, reluctant to let me go.

I glanced at Camilla, who appeared to have turned to stone. Her clenched teeth did little to hide her resentment. I felt a bit like Cinderella looking into the face of the wicked stepmother… well if the cap fits. He turned to the wife and said he was taking a break. He needed to sit and recover from the shock, and what better way than to sit with his daughter and catch up over a cuppa.

Once seated in the café, I told him some cock and bull story about a marriage and separation - a spur-of-the-moment thing... but one should never lie, as one usually gets found out. Well, they do with me because I do not live behind lies.

Dad asked many questions but failed to give me time to answer before he was laughing and adding another *"Bless my soul"* while glancing around the café as though everyone was in on the surprise. I had barely touched my drink when he glanced at his watch and jumped up, realizing he'd been gone long enough. He knew there would be questions. But was he aware that the wife did not share his enjoyment at seeing me? I suspected not.

I remembered my reading with the sand reader regarding letters never reaching their destination—something the good wife would not want to surface. But as a schemer, she would have had no problem lying about such matters. Deceit and lies were two of her many talents. What a pity she'd gotten her claws into my dad because he often spoke of retiring from the Forces. His dream was to become a Beefeater or Yeoman of the Guards, as they are known today. To become a Beefeater, you had to be an ex-serviceman and have served a minimum of 22 years. My father exceeded that by far.

Having always been interested in British history, he knew as much about the Tower as anyone. In fact, Camilla once said, after their evening meal, Dad was talking about the Tower and placed salt and pepper shakers, coasters, and anything he could find over the table, representing various landmarks. An hour later, they had the complete map of the Tower. Dad was in his element when talking about history. But buying himself out of the forces, he never fulfilled his dream, as Yeomen lived on the premises with their families. He would have been in his element.

I have watched documentaries and appreciate what an amazing experience it would be to live in a medieval castle steeped in history dating back to 1066 and haunted by those who had committed treason. Perhaps it would not have appealed to Camilla—and for good reason.

There is a ceremony that takes place every evening called *"The Ceremony of the Keys."* It happens precisely at 9:30 when the main gates are locked. It is said to be the oldest military ceremony in the world, dating back over 700 years.

Every Sunday, Nan and I ate with Joan and Howard. Now that my homecoming was apparent, we expected visitors. We had just cleared away when their car pulled up and out stepped Dad, the stepmother, and Alice. Much to the annoyance of Camilla, the afternoon centered around me, but the woman could not disguise her irritation. When she wasn't exposing white knuckles through clenched fists, she was rubbing imaginary lotion into them. It's a wonder they weren't sore. This was something she always did when I was around—always fidgeting and looking at her watch... her cue to leave. How she managed to hide her hatred in the past, I will never know, but she had many faces to fall back on.

Dad and I were sitting on the settee talking when Alice came and perched herself on his lap. She wrapped her arms around his neck and stared at me—the sort of behavior you would expect from a little girl, not someone in her teens. Dad looked uncomfortable but said nothing. Camilla glanced at her watch, then Howard threw a spanner in the works and invited them for supper and a game of cards, which my father readily agreed to.

Camilla was sitting on Dad's left, and I was sitting on his right. With my left hand, I reached to pick a card from the table when he grabbed my hand. Lost in memories from his past, he frowned and tutted as he stared. The family watched in uncomfortable silence. Was it my hand he was looking at, or was it my mother's? Nan said our hands were identical. Camilla glared as though I had betrayed her... tough luck.

My mother passed away at the age of 21, and here sat her 21-year-old daughter with the same features and delicate hands with long fingers that he admired long ago. Now I'm back. Does my father see his late wife when he looks at me? Yes, I believe he does. I am a reminder of the woman he fell in love with 23 years ago. Perhaps Camilla recognizes the woman she betrayed, too. I am the thorn in her side that would not leave—her past has returned to haunt her.

Chapter Seventeen

A Child Is Born 1961

Time was getting close for my baby to make an appearance. I was scared and very lonely. I didn't know anyone and longed to speak to my friends. Dad and Camilla visited every couple of weeks, bringing baby items from the shop, with Camilla giving herself a generous discount. Never one to look a gift horse in the mouth, I graciously accepted, as I had no income other than what the government gave to all expectant mums.

Dad and Howard brought me a second-hand pram. It was the biggest Royal you could get—when the hood was up, I couldn't see over the top. The hood and apron had been replaced before purchase, so Howard removed the body and sprayed it white to match the upholstery, which, thankfully, was in excellent condition. Once he'd polished the chrome with what he used on the cars, no one would have guessed the pram was second-hand. I could never resist giving it a gentle rock each time I passed it in the hall. It was the Rolls Royce of prams, and it was mine.

On September 4th, I woke in discomfort. With the landlady's permission, I phoned Joan, who asked Howard to take me to their house. During the afternoon, I was having trouble concealing my discomfort and asked to be taken to the hospital. The staff paid little attention to me until late evening, but I was grateful when they gave me pethidine. I floated in and out of consciousness, then was awoken by someone shouting. What was that bright light? Who are these people, and why are they pulling me around? Then I heard the most amazing sound of a baby cry. A nurse came and placed this little bundle in my arms and introduced me to my son. I was overwhelmed. I had never known love like this in my whole life. I cradled my baby for a brief moment before he was whisked away.

My son arrived on September 5th and weighed 7lbs 12oz. By the time I reached the ward, it was buzzing with staff rattling around with the medicine trolley. Then the breakfast trolley arrived, followed by crying babies wanting to be fed. All I wanted was to sleep, but I realized there was little chance with so much activity. Then, a nurse wheeled my son in and placed his crib beside me. I gazed at my baby. I desperately wanted to hold him but was not allowed out of bed.

They say newborn babies can't see, but my son was staring up at me with the bluest of eyes. I felt so proud, having given birth to a fine and beautiful baby. I marveled at how, just yesterday, this miracle was tucked up inside me, and now he was lying here beside me. I couldn't wait to show him off. I looked at the other mums and wondered if they felt the same excitement. But they looked far too casual to feel the same joy. My baby wasn't screwed up and wrinkled like babies were supposed to look. My baby had rosy cheeks, olive skin, and blue eyes. He was perfect.

I hated the hospital. None of us were allowed to touch our babies until staff gave their permission. We had a certain time for feeding, then we had to put the baby down. If the baby was a slow drinker or fell asleep, we had to put the baby back in the crib, where he or she would stay until the next feed. If the baby cried, the nurse would whisk the crying infant to the nursery. If baby had a wet or dirty nappy after being changed, the baby had to keep it on because you were not allowed another nappy until the next feed. Any baby that cried during the night got whisked away to the nursery, where they cried themselves to sleep.

One night, they took my son. I heard him crying, so I pulled the covers over my head and cried, too. I was desperate to comfort him, but none of us were allowed anywhere near the nursery. Having a baby is supposed to be a happy time—a time of joy—but I was constantly fighting tears. I persevered for six days and then discharged myself. The staff became hostile and refused my baby a bottle or a dry nappy. I was ordered out of bed so they could prepare it for the next patient. Perhaps I wouldn't have taken such drastic measures if they had shown a little kindness. Everyone looked on in silence. I was the only mum who didn't have a male visitor, so they may have guessed I was single, which would explain their frostiness.

Dad and Camilla visited on Sunday, but having discharged myself, they were made to wait outside until I was packed and ready to leave. Camilla and I were sitting in the back of the car when she began to rock back and forth. She couldn't wait to hold my baby. I am not one to hold a grudge (tongue in cheek), but seeing as they had bought most of his layette, I handed my son over and watched... *"Don't hold him too tight... lift his head... don't rock him... mind the door handle."*

Once home, I felt relaxed, knowing I could hold and comfort my baby whenever he needed me.

It was a few weeks before I took him out in his pram. If we got caught in a shower, I wiped and polished the pram as soon as we arrived home. I owned the Rolls Royce of Prams, with amazing suspension easing it up and down curbs so I didn't disturb my passenger. Unable to see over the hood, I often crashed into ice cream stands and sent them clattering to the ground.

As a new mum, I was coping well, but Nan was never far away with sensible advice, always there if and when I needed it. With her years of knowledge and experience, I knew I couldn't go wrong— she had raised her family successfully me included.

When I moved my son into a "big boy's" cot, I used to creep in and sit on my bed so I could slide my hand through the bars and rest my finger in the palm of his hand. As soon as he felt my finger, he'd clamp his little fist shut. Nan would often creep in and whisper that she was about to make tea. I have so many beautiful memories that will stay with me forever.

I named my son Craig Hawkins.

Chapter Eighteen

George Johnson

The landlady reminded Nan that she did not want children under her roof, so we found a ground-floor flat near Howard's workshop. Our new home was at the back of a large pre-war house, the entrance was down a narrow sideway that was a bit of a squeeze with my pram. Our kitchen/diner was drab and needed a facelift, so Howard offered to pay George to decorate, provided we supplied the materials—which suited us. It also suited George, who was a gambler and never missed an opportunity to increase his wage packet. Plus, there was no traveling; George passed our house on his way home—he lived at number 38, just a few doors down, so it couldn't have been easier.

Next to the kitchen/diner was the lounge, and our bedroom was at the back with French doors leading to a beautiful garden where I could wheel Craig out for his morning naps.

Howard told us that George was married with children, but his personal life was none of our business—he was just there to transform our kitchen. George was no stranger to me. He was always in the car when Howard picked me up on Wednesdays. He was a nice-looking guy with reddish-blond hair, a lovely smile, and a fine set of teeth. He never missed an opportunity to wink when I looked his way. I missed being around people my own age, so I enjoyed the brief attention every Wednesday. And now, this smiley, flirty guy was going to transform our kitchen.

Around this time, my father and Howard received a letter stating that their wealthy Uncle John in America had passed away and left a fortune. Uncle John's siblings had all passed, so his nieces and nephews stood to inherit his wealth. Howard and my father were two of the nephews, there was a lot of excitement within the family as they spoke of their newfound millionaire relative.

Nan greeted George on his arrival with a cup of tea, then left us to strip the walls. Before we knew it, it was 8 o'clock, and we'd barely done anything. Within a week, George was talking about his marital problems. He said he hated going home sometimes because he and his wife argued. He added that if it weren't for his little girls, he would have left home long ago. I was flattered that he trusted me enough to talk openly about his personal life. Most of the conversation was about his marriage.

We were into our third week, and the kitchen still wasn't finished. Nan would poke her head around the door to tell us to keep the noise down so we wouldn't disturb Craig. George seemed to enjoy the time he spent in our home, even if he was decorating. Howard said their marriage was far from solid—George and his wife were always separating. She was either walking out, or he was leaving her.

We eventually finished the kitchen, but George was still stopping by for a cup of tea on his way home. One night, we were disturbed by Lucy banging on the door. *"I know you're in there, George! Don't bother to come home! I have a witness here—I'm calling my solicitor in the morning. I'm divorcing you!"* Then she stormed off, leaving the gate open. The outburst took George by surprise. Nan came in to see what all the noise was about and looked none too pleased when I told her. George stubbed out his cigarette, then put on his jacket to face the music. I wondered what awaited him—poor guy.

The following day, I was feeding Craig his lunch when George burst in, *"She's leaving! She's leaving! She's leaving!"* he said dancing around the kitchen table, he had seen the van outside with Lucy and her father loading it up. True to her word, Lucy was leaving.

It wasn't until George received the divorce papers that he realized Lucy was serious. She got herself a job with the solicitor handling the divorce, and as an employee, she would likely get perks and be prioritized over other cases. Smart lady.

I wrote to Connie with our new address and mentioned how George had transformed our kitchen. I also told her about the problems George was having at home. She saw danger in the situation and warned me of impending doom.

I never saw George again. He tried winning Lucy back with letters and flowers. He even hung around her parents' house at night, hoping to speak with her, but she wouldn't see him. She returned his pleading letters and refused all contact (this information came via Howard). George had cheated on her once too often, and I was the last straw. But there was no affair—just harmless flirting. Besides, Nan was always in the next room, so an affair would have been impossible. She was constantly walking in with her empty cup, eager to see our progress or telling us to keep the laughter down. We had been in the flat for four months when we were forced to move because of the woman next door, whom we'll call Mrs. X. She played merry hell with everyone. She had been in and out of the mental hospital and had just been released on medication. She was a danger to herself and others. Why they continued to release her into society was beyond me. She was always throwing empty liquor bottles over the fence and then screeching with laughter. It was only a matter of time before she aimed one at the pram. Until Nan found somewhere safer, she suggested that Craig and I stay with Joan.

Nan decided to take the day off work to visit William's mother-in-law, Ethel. It was here that she met Crystal, whom she had not seen since she was a child. Crystal enjoyed catching up over the fun times we spent at Christmas. She was surprised to learn I had a son and was keen to know more, and Nan was more than happy to oblige. Hearing my social life was non-existent, she invited me to spend the weekend with her and her Polish husband. I called the following day and arranged to meet her at Fenchurch Street on Friday. I recognized her immediately; there was no mistaking that broad grin.

Crystal brought me up to date with her news. She had been married for a year and lived in a large, swanky flat in Maida Vale. Stan—10 years her senior—had been a bachelor until he met Crystal, so he knew his way around the kitchen well and had dinner on the table when she arrived from work. Stan loved introducing guests to his Polish dishes without appearing intimidating in any way, shape, or form, but Crystal could not boil an egg, which she happily confessed to. As a youngster, she was banned from the kitchen because she was clumsy—she would either drop, spill or break things. Only when it was time to serve was she allowed to collect cutlery. Consequently, she had no kitchen skills until Stan came into her life.

We entered the flat and were greeted with the amazing aroma of Stan's Polish curry. It wasn't hot but beautifully spicy—the curry accompanied his homemade onion chutney.

I enjoyed my weekend with these fine people—not that we did anything special except sit around talking over drinks, eating leftovers, and playing records, something I had not done since my days in Canada. I was pleased when they offered to drive me home to Joan's, where Nan was waiting with Craig. Joan and Howard had not seen Crystal since she was a child, and I was anxious for them to see what a lovely person she had grown into and introduce them to Stan. A couple of weeks later, Crystal wrote to say she had holiday owing and invited Craig and me to spend the week with them. I did not hesitate in accepting her kind invitation and spent all week preparing.

They arrived just after lunch on Saturday. I watched Stan strap Craig's cot to the roof of his Vauxhall. Then, he loaded the boot with the mattress and the rest of our luggage. Once Craig had eaten, we were off.

Sunday afternoon, Crystal introduced me to her old flame Elliott, who called 'unexpectedly.' I was amazed Stan did not mind knowing he was an old flame, but this is where trust comes into a relationship. Elliott was a real gentleman; each time I sat, he held my chair. When I reached for a cigarette, he was there with a lighter. After our first meeting, Elliott visited every evening until it was time for me to return home. I was delighted when he asked if he could visit at the weekend when his shift finished at midnight.

I liked to wake early Saturday morning to see him sleeping in the front seat of his car with a blanket.

A few weeks later, he took Craig and me to meet his parents, who lived in a converted mansion. We drove through these tall iron gates to their apartment, which was hidden by trees and shrubs. It looked very grand. His parents made Craig and me welcome. Then his mother showed me to my room, which housed a single bed and a cot...they were decent people and a little old-fashioned, so there would be no sharing beds under their roof. Back home, life with

Craig returned to normal with Elliott visiting at weekends. One night, we had just finished a late-night snack when my aunt said they were retiring. Elliott followed them upstairs to get his bedding but was gone for ages. I wondered if everything was okay, then I heard him on the stairs. He walked in, threw his bedding on the armchair, and came to where I was sitting. He said Howard had cornered him on the landing and gave his permission for Elliott to have sex with me. I was speechless. Surely, that decision was mine to make, but Howard said something else that really concerned Elliott. All he was prepared to say was, *"If your uncle continues to speak about you the way he does, it will be detrimental to your future and could change the person you are."* I'm not sure if that makes sense, but those were his words, so whatever Howard said must have been pretty bad to have disturbed Elliott the way it had.

Nan and I eventually moved into a first-floor flat just off the seafront. It was a large pre-war converted house. We had a small kitchen adjacent to the bathroom and a sitting room. The bedroom was big enough for a double bed and Craig's cot. It was a little small, but at least we were together. Elliott was still visiting at the weekend, but with nowhere to sleep, he stayed with Howard and Joan. Howard usually cooked a late breakfast on Sunday and insisted Elliott ate before leaving, so I never saw him until the afternoon.

One Sunday, Elliott was about to leave for home, then said he had to pick something up he'd left at my aunt's. I thought nothing more until Wednesday when he failed to phone. Puzzled, I waited for the weekend, but he never arrived. So, I called him and was shocked when he said he would not be coming to Southend again. He said goodbye and hung up. I could not understand his change of heart when, six days earlier he was warm and caring as we kissed before he drove away. Hurt and bewildered, I accepted his painful rejection.

Crystal was amazed when I told her. She knew Elliott was smitten, so to have ended the relationship without explanation did not make sense to her either. But she had reservations about Howard and revealed something else that shocked me.

Apparently, the day Craig and I returned from our week with them, Stan was upstairs assembling Craig's cot when Howard said something offensive about me. So, Stan quickly put him in his place. Stan was smart enough to recognize jealous slander. He was a man of the world and knew I was respectable; otherwise, he would never have made me welcome and encouraged my visits.

Elliott was a gentleman and treated me like a lady, whereas Howard was crude and enjoyed making inappropriate advances, knowing it repulsed me. Perhaps Howard was envious of the happiness Elliott and I shared…perhaps he was jealous of the future that lay before us? I think he was jealous of any man who was attracted to me, and as he was the last person to speak to Elliott, I am convinced he was responsible for his hasty retreat.

At the time, I was unaware of how Howard spoke ill of me. Perhaps I could have defended myself, but then—how could I defend myself if I had no knowledge my reputation was under attack?

I missed Elliott and our weekends together. Craig and I could have had a future with him and his fine parents, but Howard's jealousy got in the way.

An update on Crystal and Stan—they eventually divorced, and Crystal flew to Australia to be with her parents. I never knew what happened to Stan.

Chapter Nineteen

The Proposal 1963

I was doing a little casual work in a restaurant along the seafront every Sunday from noon until 6 pm. One morning, I boarded the bus and was amazed to see the conductor was none other than George. He was busy dishing out tickets, so we never spoke, but as I left, he passed on his regards to the family. A few weeks later, I made my way to Joan's, where Nan was waiting with Craig. I let myself in as Nan called, *"There's someone waiting to see you, miss."* I poked my head around the door and was surprised to see George. We talked casually for an hour. Then, he offered to drive us home. On the journey, he told us he was divorced and living the life of a bachelor. George dropped us outside the flat and asked if he could see me on Wednesday, which was his night off. Three weeks later, he proposed, and I accepted.

I was still spending Wednesday afternoons with Joan. We were discussing my upcoming marriage when she wisely asked, *"What would you do if Johnny called and wanted to see you and Craig?"* She gave the question a moment to sink in, then continued, *"And what would you say if he asked you to marry him and take you back to Canada?"* I was speechless. She knew I was getting married for all the wrong reasons, but I didn't want to be that unmarried mother with everyone whispering behind my back. This was my chance to rectify my mistake. Besides, I didn't want Craig to grow up as an only child; I wanted him to have siblings and a father who came home at night. Anyway, getting married for companionship rather than love might actually work.

With no money, I chose something from my wardrobe. There were no invites because I didn't know anyone. As of yet, I had not met his mother or stepfather, so it didn't bother me that he didn't want them to attend.

Nan moved in with Joan, and the flat we once shared became our home. But within days, my husband was staying out at night. His first excuse was that the keys to his stepfather's garage were lost, so he had to sleep on the premises. I can't remember his other excuses, but married life was nothing like I expected—it was over before it began. George found fault with everything and was unreliable with money. One week, I had no housekeeping because he said he'd lost his wage packet. Another time, he took the rent money and book to pay the landlord. He came home the following day and said he'd lost the money. Being a gambler, he probably lost it in the betting office so Craig and I survived on whatever was in the pantry.

Within the month, I suspected I was pregnant. George denied the baby as being his—cheeky bugger. I didn't know anyone, although my pregnancy had not been confirmed, I recognized the symptoms. George made life as difficult as possible. He complained if his meal was not ready, but how could I have a meal on the table when he came home at all hours and sometimes not at all? I suspected he created rows as an excuse to go elsewhere. One morning, I was reading a letter from Johnny, who wrote asking for pictures of Craig. George came home unexpectedly (having been out all night) and used the letter as an excuse to cause another row, which upset Craig.

With no regular money, Nan got me a part-time job in the shirt factory. I was operating the button and buttonhole machines. Nan worked at Joan's as their outdoor machinist.

I was getting used to my husband staying out then one night, I woke as the bedroom door creaked open - in the darkness, I saw a silhouette looming then George leapt onto the bed. He tried to goad me into an argument but I did not reciprocate so he slapped my face…I was startled and upset so I spent the night in the armchair. The following day, one of the women noticed how quiet I was. She asked if I was okay and I burst into tears. The girls gathered around then the supervisor appeared, by which time I was sobbing. I never show emotion in public so I surprised myself with my tearful outburst.

George barely supported us so I avoided the milkman - it was only a matter of time before he stopped leaving my daily supply. When Nan realised we had little to eat, she started bringing food parcels with instructions not to give any to him if - and when he returned. I left the factory when it became difficult working the machines and juggling my time with Craig and Nan's work. I applied for help and was relieved when I was given a weekly allowance.

One afternoon, I answered the door to this well-dressed lady who I suspected was his Mother. Gladys wasn't a bit as I expected, so I was weary as to what to say to this stranger. Would she have a sympathetic ear, I wondered - probably not so I allowed her to do the talking. Gladys was surprised when I told her we were married. She talked a lot about his wife Lucy and said George had many affairs while they were married, then she said something rather odd…apparently, she told George *if you ever hurt that girl, I'll kill you;* what a strange thing for a mother to say, I can't imagine what the purpose of her visit other than curiosity because I never saw her again, further-more she never enquired over the child I was expecting.

I will never forget the Saturday Nan called with another food parcel. *Come on, Miss, I want to know what's been going on.* The girls had obviously told her about my tearful outburst. She never let up until she'd prized every detail out of me. *You just wait till I see him the bugger I'll give him something you see if I don't* I had never seen her so angry I wondered what she had up her sleeve then George walked in having been out all night...poor timing George, he beamed when he saw Nan but it didn't take her long to wipe the grin from his face, after a few choice words she gave him a shove, he turned to leave then realised she was close behind so he quickened his pace and ran downstairs, before he could reach the street door she grabbed Craig's push chair and rammed it into his legs, I watched as he tried dodging the pushchair but she had him trapped *So you've been hitting this girl have you...how dare you hit her she's done nothing to deserve it,* RAM *she is a good girl and far too good for you ya bugger, what sort of a thing are you to hit her when she's pregnant,* RAM *you're nothing but an animal you should be bloody well ashamed of yourself* with the push chair firmly in her hands I watched him jump from one foot to another trying to ward off the attack *Well I won't have you treat her like that your nothing but a bully, well I'll hit you and see how you bloody well like it,* RAM *and if you ever lay a finger on her again I'll brain you* (whatever that meant) he continued waving his arms and jumping about trying to dodge the pushchair, I watched in awe...how brave was this woman? I marvelled at her fearlessness as Craig's pushchair made contact until eventually, he escaped. He ran down the footpath like a bat out of hell, jumped in his car and disappeared. One thing for sure he would not mess with her again.

This fiery woman was prepared to go to any length to protect her granddaughter. Perhaps she was reliving her younger days when she herself had lived with abuse, but she didn't have a grandmother to turn to—unlike me.

Uncle Howard told me where my husband was spending his nights and offered to drive me to the address. He watched as I walked up the path and rang the bell. A woman answered, so I asked to speak to George, but she said he wasn't there. *"Well, when you see him, could you tell him I have some money for him?"* Amazingly enough, he appeared. *"It's okay, George. I only wanted to know where you're living, that's all."* I walked away without looking back. Now, I was the woman on the doorstep asking for my husband, but with one huge difference—I did not love him.

A month later, George begged me to give him another chance. Perhaps I had misjudged him, maybe this other woman was just a fling. So, I agreed—much to Nan's horror and dismay.

We moved into a ground-floor flat on Huntingdon Road. The owner was an elderly woman who lived upstairs, but in less than a week, my husband was staying out nights.

Nan had moved back into her flat and was caring for Craig while working from home, just as she had done with me years ago. I looked forward to Sundays when she brought my son to visit, but as the evening grew closer, I became depressed knowing it would be another week before I would see them again. I used to walk them to the bus stop, feeling low. Then I'd see the bus turn the corner and hold onto Craig for one more hug, one more kiss. God, how I hated seeing the bus disappear with my two favorite people on it. One Sunday, I jumped on the bus as it was about to pull away. I picked Craig up, sat him on my lap, and nuzzled my face into his little neck.

I had no money, but Nan was more than happy to pay for me… now, it was my turn to stay out all night.

I was peeling potatoes when the news broke that President Kennedy had been assassinated. That night, I ate alone and went to bed early, but I was woken in the early hours by someone climbing in through the bedroom window. I tried to make a dash for the door, then realized it was George—drunk. I didn't engage with his goading, so he punched me in the face. Thank goodness Craig was with Nan, so he didn't have to witness these upsetting scenes or my tears.

The following day, Nan and Howard helped me pack. I couldn't wait to go home, to have the stability of a normal life with the two people who meant more to me than anything. I would later learn that George had been watching us pack through the pantry window where he had been hiding. I couldn't help but wonder who had told him about my plan to leave... hmmm.

Upset by the latest events, I phoned my father and asked if we could meet the next day. I needed some fatherly advice. He was waiting for me on the platform when I arrived. Smiling, I walked over, but I didn't get the greeting I expected. His expression was sombre as he shook his head from side to side. It was the wife.

Dad walked me to the car where Camilla sat, her nose buried in a newspaper. I greeted her as I climbed in, but she ignored me. I knew our journey was going to be difficult. As soon as we arrived home, she scurried into the kitchen like a rat, slamming cupboards and crashing about.

Father took me into the lounge/diner and placed a chair in the bay window, then pulled up a chair for himself. Leaning towards me, he shook his head and blew imaginary bubbles but never took his eyes off the serving hatch—waiting for instructions. I told him about my predicament, but it was clear he wasn't listening. Then she called him to the kitchen, and he took his chair to the table, eating what she had prepared. The meal must have choked him, having to eat in front of his pregnant daughter without offering her a drink. After gulping down his food, he took his plate to the kitchen, where she was still slamming things around and muttering.

Dad returned and said they had to shop but would drop me in the market so I could catch my bus home. The bus was an hourly service – fingers crossed I would not have to wait long. He helped me out of the car, kissed me on the cheek, and drove off.

I had been rejected because Nan called into the shop a few months ago and spoke to my Father without *her* being present. All Nan did was praise Craig and myself, but in doing so, she played into the hands of the devil woman who accused us of grovelling for a slice of Dad's inheritance. Just for the record, my Son did not receive a bar of chocolate.

Disappointed with the rejection, I made an appointment with a solicitor in town for the following week. Mr. Beecham was lovely; he could see I was nervous, but he put me at ease from the moment I walked in and made Craig comfortable with some toys. He talked about his little boy, who was about the same age. Mr. Beecham said I was not eligible for a divorce for three years and suggested I apply for legal separation.

My case was heard at the Magistrates' Court. George was asked if he would like a duty solicitor, but he refused and said he would be representing himself.

Mr. Beecham introduced my case to the Court. George was called first. He tried to discredit me and said some horrible things, none of which he could prove. He told the Judge I was writing to old boyfriends in Canada, which infuriated him, and he was not prepared to give our marriage another chance as I was untrustworthy. He tried to make me look guilty when all he succeeded in doing was incriminating himself.

When it was Mr. Beecham's time to speak, he expressed to the Judge that there was one man I occasionally wrote to, and it was my little boy's father who was within his rights to enquire after his son. Furthermore, there is nothing suggestive in the letters. *I have them here, My Lord if you wish to read them…* I don't think the father poses any threat to this case, living so far away. *Besides, it is not my client that is untrustworthy, My Lord, but Mr. Johnson himself.* Mr. Beecham told the Judge that George was living with another woman and had been doing so throughout our marriage. He spoke about the abuse and how Craig and I had been left with no food or money, and if it wasn't for the Grandmother, Craig and I would have gone hungry. The Judge listened as my adviser described how George had driven me out of the home. He spoke until all the facts had been presented to the Court.

The Judge asked George to stand. "Deserting your wife in her condition is despicable." George was standing with legs astride and arms folded. *"If your Honour pleases, I did not desert my wife. She walked out on me."*

The Judge silenced him with his gavel before responding with a raised voice.

Mr. Johnson… your wife gave you every opportunity to behave like a husband, but you made a mockery of the marriage. You tried and succeeded in driving her out of her home, which she was reluctant to do. I find your behaviour appalling.

The Judge studied the face of the man standing before him. *YOU* said the Judge sternly. *YOU are responsible for your wife leaving the matrimonial home because you drove her out… she left against her will when you made it impossible for her to stay.* Taking a moment to observe the offender, the Judge served his sentence.

I hereby find you guilty of desertion. Now, about maintenance – to avoid you having any contact with your wife, I order you to make weekly payments to the Court for her to collect until such times when the child is born. Then, it will increase. If you fail to make regular payments, a warrant will be issued for your arrest. I hope that is clear.

The Judge banged his gavel on the Bench... *Court adjourned.* George stormed out in anger.

Mr. Beecham concluded that the reason he wanted to give our marriage another chance was to drive me out so he could accuse me of desertion, but his plan backfired. Thank goodness the Judge – with the help of Mr. Beecham – was wise enough to see through him.

I never knew what happened to Lucy and his daughters, but they were well shot of him.

Chapter Twenty

My Son Robert

We moved from our one-bedroom flat into a ground-floor flat close to town, which was so much nicer. We had a sitting room, two bedrooms, and a garden. Unfortunately, the kitchen was in a terrible state. The previous tenants had a personal issue with the landlady and did a lot of damage before leaving. They wrenched cupboards from the walls, leaving holes the size of golf balls. The floor was covered in bitumen where tiles had been ripped up, and wallpaper had been ripped off the walls. What they left was greasy and discoloured. What little knowledge I had from watching George decorate was going to come in handy. Fortunately, I was never one to turn my back on hard work and loved a challenge. Personally, I think the owner should have made the flat liveable or helped with the cost at least.

It was ages before I made the kitchen presentable, where we were able to eat at the table. The praise I received encouraged me to start on the hall. Then I decorated my bedroom. It was tough going, but once finished, the flat looked a lot different from when we first arrived, and it was our home. I was putting my bedroom furniture in place when my baby decided to show an interest in the outside world. Exhausted, I retired early but was glad when dawn broke. On April 24th, the midwife arrived with the forms for me to take into the hospital to say I was booked for home care and to discharge me after 24 hours. She noticed I was still in discomfort from when she arrived and asked Nan to phone the ambulance immediately. I could not understand the urgency, but within minutes, we were on our way to the hospital with blue lights. Half an hour later, my little treasure arrived, weighing 7lb 7oz. This little guy had the most beautiful eyes. He had fair skin, freckles, and reddish-blond hair. I couldn't wait to introduce Craig to the little one.

I was discharged on Monday afternoon and driven home by ambulance. The nurse handed my son over to Nan as Craig ran past my open arms and asked if his baby brother could play with him in the garden. I named my son Robert – Robert being my Father's middle name.

Robert was 5 weeks old when Dad and Camilla turned up unannounced as though nothing had happened. Dad followed me into the dining room and discreetly tucked a £5 note in my hand and told me not to say anything.

The following year, Camilla told us Alice was getting married and wanted Craig as pageboy. She went into detail about his outfit, but there was no mention of Nan or Robert. If it hadn't been for Craig, I would not have attended.

The wedding party was in full swing when Dad took me outside to speak where it was a little less noisy. But it was chilly, so we sheltered in the pub next door and had a quiet drink. When we returned, he took me in his arms and whisked me onto the floor (the last time we danced, I was in the arms of both parents). Dad told me he'd bought Alice's wedding dress but had always dreamt of buying my bridal gown and walking me down the aisle. Then he picked me up and swung me round and said how much he loved me, but he didn't realise the music had stopped and everyone was watching. Then I noticed Medusa glaring at us and rubbing her hands together. *Tut-tut, what would people think, seeing Allister dancing with his daughter?* My tipsy father would have felt the wrath of her tongue the following morning.

Robert was 12 months old when I started work in the canteen at the airport. The canteen was for the workmen and was situated in the hangar, which could be pretty noisy when they were testing the engines. My hours were 5 p.m. until 10 p.m. I got a lot of attention from the men, but there was only one I was particularly drawn to, who reminded me of Johnny. The only difference was – Johnny was reserved and did not have a chat-up line, unlike Terry, who didn't waste time making his move and offered me a lift home. Terry confided in me about his home. He told me he was separated but still lived at the house, which was up for sale. He had been advised not to leave the property until a sale had been secured because he could lose everything. I admired his honesty and looked forward to lifts home if his shift coincided with mine.

Terry introduced me to Norma and Collin, who both worked days. We occasionally visited them in the evening if my shift coincided with Terry's, but I always left their flat tipsy. Collin was over-generous when mixing drinks, and I could not afford to be nursing a hangover with my boys to care for, so I began making excuses. Eventually, I stopped going.

I handed in my notice after 12 months when I discovered I was pregnant. Nan was far from happy but accepted the pregnancy better than I thought. Seeing how effortlessly I coped with my boys put her mind at rest, although she could not deny her disappointment at seeing me with another baby. I suspected my next addition was a girl because the whole pregnancy was different. Six months into the pregnancy, I ended the relationship when I suspected Terry was seeing someone else.

I answered the door one evening and was surprised to see George - Howard had told him I was pregnant. Perhaps he wanted to see for himself so he could get his maintenance reduced. Never mind, he was still living with another woman, dam Howard for opening his mouth. George used Robert as an excuse for his brief visit but paid little attention to our son. He stayed about 15 minutes, then I offered to walk part of the way as I had a birthday card to mail…as we walked, he revealed an appalling secret…

You know - when we married, I never loved you in fact I despised you. Lucy was the only woman I ever loved. She divorced me because of you - she thought we were having an affair, YOU were the reason she walked out and I hated you for that so I made up my mind to hurt you the way you hurt her - I only married you so I could make you suffer the way you made her suffer, I wanted you to feel the same hurt and pain you put her through, I decided long ago I was going to drive you in the ground and destroy you the way you destroyed her - I despised you then and I despise you now then he walked away…I was speechless. His malicious tongue cut deep into me like a hot knife through butter. If I live to be 100, I will never forget his intention of wanting to destroy the mother of his child. It's a pity I never got a chance to tell him I never loved him either but I was reeling from the shock which hurt more than anything he had put me through during our farce of a marriage. I didn't think it was possible to hate someone enough to marry them purely for revenge. That is as low as anyone can possibly stoop. What a pity he wasn't man enough to take responsibility for his actions instead of blaming me. He was the guilty one who enjoyed taunting his wife. All I was guilty of was soaking up the attention. Nan was speechless; she spent all evening shaking her head and muttering her indignant views; she was fuming; no wonder George looked shifty when he called that evening. Perhaps he remembers their last meeting, in which case he'd do well to avoid her. If she knew where he lived she would have shot round there.

Now I know why his mother said *if you hurt that girl, I will kill you* she knew what he had planned. She was warning me of the tsunami that was heading my way further; she never enquired about her grandchild. Showing any interest would have been futile. She knew the marriage was doomed but blind to his faults, she would not betray her only child who she loved deeply; unfortunately, he was not worthy of her love.

I remember his mother telling me how George used to bounce back to Lucy after his affairs. The first time was when she was expecting their first child - Claire was 10 months old when he returned. Lucy must have loved him deeply to forgive him time and again...until the night she came face to face with me who she assumed was having an affair with the man she loved. The ironic thing is we were not having an affair; we had never embraced or even kissed. Nan was in the next room and was always walking in unexpectedly. George teased his wife repeatedly until she believed we were in a relationship. He enjoyed making her jealous but his teasing backfired and he's lived with the torment ever since. He got his comeuppance. How's that for retribution? What a jerk.

Through Howard, I am led to believe George told Lucy he had not been unfaithful but she did not believe him. If I had been called upon, I would have been happy to declare his innocence but George got what he deserved. He lost the only woman he ever loved and the torture has troubled him for years but instead of taking responsibility for his actions, he chose to seek revenge on me but I was a victim, the same as Lucy.

He who lives by the sword - shall die by the sword.

Connie and I kept in regular touch; I wrote every episode of my life and mailed it off. I knew her reply would be stern - always lecturing me but in the nicest way and with love. She was appalled with the situations I succeeded in getting myself into. Quoting her letter: -

Olivia, for Christ's sake, what is going on over there? What the hell…you get shot of one arsehole, then you pick up another. What the hell is this Terry guy up to anyway, treating you the way he does? I'm surprised you allowed the creep into your life after what that bastard husband did to you, you are so naïve my God your poor Nana must be beside herself, listen to me sweetie, you have been starved of true love and affection for so long you readily accept any poor imitation from those ignorant bastards…honey they don't deserve you, now you listen to me okay, you get those little kids into some sort of crèche, wipe your arse and find a job then perhaps you will meet someone decent that is worthy of the love that you have to give so before it's too late ditch those no good son of a bitches, you are too good for those slimy bastards they are not worthy of you or the love you have to give, they are destroying that beautiful person that we know and love, come on honey pull your socks up, if you want to come back to Canada Ivan and I will help all we can, you think about everything I have said and keep this letter handy, read it - and read it some more, those fucking creeps need a kick up the arse, if you were here with us Ivan would sort them out for sure, my heart bleeds when I think of the pain you have endured needlessly, come home to us sweetie we will look out for you, okay darlin' end of lecture. Now…how is your Nana doing? She is a beautiful lady. Don't forget to say hi from us.

I sailed through my pregnancy with the exception of a little nausea in the early mornings. I had arranged for a home delivery, and then on March 17th, I took my boys to the surgery with suspected chickenpox and to inform the doctor that my contractions had started. The following evening, at 7:45, my little girl arrived, weighing 7lb 9oz. She had the biggest dark eyes, long lashes, and thick curly hair. I could hardly believe I had the little girl I had always wanted. Unfortunately, my boys were unable to meet their baby sister when it was confirmed that they both had chickenpox.

I named my daughter Tiffany Elizabeth, with Elizabeth being my mother's name. I couldn't wait to shop and buy pretty dresses.

Chapter Twenty-One

Collin Wainwright 1967

I met a lovely couple with two children the same age as my boys. I liked Jill from the moment we were introduced and was delighted when she invited me to join them on Saturday evening for drinks. On my arrival, Bernard guided me into their warm sitting room where Jill was sitting by the open fire. We drank homemade wine and talked about children, hobbies, food and gardening until it was time for me to leave then Jill suggested meeting during the day so we could introduce our children.

Bernard was a self-employed carpet fitter and Jill took care of their home and family. Every Thursday, she baked starting with the family fruit cake and little cakes for lunch boxes. She shopped economically which is something I had not had much experience with. She cooked tasty delights like stuffed marrow cheese soufflés and grew most of their vegetables. It fascinated me to see her wander down the garden with a sharp knife and colander and return with something fresh for the pot. I could ask her anything about cooking she was always ready to share tips without being a know-it-all and never bragged. Jill and Bernard were self-sufficient rather like Felicity Kendal in 'The Good Life'.

Sometimes Jill spent the afternoon with Nan and me but I did not have her kitchen skills so there were no fancy cakes to offer with our tea. Nan was pleased I had made friends with this fine couple now that Crystal was no longer in my life. Nan enjoyed Jill's visits as much as me, it was the only time she turned off her machine.

It was late afternoon when Nan and I took the children for a walk along the seafront. We brought chips to eat on the way home and noticed they were advertising for evening staff. I applied and was hired with an immediate start. A perk that pleased Nan was - they sent me home with fish and chips.

One evening, I was about to leave when the heavens opened, with no coat or brolly decided to visit Norma and Collin. I had to pass their flat anyway and it was less than 5 minutes away; relieved to see their lights on, I knocked.

Collin guided me into the sitting room before telling me Norma had gone back to her husband. I told him the saga of Terry while he tucked into my fish supper. I struggled through my drink then he drove me home.

After my random visit, Collin started calling round and pestering me for a date, cripes he was the same age as my father. In fact, it was because of his age I felt safe in his company. I reminded him I was not interested in dating anyone which I made very clear the night he ate my fish supper but not wanting to offend him, I made a lame excuse about not being fair, leaving Nan. Collin was not about to be put off and suggested getting a sitter so she could join us...my heart sank. Each time the doorbell rang, I cringed then I noticed he was more attentive towards Nan so the family began teasing her about having a toy boy which amused her - she thought he was charming.

It was a couple of weeks later when he mentioned taking us out again. Now that Nan had got to know him, she seemed keen on the idea and said she would speak to Edith, our neighbour opposite. Edith was a private person who did not mix but would call across and ask after my children if she saw either one of us. When Nan spoke to her, she jumped at the chance of babysitting. With no family of her own, she said we would be doing her kindness, Collin was delighted.

We spent a pleasant evening at the Chequers pub in the village of Canewdon. It made a change getting dressed up for an evening out because Terry never took me anywhere, we made ourselves comfortable by the open log fire and left Collin ordering drinks. When the last orders were called, he disappeared and returned with Cointreau for Nan and myself. The pub was almost empty when we staggered outside and fell into his car.

Collin invited us out for lunch on Sunday but we always ate with Joan and Howard so he offered to drive us there and pick us up that evening. Nan said it was a kind thought and invited him for coffee on our return. Collin spent the evening talking about his family and confessed he was the black sheep. He did not keep in touch with anyone especially his daughter Pauline. The last he heard, she was living with her Mother who - between them cooked up some cock and bull story about rape to get him put away but it failed to impress the Judge and the case was thrown out. Collin also had two sons. Barry lived locally and Leslie lived in Clacton with his wife. Collin did have a sister Rita who he hadn't seen in years then there was his brother, Simon. Other than that he was pretty much isolated. Nan yawned and looked at the clock. He apologised for keeping us up and left.

I was angry when he started walking round the sideway; my heart sank seeing his mop of white hair above the fence heading towards our side gate just as Terry used to. I resented his visits and disappeared which wasn't easy in our little flat, then he began buying treats for our tea so Nan invited him to join us then he offered to do chores.

Eager to make headway, he took things one step further - he arrived in despair and told Nan he had to be out of his flat by the end of the week. He'd been searching for somewhere all day but had found nothing...he spent the entire evening pulling on Nan's heartstrings but I wasn't buying into his story. *I don't know what I am going to do* he said with his head down, looking forlorn. He continued his tale of woe until Nan offered to put him up for a few days, the change in his expression was alarming he couldn't thank her enough. Oh Nan, what have you done? I mourned but it was too late.

Collin and Barry arrived Friday evening with his gas cooker and cocktail bar and covered them with tarpaulin outside. They put his double bed in my bedroom and spent the rest of the night back and forth until he'd crammed everything he owned into our flat; that night Nan made him a bed on our three-seater settee. A couple of weeks later, he said he'd lost his job...well it didn't take much to figure that with no job, he would not be moving anytime soon could it get any worse, having secured a place in our home he made his intentions clear it was me he was interested after all, he followed me around and interfered with my routine. I woke one morning to find him in the kitchen doing the family wash in our twin tub. I cannot remember Nan's reaction but I found it intrusive.

Another time, he shut himself in the kitchen, cooked dinner, and cleared away. Mrs. Softly from upstairs thought we were lucky and said he was too good to be true, but my space was being invaded, and I didn't like it. If I went into the kitchen, he'd say, *Are you going to make Tiffany's bottles now, darling?* (Of course, I am, you bloody fool, and I am not your darling.) I muttered, slamming the door. If I looked in a drawer or opened a cupboard, he wanted to know what I was looking for—maybe he knew where it was, or maybe he could help me find it. Sometimes I'd turn, and he'd be behind me. It startled me to see him leering down at me with a grin. I was completely baffled when he said he loved me... but how was that possible? He didn't know me. He had never held me in his arms, neither had we kissed... *perish the thought.* So I did everything possible to avoid being left alone where he could whisper sweet nothings. When I refused his advances, he got nasty but made sure Nan never heard. She thought he was charming, and he wasn't going to jeopardize her image.

Collin loved to gossip. I was shocked when he told our neighbors, *I won't be happy until I have made that girl my wife, but there will be no children because I am sterile due to an accident many years ago...* What the hell? I was furious with him for discussing something so intimate with our neighbors. I did not want a relationship with him or with anyone. I was happy on my own, but he insisted I needed someone to look after me and that my children needed a father. I could feel the carpet being dragged from under my feet.

He wanted to know everything—where I went, what I was doing, and why. He drove me nuts. I wished I had the courage to tell him what I really thought but could not find it in my heart to hurt or insult him. But he would not accept my gentle refusals. I could understand if I was bringing an affair to an end, but there was no affair, so where was all this shit coming from? Perhaps, living under the same roof, he assumed we were an item. If I had spoken to Nan, she may have thought I was overreacting and making a fuss, but I felt trapped. Every night before bed, Nan used to gather her knitting and fold the newspaper. I'd jump up and bustle about so I was first out the door, but it annoyed me having to wriggle out of situations where he could pledge his undying love and sterility.

Craig's teacher pulled me aside to say she'd seen a noticeable change in him. She said his mind was elsewhere and he was not paying attention, which was puzzling. Craig had always been a good student—eager to learn and coming home with ticks and gold stars. Once this was brought to my attention, I noticed he seemed pensive. I hadn't noticed anything sooner because my mind was preoccupied with Collin. Thank goodness his teacher brought it to my attention. The following day, I took him to our doctor, who made an appointment for Craig to see the child psychologist, Mr. Bevan Jones.

On the day of his appointment, Mr. Jones took Craig into his office so they could speak privately. To avoid stress, I did not ask my son what they had discussed because Mr. Jones was going to talk to me once he had completed his sessions.

I can't remember where Collin was when I spoke to Nan, but he must have been hovering. Once alone, he ordered me to cancel the rest of our appointments because all psychologists were quacks that liked to delve into your personal life. I told him it was none of his business. I could not understand why he was questioning my authority over something that had nothing to do with him. The scene he created—you'd have thought Craig was his child.

Craig had six sessions with Mr. Jones, but we never made it past three. I could not cope with the sarcasm and snide comments. I had managed to survive 27 years on my own and did not need him or his advice... but this was not advice... this was control.

Robert was only three, but he'd go into a rage each time Collin cornered me, which was usually in the kitchen. The only way my little lad could defend me was to pick something up and hold it in the air, ready to throw. Only when Collin backed away did Robert put the object down—except the time he picked up a pile of newly washed breakfast dishes. I grabbed them just as they left his hands, but this amused Collin.

The more I told him to leave me alone, the more he continued. At the time I put Robert's behavior down as naughty then realized he was distracting Collin. It was his way of protecting me. My boys had never known any life other than the one they shared with Nan and me. They had never experienced arguments, foul moods, tempers, or bitchy sarcasm. Having Collin under our roof was affecting them both… I failed to see he was molding them.

I was relieved when he said he'd got a job, so Nan began dropping hints about him moving out. It was bliss not having him around during the day, but he never failed to ask for cuddles at every opportunity. Collin did not take rejection lightly and said horrible things, which were upsetting and unjustified. Any fool could see I wanted nothing to do with him, why can't he bugger off and leave us alone?

One Saturday, we went to buy new drapes. Collin insisted on coming along with the excuse of carrying shopping. He was smoking, so he waited outside with Robert. On leaving the store, I saw my son crying because he'd wet his pants. Collin had hold of his hand and refused to let him enter the store to use the toilet. Poor kid must have been frozen—a little accident that could have been prevented.

There was another incident, but it involved Craig. Nan and I were going to town. Collin said the boys should stay behind in the warm, but Robert showed off, so I relented. Craig stayed silent.

It was dark as we walked down the sideway, then we heard Collin—*You dirty little bastard!* I couldn't get through the door quick enough. I flung the door open hard, and it bashed against the butler sink, making them both jump. I fell into the kitchen and saw him leaning over Craig, who was standing on a kitchen stool looking pale and scared. My son had had an accident, and Collin was making him wash his underpants. I wondered what the hell he had put my little boy through to cause him to soil himself when he had been clean from an early age. If only I could turn back the clock.

I deeply regret leaving Craig behind that afternoon. Poor kid must have felt desperate being left alone with the one person he hated most but was too scared to say anything. My God, was it any wonder he was having issues at school? *Bless his heart.*

The bastard didn't know what to say, having been caught out. He stood, grinned at the pair of us, and said he was trying to scare Craig so he wouldn't soil himself again.

"Scare my son?!" I screamed. *"What gives you the right to scare my son?"* I wanted to punch him in the mouth.

I lifted my son from the stool, gave him clean clothes, and assured him everything was okay. Nan laid into Collin, then ignored him for the remainder of the night and the days that followed. Why she didn't insist he leave there and then, I do not know.

We remained angry for weeks, so he took matters into his own hands and asked Edith to babysit. He wanted to take us back to The Checkers, and what better way to grovel than by getting us tipsy? He made sure Nan had sufficient that night and got me tipsy too. But with all the tension he created, I needed to unwind and welcome the chance to get drunk.

We arrived home that night worse for wear. Nan made herself a goodnight drink but would have crashed out before taking a sip, and I never saw the back of Edith.

I hated using our outside loo at night because it meant walking through our sitting room, which doubled as his bedroom. Although my bladder was in good shape, I always visited the loo just before bed. I returned from the loo and saw him in bed with his arms outstretched, asking for *cuddles*. Normally, I would have left in a huff, but I was wasted and allowed him his *cuddles* and hoped *cuddles* might improve his mood. But *cuddles* went further than I expected... *Oh, what the hell,* it's not as though I could get pregnant—he's made that perfectly clear.

I often wonder if he saw me wipe my hand across my mouth as I left the room, however, I made a promise that *cuddles* were something we would never repeat.

I woke one morning with my usual stomach ache. They lasted for days, then they stopped altogether. I couldn't wait for him to arrive home. I didn't have to worry about him isolating me since that was an opportunity he never missed.

"No, darlin', you must be mistaken. You're just late, that's all... Anyway, it's impossible because you know I am sterile."

The horror of being pregnant by the scheming bastard angered me beyond belief.

"Sterile, my arse! You're no more sterile than an alley cat, so stop treating me like an idiot—I know what I'm talking about."

We argued quietly out of Nan's hearing. This had been his plan all along, and he was gloating, having hit the jackpot. Now, he had a hold over me.

I demanded he arrange a termination immediately, but the look of satisfaction on his smug face told me I was wasting my time. I was not streetwise like most 27-year-olds and did not know the first thing about terminating an unwanted pregnancy. And doctors did not agree to abortions.

When he failed to help me, I insisted he break the news to Nan. She was devastated and wiped the floor with him. Every time she opened her mouth, she swore, but it was *water off a duck's back.* Collin took the tongue-lashing rather well—he probably thought the verbal attack was worth it now that he had me where he wanted.

I saw the pain on Nan's face, and her eyes were raw. Each time he got off his arse, she glared at him. I wondered if he felt her eyes piercing the back of his head but realized he was too thick-skinned to feel anything other than satisfaction.

He was a manipulative, scheming bastard. He knew how to achieve his goal with the utmost impact.

It was weeks before she started talking to him again, but there was nothing he could say or do to win her over. Not this time.

Nan and I visited Joan every Sunday, but due to my circumstances, I stayed home and dreaded being left alone with him. This should have been a happy time for me with my children, but things were different now. The flat had lost the ambiance it once had—nothing felt the same, and I hated it. *I hated him.*

We argued. I told him to get the hell out of our home, but he remained.

Nan was out the night he put his arm around me. When I pushed him away, he told me I was being unreasonable. I lost my temper and threw our coasters at him, then my wooden ashtray, then a jar of peanuts. I threw more, but I can't remember what—only that I made contact with each aim. Not until then did he keep a safe distance. But what a shame I had to lose my temper before he left me alone. Any decent man would have packed his bags and got the hell away—but not him.

Looking back, I realize there were a few ways we could have got shot of him. We could have contacted the landlady and asked her to evict an unwanted guest who had overstayed his welcome. We could have shoved his stuff in bags and thrown them out like they do in the movies. In fact, Howard could have told him to shove off. Collin, being a coward, would have packed his bags.

Nan and I always spent Christmas Day with Joan and Howard. Collin offered to drive us but had not been invited. I didn't know where he went as long as he was out of my sight.

After our meal, we were in the sitting room discussing Collin then Howard told me Collin had visited my father and told him I was pregnant. I was *hopping mad.* Jesus, there was no stopping the son of a bitch! I was going to speak to my father, but I would do so in my own time.

Joan and Howard were not on the phone, so I marched to the call box across the street, but there was no answer.

Collin picked us up as arranged. I got my children into bed, then shut him in the kitchen.

"So you've been to visit my dad? How dare you tell him I am pregnant without consulting me! I will decide who to tell and when. And what gives you the right to visit him anyway? You've got a bloody cheek! Why can't you stay out of our lives?"

He denied the allegations, so I stormed out and headed for the phone box, hoping my journey would not be in vain. Thankfully, it was Dad who answered.

I briefly wished him *Merry Christmas,* then asked what Collin had said about my pregnancy. His reply left me speechless.

"We haven't seen Collin in ages. It was your uncle Howard who told us you were pregnant—and that the baby belonged to the carpetbagger."

I was so shocked I said goodbye and hung up.

By the time I arrived home, Collin had buggered off to sulk, so I was able to discuss the phone call without him butting in. Nan pondered before deciding we should not say anything in case it caused trouble between Joan and Howard—then the children would suffer, and that would never do. She remained silent throughout the evening.

Very often, when there was a problem, Howard's name used to pop up. He wasn't the innocent bystander he pretended to be—or that everyone assumed. He couldn't keep his tongue still if his life depended on it. He wasn't the sort to let the truth get in the way of a good story, and it certainly didn't pay to tell him anything in confidence.

I must apologize to my cousins for speaking ill of their father, but I have lived with the shame and humiliation of his lies for years. I have done nothing to warrant his spiteful tongue other than reject his advances.

With three children and another baby on the way, I realized it was time for me to move. I reluctantly applied to the council for a larger property and was allocated a three-bedroom house.

Collin drove Nan and me to pick up the keys. As I entered, my heart sank. There was no carpet in the lounge or bedrooms, and the stair carpet was threadbare. The back door was jammed, and the butler sink stood precariously on a dark green wooden frame.

Wallpaper was hanging off the walls in the master bedroom, and the wallpaper in the back bedroom appeared to have been attacked by a bear. The garden was overgrown, and there was no line post for my washing. In fact, the whole place was a total mess.

Auntie Joan came to the rescue. Having recently bought a new suite, she gave me their old one. There were no second-hand shops at the time and certainly no charity shops to my knowledge.

Collin donated his mother's cooker, which he had neglected. The enamel was chipped and black from burnt-on food, not to mention the filth from where it had been standing outside for months. But at least he offered to decorate, fix the back door, install a sink unit, and buy me a washing machine and fridge-freezer.

The following morning, Nan and I were able to talk without him butting in. She worried about how I would cope with another baby, as she would not be around to help as she had in the past. I assured her I would be fine, but she wasn't convinced.

I told her Collin could move into the box room and do the jobs that needed doing. *He can buy what I need for the baby and take care of me when the time comes—then he will get his marching orders and be out of our lives.*

At three months, I suspected I was expecting twins. Collin thought I was mad, so he took me to the doctor, who scoffed and said my pregnancy had only just been confirmed and it was too soon to tell if I was carrying two babies.

Regarding the phone call at Christmas with my father and the *carpetbagger,* I assumed Howard was referring to Bernard. So, I decided to get it off my chest. I was concerned about the outcome but not enough to stay silent.

I arranged to visit my friends the following evening. Bernard poured a glass of wine as we waited for Jill to finish the children's bedtime story. They listened with intent.

I watched their faces slowly change. Then Jill got annoyed but gained composure. However, Bernard—known for having a short fuse—was going to confront my uncle, but Jill talked him out of it. She knew he would lose his temper and probably swing for him. She reminded him that Howard was no youngster, and she did not want her husband held responsible if anything should happen.

She said Howard had some sort of problem if he has nothing better to do than tell lies about his niece, perhaps there is a bit of jealousy there she suggested in which case he should be pitied..

There was that word again. *Jealousy.*

I was glad my friends took it as well as they did. But as Howard is family, I will continue to endure the pain and humiliation of his lies and the damage he does to my reputation each time he slags me off—which is unjustified after the many times Nan and I have bailed him out of situations but stayed silent at his request to protect Joan.

But why was he so determined to turn everyone against me?

Was it because I rejected his advances?

I have heard of *a woman scorned,* but what about when *a man* is scorned?

Chapter Twenty-Two

My New Home

I felt sad to be leaving Nan and the flat where, in the past, I had felt safe and secure with the woman who had taken care of me. She stood by me like a mother, and now I was leaving that security behind to start a life with a man who had put me in a situation that was causing her to worry. But her feelings were the least of his worries.

I felt my ties being stretched. No longer would we have our cozy chats by the fire once the children were in bed. No more sharing that morning cup of tea with a buttered scone or sausage sandwich. *"Oh, that's lovely, dear—just what the doctor ordered,"* she'd say, turning off her machine to take her cup and saucer. (She never drank from a mug.)

Nan and I decided it would be sensible to leave Craig at the school where he felt safe, in the care of his teacher, Mrs. Martin. I had to admit—she was lovely and good at her job, and Craig adored her. She thought a lot of him too. It was a comfort knowing he enjoyed school when so many children cried to stay home. Nan and I agreed to wait until summer before changing his school. Until then, he was better off where he was happy, settled, and—most importantly—away from Collin.

We arrived at my new abode in an open-back truck like Steptoe. Goodness knows where he got it from or what the neighbors thought.

Tiffany, Robert, and I shared the master bedroom. The back bedroom, eventually meant for the boys, was at the moment piled high with unpacked boxes. Collin occupied the box room—how he managed to squeeze his double bed in there was a mystery. I hated being separated from my firstborn, but there was plenty to keep me occupied with a mountain of boxes waiting for my attention.

I'd watch the clock when it was time for Craig to leave school, knowing Nan would be at the gate waiting. I missed having him around. He was my little boy, but he was very grown-up and sensible for his age.

Collin never failed to ask for cuddles each night. I used to hang around downstairs until I thought he was in bed, but on climbing the stairs, he'd always be on the landing waiting, asking for cuddles. But I had no wish to repeat that performance.

He was working full-time now, so he only had weekends to do any jobs. Consequently, progress was slow. He may have deliberately dragged his heels, knowing his days were numbered once he'd served his purpose—just as I had served mine.

I crawled into bed exhausted, having cleaned the house, tackled a box from the back bedroom, and changed the beds (*not his*). I pulled back the covers and noticed something black. Strange, I thought, since I had changed the sheets that morning. Not wanting to disturb the children with the light, I leaned closer—and saw the black thing *move.*

It was a house spider.

I dropped the covers and ran to the bathroom in tears.

Collin asked if I was okay but didn't seem surprised. His solution to the problem? That I slept in his bed while he slept on top of it. He *promised* there would be no contact.

I couldn't bear to touch the bed where the spider had made itself comfortable between my sheets, so with no other option, I agreed.

The following morning, I watched as he destroyed the mattress along with the remains of the spider. Unable to afford a new one, Collin suggested bringing his double bed into my room so Robert could have the box room. And just like that, we were sleeping together.

A few weeks later, I had a visit from social security. Someone had reported that I had a man living with me while on benefits. Strange, I thought—I had no contact with the neighbors, and for all they knew, we could have been man and wife.

It took me a while to realize it was probably *himself.*

Collin could be very patronizing at times and took great pleasure in contradicting me in front of others. When I said I was expecting twins, he corrected me, making me sound stupid. But at three months, past experience and common sense told me that flutters on both the left *and* right side at the same time *could not possibly be one baby.* The foetus was too small for that.

The medics disagreed, saying I was having one *big* baby. Collin, of course, sided with them.

When Dad and Camilla visited, Collin wasted no time in telling them I was expecting *one* baby and *not* twins. Camilla smirked.

"Oh, our doctor thinks Alice is expecting twins," she said.

Alice this. Alice that.

Alice, Alice, Alice.

That's all she spoke about. And, of course, Alice was married, unlike me.

I looked forward to Sundays when Collin would drive to collect Nan and Craig for lunch. He took over the kitchen and cooked his favorite—roast pork. After our meal, he'd clear away, leaving Nan and me to rest while the children played. So, times were *not* all bad.

He appeared to have mellowed. But perhaps it was only because his plans had fallen into place—I was pregnant, we were sleeping together, and I was dependent on him for money, shopping, and transport.

In fact, I never left the house without him.

One evening, he suggested a takeaway. My favorite was chicken curry from our local Chinese, but Collin preferred pork. He got stuck into his curry, but mine tasted bitter. When I mentioned it, he got angry and threw my meal in the bin. That caused a row.

"You've got a vivid imagination," he snapped.

But this wasn't the first time I had experienced that bitter taste in my food.

"It's just your pregnancy taste buds," he insisted.

Unconvinced, I ignored him for the rest of the night.

The following day, he buggered off. But when he returned, he was a *lot* nicer—he brought cream cakes, his usual peace offering.

I hated arguments and would go to any length to avoid them.

So, when he groveled, I forgave him.

All I wanted was a *peaceful* life.

But that made me a *pushover*.

My pregnancy was nearing its end, and my check-ups had become weekly. The midwife told me I was overdue. My next appointment was scheduled for July 4th.

At the clinic, she weighed me, then pointed to the couch and began to prod at my stomach.

"I'm having twins, aren't I?" I asked.

She ignored me and called the gynecologist. He, too, poked and prodded.

I studied his face. *"I'm having twins, aren't I?"* I repeated.

He sighed. *"I don't know, lassie, but you have a lot of lumps and bumps in there. I want you to come to my clinic tomorrow at 3 p.m."*

He scribbled on my notes—(*twins, I think*)—then left the room.

The next day, at 3 o'clock, I arrived at the clinic, where a nurse was waiting with a gown. After my X-ray, she led me to where Mr. Sutton was waiting. He examined the film, removed his glasses, and turned to me.

"Well, here you are, lassie—here are your babies."

My babies.

He told me they were small and due on July 27th—three weeks away.

I was relieved. Finally, twins had been confirmed. No more listening to Collin contradicting me in front of everyone.

A pleasure I was more than happy to relieve him of.

Chapter Twenty-Three

The Arrivals Of Twins 1968

I was due for a home delivery, but now that twins had been confirmed, it was out of the question. Multiple births need extra medics and special equipment, which my midwife would be unable to cope with if a problem occurred.

On Saturday, 20th July, at 6 o'clock, my babies were ready to make an appearance. Collin was adamant I was not going into hospital until he realized the situation was more than he could deal with and dialed 999 from the call box. Within minutes, doctors arrived with incubators, oxygen tents, and other equipment before deciding there was sufficient time to get me to the hospital.

I would love to have observed from behind nets, but I was the *main event* that afternoon and missed the excitement. I was vaguely aware of those gathered in my bedroom and on the landing, but I could hear the commotion. Then we were off—with blue lights and sirens.

After being chased through the streets by paramedics, my first daughter arrived within half an hour of reaching the hospital. She came into the world at 7:30 p.m., weighing 7 lb. 7 oz.

Fifteen minutes later, my second daughter arrived at 7:45 p.m., weighing 7 lb. 5 oz.

Collin phoned the family with the exciting news, but when he told them their weight, everyone assumed he was mistaken. My girls weighed almost 15 lb. between them—my normal weight was under 7 stone—no wonder I looked like a tank.

When the Dr. did his rounds the following morning, he looked at both cribs, flicked through his notes, and asked what I had taken to have such big babies. When I told him about *iron injections*, he offered no comment and walked away.

So much for my babies being small and arriving in three weeks—they made their appearance within two weeks of the scan.

At three days old, Collin took me and my babies' home. We were greeted by our skeptical neighbors, eager to see them.

Collin was tickled pink, being the father of twins. He was in his element—washing and sterilizing bottles, making feeds, preparing baths, and changing nappies—but he loved being in control.

Collin named the first twin Allison, and Craig named the second twin Morgan.

The day he returned to work, my home help arrived.

I opened the door to this lovely, round-faced lady with thick, curly hair. Joyce was charming. She sailed through—cleaning, cooking, washing an abundance of terry towel nappies, and tackling the rest of the laundry.

She was amazing.

Chapter Twenty-Four

Trapped

Collin sold his car and *bought* a Bedford van. Then, he built a bed behind the front seat. Their bed was the width of the van, so they could sleep end to end. If he pumped the brakes, they would have rolled from side to side like sausages in a pan. Then, he secured a child's seat for Tiffany in the front between us. Nan and my boys had garden chairs in the back, which was rather dangerous, but seat belts had not been enforced, and there was not the amount of traffic there is today.

Since the arrival of the babies, life has run a lot smoother. He was not argumentative—he was jovial and kind. Once the babies were in bed, we'd spend evenings talking about what the other had done throughout the day.

When the babies were six weeks old, we had family visiting from Canada. Their visit was not centered around me, but they liked to catch up with everyone *in between* scheduled tours. They liked to pack as much into their trip as possible.

We had just finished Sunday lunch when Collin suggested going for a drive. On our journey, he brought up the subject of marriage—a word I let pass over my head. But without thinking, I turned to Nan and casually said how nice it would be to have a wedding while the Canadians were here.

As soon as we got home, he was running around like a headless chicken, cracking jokes and attempting to sing. I reminded him I had *not* agreed to marriage, but it made no difference to his crazy performance.

Monday evening, he was full of beans when he came home. He gave me a form and said he had to return it the following day with a copy of my birth certificate and divorce papers. Then he handed me the pen, pointed to where I had to sign, and said our wedding was booked for 12th September—and he'd ordered the cake.

I felt the carpet rip from under me. I had no intention of making the relationship *permanent*, but everything had been arranged, and it was too late. I was not strong enough to challenge him without causing a scene and making him angry. *Basically, I was scared.*

So I signed the forms and left Nan to inform the family of the date and time of our wedding—*in seven days' time.*

Tiffany was a beautiful toddler. She had thick, curly hair, dark eyes, and long lashes. Everyone commented on her beauty. I used to sit her on the kitchen table with my box of colored pegs so she could play quietly while I teased her hair into ringlets, carefully putting them in place before adding a ribbon or slide. It took ages, but it was worth it—she looked every bit like Shirley Temple.

If my mother was watching, she would have been *glowing.*

When Tiffany was engrossed in anything, I could never get any sense out of her. Like any 15-month-old, her speech was limited. One day, she tipped my pegs onto the footpath. My neighbor peered over the fence and asked what she was doing.

Without looking up, she replied, *"You in a minute."*

It was said so casually—we couldn't help laughing.

Craig was a handsome boy. He looked like the *all-American kid* with his collar up and hair in a quiff. I could sit him at anyone's table—he was well-mannered, which did not go unnoticed by those who had children who were *not* so well-behaved.

Craig was about three years old when he corrected my cousins for leaving the table without asking. Another time, he told them not to talk with their mouths full. Joan prompted her family to take notice of their young cousin—but it *angered* Howard.

Robert was the mischievous one who kept me on my toes. He had an angelic face with freckles that were more visible during the summer. His blond hair looked beautiful when the sun shone.

I could send him out in freshly ironed shorts and a T-shirt, and within half an hour, he was walking through the door covered in dirt, his hair a mess.

But that's when he was at his *happiest*—when he was involved with something *dirty or greasy*.

He was an adventurous child who could see *no danger*.

I remember the time he made a *ski lift* that stretched the length of the garden. Pleased with his invention, he climbed on the fence, hung onto his ski lift, and shot up the garden at speed.

His journey came to an *abrupt end* when he came into contact with some rusty wire by the window. When he spun around, it dug into his back and left a two-inch gash.

He was *not* amused when the hospital gave him a tetanus injection—in his backside.

I am the proud mother of twins now. They were *not* identical, nor were they scrawny—but that goes without saying, given their birth weight. They were feeding every four hours and sleeping through the night. I coped well, but Nan was always on hand with the ironing now that Joyce was no longer with us.

My children were an amazing bunch. I got great pleasure walking them to the local shops. We attracted a lot of attention from passersby, who commented on my family.

They *were* indeed a handsome bunch.

And now, I have a wedding looming—to a man I did *not* love.

A man who had *manipulated* me with deception and lies.

Chapter Twenty-Five

My Wedding

I was up at dawn, cleaning and preparing food. Nan arrived early to help with edibles and anything that required attention. I left it until the last minute to dress my girls in the outfits Nan *bought* for the twins. Tiffany wore her red velvet dress with a white pinafore. It took ages to comb her hair into ringlets—she looked like a picture. Nan helped my boys into their beige trousers, white shirts, and cable sweaters, but my wardrobe was limited. I wore the suit that came out of hiding on special occasions, and there weren't many of them.

Collin arranged for Joyce to look after the girls while we were at the registry office—he had everything under control.

The Canadians were the first to arrive. The only members of Collin's family that attended were Simon and Emma.

There were no pictures taken other than those my father took in the garden and our dining room. In one picture, we were standing beside our cake, and Collin was messing about—he raised a clenched fist, indicating he was about to punch me in the face. Everyone laughed, with the *exception* of Nan, who thought it was a strange way for a husband to behave on his wedding day. She saw it as an *omen*.

It wasn't long before he was trying to control me. If only he would get on with what husbands do and leave me to get on with my duties, life would run a lot smoother, but I realized that was *never* going to happen. He spoke to me like I was totally *stupid* instead of a capable wife and mother. He criticized me in front of whoever was within earshot—which was usually the supermarket. Perhaps he thought it made him look big, but all he achieved was showing himself up—because no one likes a *bully*.

He often came home *looking* for trouble. I sometimes *dreaded* hearing his van outside. I knew roughly what time he was due home, so I made a point of being upstairs with the children—but I could feel the *vibes* as he walked in. He'd bang the street door, storm into the kitchen, bang the kettle on the stove, then slam the cupboard.

But if he was in a *good* mood, he'd call and ask if I wanted a drink.

I often wondered what had happened during the day to make him arrive home looking for trouble. I used to approach him gingerly, preparing myself for whatever might be the problem. If I asked about his day, he'd accuse me of *prying*—but if we had company, he had *plenty* to say.

I was *rarely* included in the conversation—except when he wanted a drink. One evening, I told him not to shut me out, but he told me to *grow up* and act my age. Another time, he said I read too many books.

I didn't *have* any books.

One evening, I was bathing the babies in front of the fire when Collin got up to answer the door. He returned when no one was there. No sooner had he sat down when the bell rang again. He flashed me a *dirty* look and rushed to the door, but the street was deserted.

He returned with a scowl and accused me of having a *boyfriend*—saying the knock was my signal to meet him.

Goodness knows where that came from. What chance did I have of meeting anyone?

I laughed and told him it was probably kids playing *knock-down ginger*, a game mischievous kids liked to play.

The next time I saw his son Barry, I mentioned Collin's moods. His reply was one I never expected.

"It paid him to be a gentleman," he said, laughing, then added, *"His patience paid off in the end."*

What the hell was he talking about?

And why the snide chuckle?

I was disturbed, to say the least.

I looked in the mirror one morning and did *not* like what I saw. It wasn't that I didn't care about my appearance, but my days revolved around my home and family.

So, I decided to do a little *pampering*.

Besides, if he liked what he saw when he came home, maybe he wouldn't be such an *ogre*.

I washed and set my hair, applied makeup, took my only skirt from the wardrobe, and waited.

As soon as he walked in, he told me I looked like a *whore* and wanted to know who I had been entertaining.

Then he told me to *wipe the boot polish off my face* because it made me look like a *slut*.

"Only prostitutes smear their faces with that muck when they parade up and down the seafront with their handbags."

(Only he would know that.)

I said *nothing*, but the insult *hurt*.

Once the children were asleep, I took myself off to bed. I don't know what time he came upstairs, but I was woken by him climbing all over me.

It was a few weeks before I informed the rent collector of my change of circumstances.

Pete Wiles was a lovely man—I could never imagine him being *angry*. He had a smile for everyone. We could hear him coming along the street, whistling like a bird.

I handed him my rent book and asked him to make the necessary changes—from *Mrs. Johnson* to *Mr. and Mrs. Collin Wainwright*.

His expression changed to one of surprise—or should I say *shock*.

"Not Collin Wainwright?" he asked.

"Yes, that's right."

He repeated, *"Not thee Collin Wainwright?"*

"Yes. Do you know him, then?"

He avoided eye contact and made the adjustments in *silence*.

Puzzled, I closed the door.

That night, when I mentioned the incident to Collin, he said he'd known Pete from school. I was busy with my babies and thought nothing more of it—but I was *aware* of the uncomfortable silence.

The following week, I asked Pete how he knew Collin.

He said they had been *neighbors* some years ago.

I thought it strange when his story *differed* from my husband's.

Pete avoided eye contact, just like the week before.

"See you next week," he said, hurrying down the footpath.

How odd.

Where had my *friendly* rent man gone?

And why was he acting so *strange?*

I was feeling *pretty miserable* with Christmas fast approaching and no money to spare. My **£20 housekeeping** was barely enough to live on.

By the time I paid rent on the house and his garage, life insurance, and house insurance—then put one pounds-worth of silver coins in the gas and electricity meters—there was *hardly enough* for groceries.

And *certainly* nothing for Christmas.

God, how I hated shopping.

Having to *add everything in my head* as I popped items in the trolley—simply because I did *not* want the embarrassment of having *insufficient* money at the checkout.

When I mentioned my plight to Nan, she suggested getting *Provident checks* to spend at the Co-op.

The weekly payment for a **£20 check** would cost me **two shillings** a week.

Then she suggested I buy *one extra item* of food each week and store it away for Christmas.

She had *all* the answers.

Mrs. Smith was the representative in our area. She called at Nan's request so we could discuss payments. She confirmed I would pay *two shillings a week* for a **£20 check.**

With paperwork signed, she handed me **twenty pounds' worth of cheques**—which looked like *Monopoly money.*

I couldn't wait to *shop.*

If I chose carefully, I could *probably* afford a few stocking fillers—as well as *one* main present for each of my children.

I felt *all Christmassy* walking into town with my *Monopoly money.*

And I *wished* life could be like this *all the time.*

Christmas was days away, so I went upstairs to wrap the stocking fillers and to look for somewhere safe to stash them. But my excitement rapidly died when I heard him *bitching*, so I crept downstairs and listened at the door.

"Bloody bastard, kids can never do anything wrong in your mother's eyes. I'd like to teach you a bloody good lesson. Now eat that up, or I will tan your arse, then you can go to bed hungry. Look what you're doing, you're spilling it. Mind those crumbs. Now look what you've done, you clumsy little bastard. Now you can clean it up."

I startled them all as I threw the door open and asked, *"What's going on?"* He changed his tone and smiled weakly. He told me the children were dirty little bastards, then pointed to crumbs on the floor and soup on the table. He said they should go to bed hungry. Then it would teach them a bloody lesson. Furthermore, they had no bloody respect… *bloody, bloody,* every word was bloody.

So I launched back, *"Oh, really? Well, that's funny because I've been standing outside, and all I can hear is you swearing. I haven't heard them once. Anyway, if you want their respect, you need to treat them with respect because that's how they learn. You don't deserve to have a family. You should be back in that dumpy little flat all on your own."*

"Well, here's something to think about, you miserable old sod. Here is the present the children brought for you. The boys couldn't wait to give it to you, but you had to ruin it like you ruin everything, you ungrateful bastard. And for what? A few crumbs and a little soup? You make me sick."

I marched over to the tree and threw his gift at him, then took my children into the kitchen to lighten the mood. We talked about Father Christmas and what surprises he may have. The codger was quiet for the rest of the night, but not before upsetting us all.

I could not understand why he was always in a bad mood. Why on earth did he trick me into marriage when married life with children was not what he wanted? He's never satisfied until he's made us as miserable as himself. I try ignoring him, but he won't stop until he's upset everyone.

It was arranged that Nan would spend Christmas Day with Joan and Howard, and they would all come to us on Boxing Day. Well, it was the worst Christmas I had ever experienced. He stormed about with a face like thunder. He nagged the children from the moment they got out of bed. He was either interfering with my cooking or looking for his next victim.

I felt sorry for my boys, who took turns disappearing to their bedroom. Like all children, they'd been looking forward to Christmas and playing with their toys from Santa, but he ruined the entire day. This was our first Christmas as a married couple with our babies, so it should have been really special. I couldn't wait for Boxing Day and hoped Mr. Angry would put on his happy face… Actually, he didn't have a happy face.

On Boxing Day morning, Nan arrived with parcels from under the tree. She offered to help in the kitchen, but my boys whisked her upstairs to show her their Santa gifts. Once our turkey roast was cleared, Joan and Howard arrived with their family. Collin was all smiles, trotting back and forth. Neither of us had time to sit, but that's what happens when you have a house full of guests with an abundance of children celebrating Christmas.

Howard was up to his old tricks… talking suggestively, brushing himself against me, and trying to corner me. Then he was trying to kiss me—he simply didn't care. I was embarrassed and protested, *"Joan, can you please control your husband?"* She'd tell him to leave me alone. Then he'd get angry.

"What's the matter with you? I'm only mucking about. Can't you take a joke?"

I'm sorry, but being groped was no joke. Then Collin laughed, which angered me more.

I have always felt uncomfortable around Howard, even as a child. I remember when I was 13 years old, I was squatting in the garden, weeding between the pansies. Joan and Nan were in the kitchen when Howard came out, bent down to where I was crouched, and put his hand on my knee, then slowly moved it up my leg. My first reaction was to hit his offending hand with my trowel. He jumped up and went inside, rubbing his wrist. What story he told remains to be seen. Nan marched out, slapped my face, and sent me to my room.

As I passed Joan in the doorway, she called me a spiteful little bitch. But what I don't understand is why no one questioned my outburst because I was not of a spiteful nature. Like any 13-year-old, I was shy and innocent, so being slapped across the face and told I was spiteful made me feel I was somehow to blame. But how else could I have defended myself against the uncle I should have been able to trust? Someone should have questioned my attack. Now, I am a woman, and he thinks it's okay to touch me. What was I supposed to do—reciprocate? Laugh it off, perhaps?

Nan used to tell him to leave me alone, but her words went unheard because there was no strength or anger in her tone. I don't think Collin knew how to handle the situation either, but he was a coward and laughed instead of defending me. I felt let down by the husband who was supposed to love me... the husband who wanted to look after me... after us.

Once everyone had gone, Collin accused me of encouraging my uncle, which infuriated me. God, how I hated Howard touching me and I hated the trouble it caused, but I was powerless to stop him without lashing out as I had at 13.

My babies were about 5 months old when I had a miscarriage. Two months later, I was pregnant again, so our doctor sent me to the gynecologist, who suggested sterilization. I hastily agreed. I made inquiries about the pill, which was not accessible to everyone unless you were on a low income or in unfortunate circumstances. I was both. I left Collin to fill in the forms and was surprised when I was refused. I later discovered he'd lied about his income.

It's ironic to hear about women wanting babies but being unable to conceive when I fall so easily. My first encounter with intimacy was with Johnny. Within the month of my wedding, I was pregnant with Robert. It took time with Tiffany because we took every precaution. Then, of course, there was Collin, who was no more sterile than an alley cat.

Chapter Twenty-Six

Married To A Stranger

Simon called one evening to say their sister Rita was surprised to hear Collin had remarried. Anxious to meet her new sister-in-law, she invited us for supper the following evening. I was thrilled to be meeting another member of my extended family. Nan, my faithful babysitter, arrived to care for the children.

Rita, I noticed, was nothing like Collin, but the resemblance to Simon was striking. They both had the same smile and gentle approach. Rita and Jamie greeted me warmly and led me into their spacious lounge/diner with a bay window overlooking the garden. I followed my host into the kitchen through the impressive stained-glass sliding doors and was in awe of the elegant worktops and secluded lighting under the wall units. I wondered what it would be like working in such lovely surroundings. Jamie, aware of my interest, told me he built the house when they were first married. Then he rushed upstairs to get the album for me to look through once we had eaten.

With snacks out of the way, Jamie shoved the album in front of me and eagerly turned the pages, explaining what was being undertaken with the help of friends and family. Rita told me she'd designed the kitchen. *"Imagine designing your own kitchen,"* I said, glancing at my husband in the far corner. I barely recognized Simon, wearing dirty overalls and wellingtons. Rita was in a lot of pictures in dungarees, but to my surprise, Collin was absent in everyone.

Without raising my eyes, I asked, *"How come you're not in any of these pictures? I bet you were skiving..."*

If I had glanced at the family, I would have seen a few surprised faces. Then Rita broke the ice and asked if we would like more coffee. Aware that the atmosphere had suddenly changed, I was relieved when Simon looked at his watch and said it was time to leave.

Collin's son Leslie, his wife Hazel, and three boys had recently moved from Clacton and were renting a flat close by. Leslie was looking for work and asked his father if there were any vacancies at Thomas Allen. Leslie had an HGV license, so Collin said he would make inquiries.

As Hazel did not know anyone, it wasn't long before she was calling around when at a loose end, which was pretty much most of the time... every day, in fact. She said, with a chuckle, that while she was sitting in my warm house, she was saving on heating. Hazel was good company, but I dreaded the mess her boys left behind. I had my work cut out putting my house in order before Collin came home. Hazel never corrected her children, so I felt she was taking unfair advantage. I soon realized that an untidy home with unmade beds and a sink full of dishes were the least of her worries.

On Hazel's regular visits, we discussed anything and everything, so she knew I struggled financially. But she'd spend all morning in my warm house drinking coffee and was never too shy to ask for another. Sometimes, her youngest would ask for lunch, which was okay if it was something I could stretch. Otherwise, not wanting to feed my children in their company, I used to wait for them to leave. I am a generous person until someone takes advantage. But for the present moment, I enjoyed her company and funny innuendoes.

Sometimes we paid them a visit at the weekend. My children loved their flat; it was like a glorified toy shop. Hazel said their boys got more toys at Easter than at Christmas, whereas mine were lucky to get an Easter egg. It used to upset me to watch my children enjoying themselves with so many lovely toys when they had very little. I often wondered what was going through their minds because they never complained. I understood and accepted our situation, but children find these situations difficult to comprehend.

I picked up a letter from the doormat and saw the envelope addressed to Collin had been damaged by the rain, so I peeked inside. I was surprised to see his pay slip, which he normally collected from the office. So, this being sent to our home was either a mistake or divine intervention. I'll go with divine intervention.

I was staggered when I saw his earnings. No wonder the swine did not want them delivered to the house. He must laugh up his sleeve every week watching me skimp and scrape in the supermarket—unable to afford treats for my children as I juggle our finances. They did have treats, but it was him who chose what to get and when, but I was never around. It was the same with their clothes. I worried seeing my boys' trousers slowly creep above their ankles and shirts getting tight, knowing I could not afford to replace them. It wasn't too bad with the girls, who were under school age and wore hand-me-downs.

I used to complain bitterly when a birthday was fast approaching. Then my knight in shining armor would arrive home late and hand me £5, saying he'd worked overtime just so I could buy that gift or item of clothing. Then my eyes fell back to the pay slip, furious to think we had gone without unnecessarily. I was an idiot to believe in him, but I had no reason to doubt him either. After the row, he increased my income by £5, but how could he refuse? I was not greedy; all I wanted was to give my family what they were entitled to. He deprived me of the joy of buying my children their needs because I can never have the time back that he stole from me... from us. Thank goodness my children were not envious of seeing the toys and treats their friends and cousins received, which is why Nan used to help us out.

When I spoke to Hazel, she confirmed Thomas Allen paid good wages. Neither of them could understand how I coped with what little he gave me, knowing how I struggled. I wonder why she never said anything to me sooner because she loved to gossip—there was always someone at the end of one of her scandalous stories.

I made friends with some lovely neighbors from two doors away. Sid worked with Collin at Thomas Allen, which is how we met. Every morning, Pat walked my boys to school with her children, then she'd call in on her way home with a sticky bun or scone to have with our coffee. I felt awkward because the treat was always at her expense, but she understood my position. Our coffee mornings became regular, except on Fridays when she went into town to shop. Sid used to sign a blank cheque and leave it on the table for her to fill in the amount she wanted—lucky lady. Collin used to leave me £20 for food, bills, rent, electricity, and gas.

Every driver at Thomas Allen had to flush and clean their tank at the end of the day, an opportunity too good to pass. Collin and Leslie brought 10-litre plastic buckets with lids and came home with the remains of what they had been carrying. Collin arrived home one night with a bucket of washing-up liquid, and Leslie took home a bucket half-full of liquid chocolate. Our next "freebie" was when he brought home two buckets of white wine. That weekend, we partied with Pat and Sid, who supplied the food. With so much booze, I was delighted when our Saturdays became regular. I couldn't wait to climb out of my baggy trousers, let my hair down, and forget about being miserable. During the afternoon, I'd call round to my neighbour/friend and was greeted by the aroma of curry bubbling on the stove or sausage rolls cooling on the unit. This was a much-needed break on my part. Sunday morning, they'd crawl around to ours for coffee.

Collin arranged with a neighbor from across the road for her daughter to babysit. Although Linda was only 13, her mother assured Collin she was a capable sitter. We were only two doors away, and Collin used to slip home during the evening to make sure all was well—until the night Sid noticed the length of time he was gone. But I didn't much care; the longer he was away from me, the better.

I answered the door and was confronted by two policewomen wanting to speak to me about Linda. *"Was I aware she had been truanting from school?"* (What the hell has that got to do with me, I wondered.) They told me Linda had been meeting my husband up the road and spending all day with him. Then he'd drop her off at night where he picked her up. They said if she continued to have anything to do with my husband, they would contact social services and have the girl taken into care. When the police questioned the mother, she could see no wrong with her 13-year-old daughter spending all day with a married man old enough to be her grandfather. But I didn't give a damn what she did or didn't do with my husband—she was welcome to him.

I closed the door and then remembered the police coming to the house the previous week, but Collin took them outside and closed the door so he could speak out of earshot. After the police left, he drove to the station and was gone for ages. When he returned, he said it had to do with work, but he failed to mention Linda was involved.

Collin was not as innocent as he claimed. There was a lot more to this story than he was letting on. I believed very little of what he said. As for Linda's mother, she had no morals whatsoever. Her nonchalant attitude made her no better than Collin. I was daft not to read anything into him leaving to check on the children, but now my suspicions were aroused. I did question him… bad idea. He grabbed my head with both hands and bashed it against the wall. *"That'll teach me to question him about his illicit behavior with an underage schoolgirl."* If Thomas Allen had known he had been driving around with a minor in his cab, he would have been instantly dismissed. Then, the children and I would have been in an unfortunate situation with no money, but we were the last people on his mind while he was having illegitimate liaisons with a child.

The incident between Collin and Linda destroyed our Saturday evenings. Thankfully, it did not interfere with my relationship with my neighbors. But Sid, who loved talking with Collin for hours, withdrew his friendship because Pat repeated something I told her in confidence. Sid was either disgusted or shocked because he cut all ties and they never spoke again.

Chapter Twenty-Seven

My Breakdown 1972

We had a Scottish family move in next door with four children. There was another woman too, who I assumed to be the mother. The whole family worked in a pub along the seafront and were particularly noisy when they returned home at night, having drunk half the profits. It was laughable watching them staggering along the street or falling out of a taxi and tripping up curbs.

Looking up from my ironing one Saturday, I saw their daughter holding Robert by the hair. She had him pinned to the ground. I shot outside to rescue my lad but was amazed when the brat would not release him. I tried prizing her fingers out of his hair, but the spiteful bitch still wouldn't let him go, so I tightened my grip little by little until she released him. What a horrible child. Nobody liked her; she was always looking for someone to have a spat with… a nasty piece of work.

That night, we were watching the end of the midnight movie when we were startled by the door knocker. Hubby should have gotten out of his chair, but it was me who answered. As I opened the door, the drunks charged in and attacked me. I tried to fight back but was no match for them. Collin, my quick-thinking husband, lay on the floor, and then I heard someone shout, *"The old man's having a heart attack; quick, get out!"* With that, they scarpered. Collin got up and asked if I was okay. Guess he wasn't having a heart attack after all, the bloody coward. Trembling, I made myself coffee and then called the police. After I gave them my statement, they went next door. When they returned, they said there was nothing they could do because it was "domestic." But how could it be domestic when three drunks barged in and attacked a defenseless woman at midnight? It all happened so quickly that I don't really know how many there were, and Collin was too busy feigning a heart attack.

I woke the following morning to find Collin had gone to work, leaving me traumatized from the night before. I honestly don't know how I got through the day. All I remember was wandering through the house in tears and punching my face. My insides were screaming as I tried to block the attack. I pulled my hair and banged my head on the door frame, but nothing helped. I could not take any more abuse from Collin, and the attack was the last straw. I curled into a ball and rocked back and forth. I don't know what time it was, but it must have been late because the children were in bed when I noticed Collin's tablets on the TV where he'd left them. I took one, even though I didn't know what they were, which was stupid, but I was not in control and unaware of what I was doing. The blue pill did nothing, so impatiently, I took another. Still nothing, so I took another… then another.

It was daylight when I woke to find Collin and our doctor standing over me. *"So, you took a trip to the hospital last night,"* said the doctor. I denied leaving the house, but he insisted I did, in fact, go to the hospital. Again, I denied leaving the house, then I remarked about the horrible taste in my mouth. *"That said,"* the doctor continued, *"it would be the stomach pump, where they pumped you out because you took an overdose."* Attempting to sit up, I indignantly defended myself. *"I did no such thing."* Then, Collin refreshed my memory. I sunk back into my pillow as Collin reminded me how he arrived home just as I was being carted off in an ambulance, with Simon holding the fort. Like a bad dream, the attack began to creep back.

I allowed my mind to piece everything together. What about my children? Who was in charge? Did they eat? Who put them to bed? All I recall was being upset and trying to block out the pain and humiliation… the tablets… then nothing.

I would like it known there was never any question of me trying to end my life. Although I was questioned about it when our doctor returned the following morning to discuss my overdose, I told him suicide was out of the question and stressed that I would never leave my children. Not in a million years could I put them through that sort of pain. There would be no one to care for them if I were not around. Where would they go? Nan, being elderly, would have taken my boys, but my girls would have been put into care and probably separated. The very thought of them fretting for each other and pining for Mummy saddens me beyond belief, so you can scrub the idea of me killing myself—*that* was never going to happen. I get upset every time Collin threatens to have them taken from me. I would have gone crazy not knowing where they were, and he knew it.

My overdose was brought on by the attack and Collin's lack of support. I was distraught, in shock, and needed comforting. I needed help, but there was no one. Then, hubby went to work and left me to deal with the aftermath alone, so I was far from thinking clearly. But I was not suicidal—I was having a breakdown.

Once everything had fallen into place, I was mortified. I shut myself in the bedroom, closed the blinds, and spent my days in solitude. I was crushed and beaten. I did not want to see anyone, especially Craig, because it was him who found me. But where did he find me? In what state did he find me? I was told my clothes were all over the place. I was hurting beyond belief. I had no fight left in me. I pretended to sleep when anyone entered and drank the coffee Collin left by my bed. I left him to care for my girls and take them to school. Then he'd disappear for the day.

I don't know how long it was before I began wandering through the house like an intruder. When I saw his car, I'd dash upstairs, crawl into bed, and turn away from the door. I needed help, but help never came. If Nan had suggested any, he would have refused because this is where he wanted me—helpless and dependent upon him.

It could have been days or weeks before a voice within urged me to pull myself together. By shutting myself away, I was playing into his hands. So, with the house to myself, I bathed and dressed, ready to greet my children from school. I watched as they climbed out of the car, then they saw me at the door and ran into my arms. Collin looked puzzled but said nothing. He shut himself in the kitchen and left the children and me alone. They talked excitedly about school and gave me all the latest gossip. I promised to be at the gates the following afternoon to take them to the swings before tea. That night, I read them a story before they slept.

I do not remember my boys being around, so Nan must have taken them, knowing things were not right. She never failed to visit daily, but I never acknowledged her presence and pretended to sleep when she entered. She must have been worried out of her mind to see me falling apart after she had protected me over the years. Thank goodness we had recently had the phone installed. It was the constant ringing that woke Craig, who told Simon he could not wake Mummy. Simon drove round and phoned the ambulance; otherwise, I may not have survived. So, I understand how easy it is to unintentionally kill yourself with an overdose when you're distraught and falling apart.

Thankfully, I gained strength when 'someone' forced me back from where I had been at my lowest ebb. The attack and Collin's lack of support had been the final straw. I can't imagine why I never called Pat, but I was not in control of my mind that day.

I have since wondered whether Collin left the pills out for my benefit. If I had not recovered, he would have had the perfect alibi—he was driving a coach full of pensioners to the seaside.

Chapter Twenty-Eight

A Brief Affair

We had just finished lunch when Leslie and Hazel arrived, eager to show us their new car. Leslie asked why I had never learned to drive, then handed me the keys to his old banger and offered to give me lessons. Collin was not pleased by Leslie's generous offer but passed it off with a casual remark. The car had seen better days and looked like it needed a decent burial, but Leslie assured me it was a good runner. I called my heap Betsy.

Once my provisional license arrived, which Collin reluctantly applied for, Leslie took me for my first lesson. Poor Betsy—what a state! To open the window, I had to press my fingers against the glass and pull it down, then reverse the procedure to close it. Part of the door handle had been snapped off, and the driver's seat was broken. There was a block of wood under the seat so the driver could see over the dashboard. Otherwise, it took on the appearance of a recliner. I was shorter than Leslie, so the block had to be moved further forward. The paintwork was a dull charcoal instead of the black body it started out with, God knows how many years ago. But I didn't care—I loved sitting behind the wheel, and Betsy belonged to me.

When Simon called the following week, I maneuvered the conversation around my lessons. I'd already had a few with Leslie and had gained sufficient confidence, and I wanted to show Simon how much I had learned. "So, when can I take you for a spin?" I said, rattling my keys. "Well, there's no time like the present," he said, smiling. I rushed to get my L-plates and headed for the door.

I was setting Pat's hair in my kitchen when Collin walked in. I could see by the glazed look in his eyes that he had taken something and was gunning for trouble. He started insulting my friend, which is something he normally did behind her back. He hung onto the door frame, slurring insults at the pair of us, but his gaze was fixed firmly on me. Then, he picked up his dinner plate and smashed it over my head before staggering out. We could hear him falling upstairs, cussing and swearing. I left Pat to clean the kitchen while I washed his dinner off my face and hair, then I changed my clothes. Pat stayed until he was asleep, but I did not want to be left alone, so I phoned Simon, who sat with me until morning. If Collin started again, I felt safe with Simon, who knew how to handle him. I could barely keep my eyes open, but I did not want to be left alone.

It was daylight when we heard him moving about. My heart was in my mouth. Then, he opened the door. He stood for a moment, surprised to see his brother, who did not respond to Collin's broad grin. Simon raised his eyebrows and waited to see what the "old bugger" (Simon's pet name for him) had to say. But the "old bugger" was as nice as could be. Perhaps he didn't remember his performance from the previous night. In which case, why didn't he query Simon's presence at 6 o'clock?

Simon was a freelance insurance representative but would have made an excellent counselor or psychiatrist. He was quietly spoken and had a gentle approach. He was the only person who could calm Collin when irate. I began turning to Simon more than ever. He was easy to talk to and knew Collin better than anyone.

Simon often called in during the evening, but after Collin's outburst, he was calling during the afternoon when in the area. I enjoyed these times. When we weren't talking about mundane things, I was telling him about the latest row, which was pretty much most of the time.

I used to speak to Simon about Collin's behavior in his presence purely to shame him. Simon would tell his brother he was a crazy old fool and remind him that he was lucky to have five lovely children and a good wife. The husband would smile and say how much he loved me, then go overboard with "darlings" and "loves." But by the next day, he was back to being the same nasty person.

I had been looking forward to watching the Olympics, but Collin had other ideas. He spent the day trying to goad me into an argument. Determined not to take the bait, I ignored him, but as the evening wore on, I began feeling vulnerable to his endless spurring. I turned up the volume on the TV, but realizing his goading wasn't having the desired effect, he started insulting Nan and my boys. I flew out of my chair and disappeared into Pat's to cool off, returning only once I had calmed down.

Collin waited for me to sit, then began again. I shot out of my chair for the second time and stormed into the kitchen, furious that he had succeeded in making me lose my temper. I banged the door, slammed the kettle on the stove, kicked the cupboard, slammed a few drawers, then threw my spoon in the sink, which made a racket as it clattered against the dishes. I didn't care how much noise I made, stomping around like a raging bull, shouting as many swear words as I could think of. Then, I marched into the lounge, ready for battle, and came face to face with Simon. I stopped in my tracks. "Where the hell did he spring from?" I thought, then I saw Collin standing behind his brother, grinning at me. I can't remember what I said or how I reacted to the surprise.

When I next spoke to Simon, he told me Collin had phoned him while I was with Pat and asked him to come round because I was out of control. Collin said I had been in a foul mood all day and he couldn't take any more. When I returned from Pat's, he continued his verbal attack until I snapped. He then watched for Simon's car so he could let him in discreetly. That night, I played right into his hands, and Simon witnessed me having a meltdown. How clever.

I was fed up with the constant rows, so I threatened him with divorce, hoping to shock him into behaving a little more civilly. But that didn't go down well. He threatened to kill me if I tried to divorce him. First, he would tell the authorities I was an unfit mother and have my children taken away. Then, he was going to wipe my name through the gutter and make me look like the biggest slut in town. By the time he was finished painting my name black, no one would have anything to do with me.

How ironic to have the misfortune of being married to two men wanting to destroy me.

I was sitting on the settee with my head in my hands, unaware that Robert had entered, until I heard his little voice: "Take this, Mummy. It will make you feel better." My son was holding a glass of water and some aspirin. Bless his heart. How did he grow into such a caring little boy? I drank the water and pretended to take the aspirin, which would have done very little, but my son did wonders. Situations like this were far too frequent. I recall some years later, kneeling in front of the washing machine, sobbing while taking laundry from the tub. Then, one of my children came from behind and hugged me. I'm unable to remember which child it was that comforted me that afternoon. Perhaps they may recall.

The thought of having my children taken from me terrified me. It would have driven me crazy not knowing where they were. That afternoon, I cried tears of fear with little hope of escape. I didn't know how much more I could take. How could I protect my children if I was unable to protect myself? He was breaking me little by little. I can't tell you how pleased I was to see Simon getting out of his car. I blew my nose on my way to the door, embarrassed by the state of my face, avoiding eye contact and keeping my head down. I needed his sympathetic ear. He was the only one I could talk to who understood.

I made coffee, which Simon carried into the lounge. I told him about the events from the night before, then turned away. My voice began to shake, and fresh tears stung my bloodshot eyes. Seeing me struggle, he took my cup and placed it on the fireplace, then pulled me into his arms. Those comforting arms were all I needed, and I burst into tears once again. Simon had observed our situation for some time. He knew this day would come, as sure as night follows day. His compassion helped me release the sadness his brother had created unnecessarily.

When I told him about Collin's threat, he assured me there wasn't a chance in hell of my children being taken into care. "You are a good mother," he said, "and the old bugger would never be able to prove otherwise. Everyone would speak on your behalf, and the old man would end up making himself look like a fool." Then, he cupped my chin and said he was going to shock me. Before I could compose myself, he kissed me, then braced himself for the slap. But instead, I asked him to kiss me again. Simon said he'd been wanting to kiss me for a long time but didn't have the courage. But now, it seemed the perfect time to shock me.

Simon reminded me of our first meeting in 1967, when Collin drove me to town with Robert and Tiffany. I do remember bumping into Simon that afternoon, but seconds after being introduced, Collin ushered me into the car and closed the door. He continued to speak to his brother and guided him to his own vehicle further down the street. At the time, Collin had just moved into our flat, but he told his brother we were making plans for a future together — that couldn't have been further from the truth. Perhaps Collin was warning his brother off... maybe he noticed a spark in Simon's eyes when we were introduced, or the smile on my face that lingered. But feeling desperate that tearful afternoon, I may have read too much into his words. What I did know was that I enjoyed Simon's visits. His gentle approach and manner were compatible with mine, and it became inevitable for both of us that a relationship was destined to follow.

I was hungry for the affection and kindness I had been deprived of, and Simon ticked all the boxes. It didn't bother me that he was related.

I was never sure whether Collin noticed a change in me or the sudden interest in my appearance, but I didn't give a damn. Of course, there was nothing going on, but we were both aware that a spark had ignited, and it was only a matter of time before we took advantage of the situation — just as soon as one cared to present itself. Yes, perhaps it was wrong, but I didn't feel guilty about the odd kiss in the afternoon, only about the consequences if my husband found out. But why should I feel guilty? Happiness is something we're all entitled to. I understand that adultery is one of the forbidden commandments, but what my husband was doing to me and my children was also a forbidden commandment. So, that makes him guilty too. Maybe I'm trying to justify my actions, but I didn't want my children or myself to spend the rest of our days being scared and unhappy with someone who had a violent temper. My husband was driving me into the arms of another man and didn't seem to care. I deserved to love and be loved, and if my husband wasn't man enough, then so be it.

With two family members giving me frequent lessons, I was progressing like a house on fire. The next time Betsy and I took Simon out, he sat quietly beside me and allowed me to show him how much progress I had made. I checked the rearview mirror and gears before pulling away. I drove to the end of the road and turned towards the cemetery. My passenger remained silent. I continued my journey until I reached my destination, then pulled onto his drive and switched off the engine. We smiled with the same thought in mind. I arrived home on the crest of a wave.

Collin was in bed when I crept upstairs. He pretended to sleep, but I knew he was awake. I don't think he knew how to handle what was happening. By now, he must have been aware of the spark between his brother and me, but I didn't care. I counted the days until Betsy and I could take our next excursion. Nothing my husband could say or do could dampen my spirits, and I slept peacefully until morning.

Chapter Twenty-Nine

Collin's Arrest

I was thrilled when Nan moved into a flat down the road from us. The flat was much smaller than the one we once shared, but it was cosy, and I felt safe knowing she was close by. She lived at number 39, and we were at 89.

Don was the transport manager at the airport and was in charge of all the vehicles. Collin had worked for him a few years ago but had since left the company — that must have been when he "supposedly lost his job" and moved in with us.

One Saturday, Collin came home and said he'd bumped into Don, who had invited us to join him at the Flair Path that evening. I'm guessing that bumping into Don was instigated by Collin himself, because it would have been most unusual for their paths to cross. Nothing ever happens by chance with Collin. *The Flair Path is for club members only*, and I missed my Saturdays with Pat and Sid, so I was delighted with the invitation and couldn't wait to meet my husband's old boss. I was overjoyed to have been blessed with another escape.

By the time Don arrived, my girls were in bed. At Nan's request, the boys stayed up to keep her company until 9 p.m.

Don was nothing like I imagined. At 5 feet tall, I witnessed him quietly but firmly put some guy in his place for swearing in front of a woman. *Wow*. My husband could learn a thing or two from this guy, I thought. Don was there to open doors, hold your chair, light your cigarette, and help you in — or out — of your coat. I was not used to being in the company of a gentleman or being treated like a lady.

I enjoyed our Saturday at the Flair Path and was thrilled when it became a regular event. There was another man who occasionally joined us, known as 'Biscuit' because his last name was Crawford. *Biscuit* would sometimes join us, too.

Most Saturdays, Don picked us up, then he'd drive us home. Other times, we'd meet at the club to be signed in. Either way, Don always ended up at our house for coffee and was never in a hurry to leave. Collin was on his best behavior at these times. I think Don would have put him in his place otherwise, and Collin preferred his boss to see him as a good husband rather than the hateful person he was. Sometimes, we took the boys to the club, but not at the same time. Don gave them money so they could play on the machines — he was more than generous.

Nan was always around for child care, and then Don used to drive her home. She enjoyed their little chats on the short journey, although it would have been Nan doing most of the talking. Don made sure she was safely inside with the lights on before leaving. She made him promise to call in for coffee anytime he was in the area. He had found a friend in our Nan, who was a pushover when it came to a gentleman. Like me, she had been unfortunate in her marriage, too.

Don had just returned from seeing Nan's home when Collin walked in and handed us coffee. I sipped mine and recognized the same bitter taste. I sat quietly, amazed that he'd dared to mess with drugs while we had company. I thought for a moment, wondering how I could get one over on him, then decided I would have to be as cunning as my husband. I wanted Don to taste my drink. I kicked off my shoes, rubbed my feet, and asked hubby to get my slippers from the bedroom. As soon as he was out the door, I quickly went over to Don and asked him to take a sip. He took one mouthful and gasped.

What in God's name has he put in there? He said, screwing up his face.

That's what he keeps doing to my food and drink, I whispered anxiously. Then we heard his footsteps on the stairs. I shot back to my seat and thanked Collin for fetching my slippers. Now, all I had to do was swap the coffee without alerting him. I waited for them to become engrossed in conversation, then I took a sip and told him, *You forgot the sugar.*

He assured me he had put sugar in my drink. *Perhaps you forgot to stir it?* He said casually. I walked into the dining room, humming to the music on the record player. Once out of sight, I quietly put the mug at the back of the pantry, took a clean mug from the cupboard, and made myself coffee — relieved to find enough water in the kettle so I didn't have to use tap water. Still humming, I jangled the spoon noisily, pleased to think I had gotten one over on him. I returned to my armchair.

Is it okay now, darlin'? He asked with a smile.

I told him the coffee was fine.

Monday morning arrived, and so did Hazel, having dropped her eldest boy at school. I told her about the coffee and asked her to try it.

Jesus, what the hell... You need to take that shit to the police station. Don't you realize if any of the children get a hold of this stuff, it could be dangerous? What is he messing with, for God's sake?

I took her up on the offer to drive me to the station with the coffee I had transferred into a jar. Nan was on hand to care for my girls.

I gave the jar to the duty officer and asked for the coffee to be checked for its suspicious contents, as my husband had put something in my drink. They took my name and address, then I left. I should have realized that making a serious complaint against my husband would have consequences, but I had never dealt with anything like this before.

Within the hour, two police officers arrived in an unmarked car and chauffeured me back to the station for questioning. It was ages before they took me home on the condition that I did not contact my husband. They wanted to know what time he was due home because they were going to arrest him. They told me there would be an unmarked black saloon at the top of the road, and when I saw him turn the corner, I was to take my children to my friend's house and stay there. They did not want us around in case he became violent… all this cloak-and-dagger stuff scared the hell out of me.

Every couple of minutes, I was at the window. Then he turned the corner. I watched the saloon pull slowly from the curb. I ushered the children towards Pat's side gate as the car crept slowly behind him, which he was unaware of. He waved as I turned into Pat's sideway, but we kept going. Once inside, we rushed to the window and peered from behind her nets. We watched three officers follow him to the door. Then they ushered him into the back seat between two officers while the third officer drove. Collin was baffled by the arrest and kept asking why they were taking him to the station (I cannot remember how I got to hear this). Once out of sight, I walked the few houses home, not knowing what to do next. I feared the repercussions that were sure to follow.

He was gone for a couple of hours before the same officers brought him home. They searched the house, garden, and his shed. They were about to leave when the officer in charge turned, shook Collin's hand, and said he'd be in touch. The second officer placed his hand on my husband's shoulder and suggested he find me a good psychiatrist because I needed help. They wished him luck and left... I could not believe my ears... I was dumfounded.

Collin told the officers I concocted the whole story because I wanted a divorce but had no grounds, and everything in my statement was a fabricated lie. Furthermore, if there was anything in the coffee, I had put it there myself. How in the hell he came up with a story so convincing in such a short space of time? I will never know, but Collin was a master at these games.

He watched them drive away, then closed the door. He turned to me and laughed. *"You'll have to be a lot smarter than that, my girl, if you want to catch me out. They never believed anything you said."* He walked away laughing and shaking his head. I was shocked and disappointed they believed his lies, but Collin was a genius when covering his tracks. My Jekyll and Hyde husband had won again.

He often used to say with a smirk: *"Believe half of what you see and a little of what you hear,"* which sounds like a cryptic clue, but Collin loved games. The only difference was — his games were devious. Whether it took weeks, months, or even years was of no consequence. He had the patience of a saint and could deceive anyone with his charm, accomplishing anything he put his mind to because he was meticulous. Collin reminded me of a prowling cat looking for its next kill. Everything was a challenge to him. He had to prove he was cleverer than you — the victim. Nothing he said or did went without cause. His brother once said, *"His carefully chosen words were like venom trickling through your veins."* His inflated ego could turn one person against another with little difficulty. The scary thing was I never knew what he was thinking in his silent moments or what was behind his smile. I was always falling into one of his traps. He could create any situation to make me look stupid or at fault. Every scheming plot was centered around me, and I never knew when he was lying — I don't think he knew the difference.

I recently read an article from a forensic neuropsychologist who claims that a person can be mentally ill at the same time as being legally sane. Insanity is when a person may not understand what they are doing, but covering their tracks proves they are not only sane but have mental issues bordering on a personality disorder. But if you look into their eyes, they appear cold — dark and menacing. *They are evil.*

After my encounter with the officers, I didn't care whether they got back to me — not now that they suspected me as the culprit. I felt powerless with no one in authority to turn to. I never dreamed for one moment the tables would turn and I would be under suspicion. But what I didn't think of was — I could have given them Don's name and place of work to confirm everything I had said, but being scared and nervous, I never gave it a thought.

He was still taking barbiturates, which made him crazy. Once the children were in bed, I stayed upstairs but could hear him falling into furniture, knocking things over, and mumbling to himself, then calling out but not making any sense. Eventually, he'd stagger upstairs, hanging on to the bannisters or crawling on hands and knees. I don't know how my children slept through it, but they were used to these incidents. One night, I sneaked downstairs after he had crashed out and saw the armchair in the middle of the room on its side.

We had a full-size mirror on the wall at the top of the stairs. I used to stand in the doorway of the small bedroom and watch him creeping up on all fours. He looked scary.

We were not sleeping together, so I'd take my pillow and spare blanket and curl up at the bottom of one of the children's beds. I went from bed to bed, looking to see which one had the most room, but if that child became restless or stretched out during the night, I had to drag my blanket and pillow to find another bed. The only time I had a bed to myself was when one of the boys stayed with Nan. Sometimes, I was too scared to close my eyes but would fall asleep out of sheer exhaustion. I tried sleeping on the settee, but that encouraged him to sit in the armchair opposite. It was frightening to wake and see his silhouette and shock of white hair in the half-light, watching me.

It was some weeks before the officers returned with their findings. Inspector Gibson and the second officer took Collin into the kitchen while the other officer searched the house once again. I remained seated. When the officer completed his search, he came and sat beside me. I was not surprised to hear they had found barbiturates in the coffee. Then he told me I should stay cautious and not hesitate to report anything if I was at all worried, no matter how small. I simply nodded. After what seemed like ages, the officers returned with Collin close behind. As they reached the door, Inspector Gibson turned and said, *"You better keep an eye on her"* (pointing to me). *"If anything happens to this girl, we know who to look for, and we'll be down on you like a ton of bricks, so you better look after her and keep her safe. You understand what I'm saying?"*

I cannot tell you how relieved I was to know they actually believed me. They were simply playing with him — waiting for him to slip up.

Regarding the coffee, there were not enough barbiturates to kill me, but over time, it would have built up with devastating results, depending on how much I ingested. But I never consumed much because everything tasted bitter. Nevertheless, my concern was that one of the children may have gotten hold of something he had meddled with.

I have watched films where tablets are crushed and put in drinks, but what surprises me is the recipient never notices and downs the lot, whereas I was able to taste it right away. So, he must have been using a hell of a lot for me to detect it so easily… perhaps he wasn't as smart as he thought — no matter how clever, you always trip up.

Chapter Thirty

Secrets Revealed

We were about to start decorating when our neighbour knocked and asked Collin to look at his car. Down went his brush and he was gone for the afternoon. The following week, another neighbour asked my obliging husband to help fix his bike, so he trotted off like a lamb. I began to wonder if he'd instigated these incidents because they were so well-timed. Collin was always looking for an excuse to disappear and get involved with whatever the neighbours were doing. He loved to impress people with his abundance of knowledge, but I was fed up with his wisdom and lectures I had endured over the last 24 months.

I was bitching to Hazel about Collin being (a know-it-all). Her response was one I will never forget: *"He probably got his knowledge from all the books he read when he was inside."* Startled, I asked, *"What are you talking about? Inside... inside what?"* She stared. *"My God, you don't know, do you?"* Shaking my head, I asked, *"What is it I don't know, Hazel? I haven't a clue what you are talking about."* And I still don't know what she meant by inside. *"Do you mean inside as in prison... inside as in jail?"* I sat transfixed, anxiously waiting for her to continue. She lit another cigarette and chose her words carefully. She told me Collin had served 10 years in prison for premeditated murder. Hazel did not want to say any more. She said it was best if I spoke to his family. I was beyond shocked and terrified to think we were living with a murderer. I couldn't wait for Hazel to take her noisy kids and bugger off. I paced the floor wondering what I should do next. If only we could get away, but where could I go with five children? I had no money.

I had planned to spend the day with Hazel, so I applied make-up that morning. I was in the hall when he came home. He looked me up and down and called me a fucking prostitute. So, I called him a fucking jailbird. The words had barely left my lips when I froze… if only I could retract those words, but it was too late. He swung round and glared at me for what seemed like ages but was probably seconds. I had often stood up to him in the past but knew when to keep my mouth shut. I also knew when he was about to erupt because he'd scowl and glare at me with piercing eyes. His brows used to meet when he frowned. Then he'd clench his mouth tight so his lips disappeared. Through no fault of his own, his hair formed a peak down his forehead, so he looked like Dracula. In fact, his face took on a whole different appearance. I was always nervous at these times, but now I was terrified.

I wanted him out of our lives, but he made his intentions very clear that he would sooner kill me. I was scared stiff – life became impossible.

Auntie Joan and I were in the garden talking to her neighbour next door. I was telling Dot about my husband, who had been the height of conversation since the news became apparent. To my amazement, she knew about his jail sentence because her husband was working with Collin when his second victim died. Cripes! There must have been plenty of gossip circulating, which had died down by the time I became an employee. Apparently, there was nothing I could tell Dot that she didn't already know. She and her husband assumed I was aware of his past and thought me stark raving mad to get involved and even crazier to marry him. But what I do not understand is why this news never reached my ears sooner. People love to gossip, but then Collin made sure I had no contact with anyone from his past and those I did, he was always present.

Now I understand why he pressured me into cancelling Craig's appointments with the psychologist. He did not want my son to reveal that Collin Wainwright was sharing our home.

When Collin committed the crime, I was 11 years old and living a sheltered life with Nan. By the time he left prison, I was in Canada, so I knew nothing about his past. But why didn't Norma or Terry warn me? We spent enough time socializing. This scandalous crime should not have been kept from me because I had children to consider. If I had such knowledge, I could not have kept my mouth shut.

Collin continued doing crazy things whilst under the influence of drugs. One night, the police brought him home at 3 am. They found him crawling in the middle of the road and thought he was drunk. The commotion woke Craig, who helped me get him upstairs and into bed. Nothing would endure me to sleep that night. I kept checking to see if he was still alive. The bedroom was almost dark except for the soft beam from the pygmy bulb on the landing that cast a faint shadow across the room. All I could see were his thick eyebrows and shock of white hair. This is not what I should be dealing with, least of all my 12-year-old son. Collin's outbursts became more frequent and violent. One afternoon, I tried to escape another attack by running down the garden. He eventually cornered me in the lounge, picked me up like a stuffed toy, and threw me. I landed on the gas fire on the opposite side of the room. The following day, my knees were various shades of black, blue, and purple from the chrome grid on our new fire, which now had a massive dent from the impact. I don't know what my girls thought, who were under school age. Perhaps time wiped the incident from their minds.

Pat was horrified when I showed her my legs. She hid a spare latch key and left a blanket and pillow on her settee at night in case he repeated the performance or threw me out, which was something he threatened. But I could kick myself for leaving my children, failing to see the danger they were in. I assumed his anger was directed only at me but realized my children were just as vulnerable – none of us were safe.

Perhaps we could have gone to some sort of shelter, but I'm not sure there was such a thing in the early '70s. But then, we may have been separated, and I could not have coped without my children, and they would not have coped without me. Besides, once these people get involved, there's no telling where we will end up. Christ, I may never see my children again. The very thought had me in tears.

It had been months since we were at the flare path. I think the episode with the police and drugs were the cause. I missed Don, who we hadn't seen in ages. Don always greeted me with a compliment, which my husband never did. When I applied make-up and set my hair, Collin would insult me, but Don always commented on my appearance. He used to call me *flower*, *blossom*, or *petal*. In fact, I don't remember him ever calling me by name. It's amazing how a kind word and a friendly smile can make you feel special. Respect and kindness were all I ever wanted – but it was the one thing I never had.

Chapter Thirty-One

A Friendship Lost

It was no secret that Collin had a fetish for drugs. I kept my eyes peeled, but they'd turn up whenever he saw an opportunity. Fortunately, I was able to detect them, but it was hard trying to stay ahead of his sick games. I always prepared our meals, but that didn't stop him from wandering into the kitchen to meddle. Like the time I was preparing our evening meal—I took my eyes away for a moment, and on turning back, I noticed the red speck in the pan. It was the remains of a capsule that had started to melt. Unsure where the contents were, I tipped the lot away. Telling him to stay out of the kitchen would have been futile and probably caused a row, so I kept my mouth shut. Later that evening, I saw another red speck in the jar of coffee mate (*that only I used*). I left it until he was upstairs, then tipped the lot away. Either he was becoming careless, or he was hoping I would run to the police with my latest findings. But if I had gone to the station each time he did something stupid, the police might have thought I was crazy or stupid. Perhaps that was his intention, so I chose not to report the repeated incidents and the problems they created.

Pat phoned every morning to check on my safety. As soon as I answered, she'd say, *Okay, see you later,* then hang up. If he picked up, she'd ask for me—all she needed was to hear my voice to know I was safe. If I was okay, then so were my children.

As we never closed our blinds at night, I often saw Don drive slowly past. Other times, I'd see his car parked a few houses away. Collin thought I was stark-raving mad because Don lived in the opposite direction. It was years later I discovered Don—concerned for my safety—did, in fact, drive past most evenings. He'd either leave his car up the road and walk back and forth or park across the street until he saw me.

One night, I answered the door to Inspector Gibson and a couple of officers. I led them into the sitting room as Collin was rising from the settee. They asked to speak in private, so he took them into the kitchen. When they returned, Collin looked worried but hid his concern with a stupid grin. As they reached the door, Inspector Gibson turned. *I'll get something on you one day, Wainwright, you wait and see. I don't care if it takes me a lifetime—I will find something to pin on you.* He pointed towards me. *You better guard her with your life and make sure nothing happens to her because I know where you live, OK.*

I was getting used to the law dishing out these verbal threats. Aware of Collin's track record, they knew I was in danger. Collin assured me their visit was nothing to worry about. He said they were looking into an incident regarding a caravan that had been dumped before being set alight, and his car had been seen in the area. Leslie said they were looking into stolen goods from Thomas Allen. I never did get to the bottom of that—I had other things on my mind.

Simon often called in when he had papers to deliver in the afternoon. Sometimes, he took me and the girls along for the ride. I loved those little trips—it was a treat being able to relax instead of being on edge all the time. Unlike Collin, Simon took everything in his stride and always had a kind word. He was very patient because all I did was talk about the latest row. If he got fed up with hearing me bitch, he never complained. But I needed someone I could unload onto other than my friend Pat—that is until Sid took her to the doctor's.

Pat had become tearful, depressed, and had trouble sleeping. Once inside the surgery, she burst into tears. The outcome was—she was *living my life with me*, and it was making her ill. So Sid told her it was time to stand back and not be so involved. I was upset and felt rejected, wondering how I would cope without her. Selfishly, I needed her friendship and support. I was unable to confide in Nan because of her age, but she was far from stupid. She knew there was trouble in our house, even though I did my best to hide most of what was going on. I'm sure the children told her stuff—by her comments and the way she glared at the husband when he wasn't looking. How much she knew depended on what my children told her and what she herself witnessed. The only other person I spoke to was Simon.

Although Pat had withdrawn her friendship, she continued to phone every morning to check on my safety. But I missed our morning chats over coffee and escaping into hers when he became violent. Regrettably, the saga of my marriage was too much. I never knew if she took her latch key in or left it out for any emergency.

With Simon in my life, I found the strength needed to take that first step to freedom. I had put off making the call out of fear, but now I felt able to cope. All I needed was another outburst, and I knew I would not have to wait long.

Peace reigned for 24 hours before it became necessary to contact the solicitor. But on the day of my appointment, I got cold feet—until Nan reminded me it was our only means of escape.

I entered the building and introduced myself, then wondered if I was being a little hasty. When I made the appointment, I was full of determination, but my confidence had suddenly died. I was about to leave when a lady appeared and introduced herself. Mrs. Lamb took me into her office and said she would be handling my case. An hour later, she guided me back to the reception and said she would be in touch. I walked away, having taken my first step to freedom.

Unfortunately, it was my husband who picked the letter up from the doormat. I had hoped it would arrive when he was out so I could arrange for Simon to be with me, but nothing worked to plan. He never completed reading before he was stomping about in a rage. I crouched on the settee, waiting for the first blow. Then he marched to where I was huddled until his face was inches away and whispered through clenched teeth, *If I can't have you, I'll make sure no one else does—because I'm going to kill you.*

When I told Mrs. Lamb, she assured me it was an idle threat that all husbands say when faced with divorce… but I knew different.

My driving lessons came to an end when he gave my car away because he said it was not roadworthy. When he put the clutch down, his foot went through the floor. I believed him at the time, then realized it was another lie—having spotted *Betsy* being driven through town. But by getting rid of my car, I was unable to leave.

Chapter Thirty-Two

Collin's Heart Attack

I cannot remember why we visited my Father because it was something we never did without an invite but we paid him a visit…sorry them a visit.

It was over tea that Dad mentioned a particular letter he had written to me when I was in Canada. He went into detail of its contents - puzzled, I told him I had never received such a letter and the 'devil woman' jumped in and spoke defensively. *Well, I know he wrote it because I mailed the letter myself;* it amazed me how she remembered that particular letter from 20 years ago and at short notice - but how did she know that 'particular letter' was the one in question unless she'd read it before destroying it, my reading with the sand reader sprang to mind.

Camilla didn't waste time bragging about all the things she and Dad brought for Alice's little girl and Duncan's pregnant wife, not to mention her nieces and nephews, brag, brag, brag then there was their recent holiday she thought I might be interested in…yawn…yawn. I was glad when it was time to leave so I took our cups into the kitchen. This gave her the opportunity to show off her new cooker. I was still using the cooker that belonged to Collin's mother, running my fingers along the front of their shinny cooker, I innocently said, 'I would love a nice cooker like this.' *Oh, go on with you; you don't do too bad* she snapped. I withdrew my hand as if the stove were hot. That remark hurt; what did she mean, for goodness sake? I had nothing compared to them, my cooker was old and in bad shape and I was still sleeping in Collin's old bed with his dirty mattress that God knows how many women had slept on, I had nothing decent in the way of furniture and nothing new to wear neither did my children but then - Alice and Duncan were lucky that Dad's inheritance helped fund their lifestyle so they could look down on those less fortunate, I was told Dad paid for the deposit on Alice's house meanwhile Nan, Craig and I were living in a one bedroom rented accommodation, Dad also set Duncan up in business and now the lucky guy was driving a Rolls Royce with a private number plate, Camilla couldn't wait to tell me Duncan brought Dad a private number plate for Christmas but that was the least he could do, he was a Father to them I had been denied, cheeky bitch telling me I don't do too bad, did she know what hell we were going through of course not…was she interested….not in a million further-more I did not want her knowing. I may sound like a bitch but I'm not really…pissed off, yes…but I'm not a bitch. If I have given the impression I dislike the woman, then you're not wrong.

I was shocked when Leslie phoned to say Collin had had a heart attack at the wheel of his truck; he'd been experiencing chest pains for some time which our GP said was anxiety - any anxiety would have been brought on by his own actions.

A colleague from Thomas Allen visited me and kindly left his number should we need anything. Leslie called in each day and so did Simon who did not take advantage of the situation. One afternoon, we were talking about life in general when Simon said I should write a book. Laughing, I told him I would have nothing to write about. *I don't know so much,* he said, tapping my forehead; *you have a mind full of information up there - there's a great deal waiting to be said.* I casually brushed it off; *perhaps one day, Simon, when I am old and grey,* I laughed at the remote possibility of writing my memoirs but he was right. There is much to be said.

Collin was discharged a week later, having told staff that his wife "yours truly" was a nurse and would be looking after him...I was furious to think I was expected to nurse the husband I was planning to divorce.

He was about 5/6 weeks into his recovery when I was aware of the change. He was considerate and kind, he brought in washing and helped with dishes. The sudden change in his behaviour caused me concern.

I was getting the children ready for bed when he mentioned our lack of space and said we could do with an extra bedroom, he suggested going to the Council to see about a four bedroom property, he waited for my eager response then said he would apply first thing Monday on condition I drop the divorce because he wanted to give our marriage another chance and promised faithfully to change his ways, I knew there was a catch - yes I wanted to move but giving him a second chance was the last thing I wanted, he was unpredictable and violent and I was scared but on the flip side he did have health issues that needed to be taken into consideration, after giving it some thought I reluctantly agreed, I suspected he may have some trick up his sleeve so I needed to be a lot more vigilant, he was thrilled when I agreed to his terms but rekindling our vows depended on him finding a property, I was adamant about a four bedroom house so I had every faith in him because he always got what he wanted - he could charm the carcass from a vulture. The following morning, he put our names forward for an exchange.

I contacted Mrs. Lamb about his proposition who suggested I put the divorce on ice for six months. If, within that time, he slipped back into his old ways, we could pick up from where we left off but after six months, I would have to start over. She assured me he would probably fall back into his old ways within a few months - I was giving him weeks.

I was pleased to be leaving the drunks next door. Since the attack, they looked down on us as though we had wronged them. I couldn't wait to leave Vic and June. They lived on the other side to the drunks – they too were a troublesome bunch. Their kids used to aim tomatoes and all sorts at our windows and door when it was open, their mother June thought nothing of shouting abuse from across the garden, not the sort of behaviour you would expect from a grown woman naturally, her children followed suit, abuse was something we did not need we had enough of that at home. I was never sure whether Vic knew how his wife behaved while he was at work - I suspected not so I decided to get my own back.

I had watched Vic for weeks making a picket fence for their front garden; he meticulously screwed each slat into place before painting them white. I looked on in admiration, wishing my husband would do something like that for us but I would have settled for him being nice. Earlier that day, their kids had been hurling abuse at my children so I had no choice but to bring them in. I was furious when hubby refused to do anything so I took matters into my hands. I waited for darkness and made sure my children were sleeping, then I took a brush full of red paint and ambled along the street, dragging the brush along the fence. I repeated the performance until I felt satisfied. Now, all I had to do was wait until morning to view my handy work normally I would never do such a thing but there is only so much a person can take and this family had pushed me too far. There was no damage done to the fence but Vic had to get his paint pot out again.

The downside to the move was leaving Nan; she moved so she could be close and now we were leaving her behind. Nan and I agreed that Craig should stay with her until half term then he could start his new school after the holidays - plus he had privileges with Nan, he would have been denied at home.

Chapter Thirty-Three

Our New Abode 1973

It was a few weeks before we received the letter to say we'd been allocated a four-bedroom townhouse. It was in a bit of a state and needed complete decorating and new carpet which Collin happily paid for. Life was a lot easier now he'd got his own way. He ignored Dr's orders and bustled about rolling carpets and lifting boxes. Being the sole owner of the shed, he packed that up and helped the men load the van, including a 'broken pick-axe'.

With an extra bedroom, it didn't take long to get straight. We had a bedroom and W/C on the ground floor – a lounge and kitchen/diner on the first floor. The top floor had three bedrooms and a bathroom. We also had a driveway with a garage that ran under the lounge, and our back garden was small with a side gate.

We settled Robert and the girls in their new schools but I was concerned when they put Morgan in a different class to Allison. Morgan had always been clingy and didn't settle easily being separated from Allison who was the stronger twin. I spoke to their teacher but cannot remember the outcome.

I can't imagine what I had done – or didn't do to make him so angry but Collin was holding my head and banging it against the frame of the street door but he quickly disappeared when our neighbour came to intervene. A few weeks later, our Dr sent me for X-rays because of the persistent pain in my neck and head.

Another of his violent outbursts was just after I had tucked the twins in their beds, a short time later I heard them running around, I was on my way upstairs - aware Collin was close behind I quickened my pace but he caught up with me in the bedroom picked me up and threw me with amazing strength I sailed across the room and through the door without touching the sides I continued my journey until I hit the banisters, I was about to roll down stairs then grabbed the handrail, I recovered from what could have been a serious accident then I noticed Robert at the bottom of the stairs looking up at me, poor kid must have been terrified and God knows what my girls thought, by morning my hand was swollen and painful so he took me to our surgery, Collin was sitting beside me when I explained the attack, our Dr raised his eyebrows and told hubby he needed to calm his temper, everything happened so quickly I do not remember sailing through the air only hitting the banister and seeing Robert at the bottom of the stairs, I don't know where he got his strength from.

I answered the door to a gypsy selling wares. She looked to where Craig was standing and said *keep an eye on him; he's hurting inside - keep the blond boy close and no harm will come to you and he will always look after you* Robert was blond but he was at school…impressed by her knowledge I kept her talking hoping for more news, she went on to say:- *no man would break your heart but your children will and there will be another man in your life but a dark haired woman will always be in the background.*

I was uplifted to think another man meant Collin would soon be history and true romance was on the horizon and hoped the dark-haired woman was someone innocent like a child or an aging mother. She ended her message with a warning to watch my husband when he makes my drinks…clever lady.

Joan phoned to say George wanted to see Robert. I was to take him to her house on Saturday at 3 pm, we arrived well before time and patiently waited. I watched the hands tick slowly by then Joan answered the phone…it was George to say he couldn't make it, she handed the phone to Robert who was on the phone for less than a minute then he wandered off deflated, we travelled home in silence and Robert never spoke of the incident again, the rejection must have hurt deeply. Nan was furious and wanted to give George a piece of her mind but did not know where he lived, Howard knew because their paths often crossed.

It was a year later when George made contact again to say he wanted to take Robert to the zoo. Understandably, I was concerned in case he failed to arrive and I would be left to pick up the pieces but - he turned up and took one excited little boy to the zoo along with the woman in his life and their two children. I never asked Robert what they talked about and he never said whatever they discussed was between Father and Son but it left me wondering if George took the opportunity to tell Robert I was responsible for the distance between them because Robert has accused me more than once of preventing Father/Son relationship which could not have been further from the truth, if I were responsible I would not have agreed for them to go to the zoo, neither would I have taken him to Joan's the day he never turned up, further-more he never made contact again.

George eventually passed away but did so without knowing what he missed. I am more than proud of everything Robert has achieved from years of hard work. He runs a successful business, keeps his books straight and holds the deeds to his bungalow which he achieved without any help or encouragement from his poor imitation of a Father. Unfortunately, Robert and I clash; trying to hold any form of conversation with him is like wrestling with a bear but he's fine with everyone else. It must be a Mother/Son thing.

Jumping ahead, Robert is now an adult and in a split relationship with a young daughter. He knows only too well that when a Father wants to see his child, wild horses won't keep him away.

Since Collin's heart attack, we survived on disability allowance. It was a struggle making ends meet but I was used to juggling our finances. Collin was always looking to escape from family life so he went job hunting. It didn't take him long to find work in a petrol station. He had just left for work when I answered the door to the Inspector which surprised me being as we had not informed them we had moved then I remembered Inspector Gibson telling Collin he was keeping an eye on him. Perhaps the inspector had passed the old house and noticed different occupants and contacted the Council as to our whereabouts. The inspector must have seen Collin leave. Otherwise, he would not have knocked without making things difficult for me. I led him into the kitchen, then he opened a paper bag and handed me the empty coffee jar with the label 'exhibit one.' I assume the jar was an excuse to check on us; otherwise, why return an empty jar he could have thrown away but it was comforting to know they were keeping an eye on us.

Collin - like everyone got paid at the end of the week, by Friday, our cupboards were empty as was my purse. I'd watch the clock, hoping he'd arrive home soon. Even then, he only gave me sufficient to buy something for that evening then I had to wait until Saturday for his giro by which time he'd left for work. Hazel told me to forge his signature and get to the post office before they closed but I never did in case I got caught.

One evening, I was talking to Mable who lived at the end of the close, when Morgan came and asked when we were going to eat because she was hungry. I told her as soon as Daddy gets home, I will go to the shops - I feebly smiled then Mable opened her purse and gave me £5 and told me to hurry to the supermarket before they closed. She was cross and told me to knock any time I needed money for food. Bless her. I was so grateful.

Collin continued going off into the night, topped up with whatever he'd taken - coming home all hours and falling about. I don't know how he managed to work the next day. Hazel told me to shove him downstairs and finish him off. *It's not your fault if he keeps falling over, is it?* She said, laughing. I told her *with my luck, he probably wouldn't die,* still laughing. She replied *you'll have to make sure he doesn't get up then.*

I became friendly with Julie from across the road. One day, she asked if I could keep an eye on her two children until she returned from work; she often stayed for coffee when she collected them, one afternoon she told me about a strange guy she'd seen hanging around when she came home after a night out, Collin appeared from no-where and paid great attention - encouraging her to release more information about the prowler/peeping tom.

A couple of weeks later I saw Robert playing with a pick handle he'd found in our garden so I threw it in the sideway, a few days later it was back so I threw it out again then I saw it in the road, a few days later it was in the sideway then back in my garden, the pick seemed to turn up every-where to the point I began looking for it when putting out washing or walking the girls to school - then it disappeared altogether.

I often heard Collin creeping about during the night, always sneaking about while everyone slept. The following day, I heard him telling our neighbours he'd seen a strange guy peering in their downstairs windows. I thought he was seeking attention, unaware it was part of a sinister plot.

It was no secret to the family that Emma wanted Simon to walk her down the aisle but he was reluctant to make any form of commitment; a wife was not going to fit into his casual lifestyle plus there was our time together so I was surprised when he paid us a visit and said he was getting married at the end of the year, Collin congratulated him then turned to me *Excellent news isn't it darling* to which I had to agree, I suspected Collin was somehow involved by the look on his face – it spoke volumes (*well that'll stop your little caper won't it my girl - just as I put a stop to the driving lessons*) I later discovered Collin told Emma about the affair…I should have guessed. They say all good things come to an end and I was used to my happiness surviving for only a short time. Perhaps things would have been different when we first met but we never got a chance to find out. Collin made sure of that, too.

Chapter Thirty-Four

A Robbery At The Garage

I answered the door to a police officer who said the garage where Collin worked had been robbed. Two youths had bashed him over the head, stole the takings, and driven off in a white car, and my husband was in hospital with a possible concussion. I tried to look concerned, but the officer assured me he was ok and would be released within a few days. I closed the door. *Never mind, he's not here now*, I whooped, running upstairs with my little dog Peppy at my heels.

Collin was released the following morning but said nothing of his attack. He had been home a couple of hours when two officers arrived and took him back to the station because they were not satisfied with his statement. He returned a few hours later and said they'd found the missing cash under the till where he'd stashed it, and they were charging him with theft, so now he needed a solicitor to represent him. He left for town and returned a few hours later with the relevant forms to apply for legal aid and a form for our weekly expenses. Due to his failing eyesight, he asked me to do the honours… I was filling in the form with our expenses when he asked me to make our outgoing greater than they were by adding a catalogue we didn't have. Half an hour later, he placed the forms in his wallet and left for town.

On the day of the hearing, I sat in the gallery along with Joan and Howard and a few of our neighbours who — by now — were aware he was not as holy as he led them to believe. Collin entered the court, fumbling like a blind man. He was led into the dock with hands outstretched in case he tripped. Then the clerk gave him the Bible and spoke for Collin to repeat (*I declare, etc*). Once he had been sworn in, he cupped his ear and tilted his head as though hard of hearing. Because of his heart condition, the Judge said he could sit if he wasn't feeling well, then they offered him a glass of water... his performance required an Oscar, but the trump card was when his solicitor addressed the court and produced *MY* letter in *MY* handwriting. She told the Court I was running up expenses that he was unable to meet, which forced him to work whilst on benefit. She told the Court I took his weekly giro and left him with no money to buy a little tobacco. The poor man was unfortunate to be married to a woman who had destroyed his self-esteem and taken his independence. She made me out to be the wife of hell and had the entire Court feeling sorry for him. I was stomping at the bit and had to be silenced by my entourage. The Judge looked towards the gallery and demanded silence. I was livid. *I* was the one with no money — skimping and scraping every week, trying to make ends meet.

Collin was charged with theft, forging a robbery, and working whilst claiming benefit but walked away a free man — something only he could achieve — and I helped him put a noose round my neck.

I was concerned over Craig, who appeared distant — more so than usual. He was reluctant to talk about what was bothering him, so I decided to get medical advice. I contacted the surgeon and told the receptionist of my concern. She said the Dr would visit once he'd finished surgery. Within the hour, the Dr arrived with a couple of social workers who asked to speak to my son in private. Collin and I stayed in the sitting room while Craig — a little puzzled — led them into our kitchen/diner. Half an hour later, they returned and said my son was bordering on suicide and being taken into care.

Suicide! I screamed in alarm. I could not believe what they were saying. The very thought of my son living with total strangers horrified me. I told them he could stay with my Nan, who he adored. They replied sternly that my son was at breaking point and would be leaving right away, but I was adamant he was not going to strangers and told them he would never survive. I would never rest, neither would Nan, if she thought for one moment he was suicidal and living with strangers.

Craig was upstairs packing as I continued to beg them not to take him into care. Collin remained seated, listening to my pleas. Then, *if you won't let him go to my Nan, please let him stay with my Auntie,* he loves it in her house… it's a happy, carefree home. He has cousins there and my Auntie would look after him like her own. *Please, please don't take him to strangers.* Craig would miss his family, and the consequences would be far greater. They could see that I was not the problem as I continued to plead — thank God they agreed. I called my Aunt, who I knew would not refuse my son. Furthermore, I could see him whenever I wanted. The officer said Craig would be unable to return while my husband was living on the premises (*speaks volumes*).

How in the hell did it get this bad? How did I not notice what was happening right under my nose? This was my worst nightmare — that the bastard husband was responsible for. *He* had done this to my son. My darling boy never spoke of his feelings, never told me how unhappy he was. In fact, he never complained about anything… never.

I contacted my solicitor, who applied for an immediate injunction to have Collin removed from the premises. Collin went to his solicitor and had the injunction overturned. He came home laughing and said, *you'll have to try another trick because that one didn't work. Trick?* This was no fucking trick. If there had been a fraction of decency in him... one iota of decency... he would have left the house so Craig would not be parted from his family... but separating me from my boys was part of his plan.

I feel unbelievable pain for the hurt and sadness Craig suffered. I did not realise just how much damage the bastard did to my firstborn — and to think, when he was a baby, I promised to protect him always. Over the years I often spoke to my son when things were tough. He was sensible and grown-up, which is why I used to bitch when I was troubled, but I never realised the burden I was putting on his young shoulders — unaware he was taking everything to heart. It was so very wrong of me. I wish my son could have found the strength to talk to me about his troubles and the pain in his heart as I spoke freely to him. If he was unable to speak to me, he could have confided in our Nan, who would have moved heaven and earth to help him. I used to blame myself, but soon realised if he could not speak to our Nan, then he was unable to confide in anyone, so I released myself from guilt. Craig, being the eldest, had seen and heard far too much for his age, resulting in depression and suicidal thoughts.

Collin began moulding my boys from the moment he entered their lives. However, Robert was made of stronger stuff and often challenged Collin, like the time I was bringing in washing from the garden. I cannot remember why Collin was angry, because I never put a foot wrong, but he was shouting at me and raised his arms in a threatening manner. Robert came charging in with a garden fork like a soldier with a bayonet and screamed. *You leave my mum alone!* Collin pushed me aside and lunged at Robert. *Let me get the bastard boy. I swear I'll kill him one of these days.* I dropped the washing and stood between them with arms outstretched until the evil one strode upstairs, mumbling threats. My protective lad was no taller than 4 ft.

Chapter Thirty-Five

Leslie's Warning

My heart was not in the reconciliation. It never had been; it was time to start the ball rolling again... no longer was he going to keep me on a tight leash. I wanted my freedom. I contacted my solicitor six weeks before my cooling-off period — all those promises to turn over a new leaf had been lies. It didn't help knowing of my affair, but it was him that drove me away in the first place. I *accepted* life without love; all I wanted was the respect with a little kindness.

Mrs. Lamb greeted me and said she'd been expecting me. I was about to tell her about Collin's past when she raised her hand and said whatever happened before the marriage was inadmissible, but we were living with a murderer so it has everything to do with the case. I was determined to make her listen if it was the last thing I did.

Leslie was visiting daily because Nan had asked him to keep an eye on us. I had just served coffee when Collin began talking about the night stalker. He went on and on and said he'd seen him peering in the downstairs bedroom window, which was where I slept. Then he left the table and went upstairs to get his tobacco. Leslie leaned forward and whispered, *Watch him, Olivia; he is up to something... you think about it, right... he's as blind as a bat and waiting for eye surgery, so how can he see anything out there? That worktop is really wide and don't forget the wide window sill — he would have to climb on the work surface and press his face against the window.*

Even then, there's no way he could see your window. It's too dark... pitch black. He's definitely up to something. Leslie watched my expression as things began to fall into place. Then we heard him on the stairs. I whispered to him not to leave without me. After our second coffee, Leslie grabbed his keys and said he was heading into town. I pushed my chair back and asked if I could hitch a ride, as I had things to do myself. Collin did not challenge me in Leslie's presence.

Once in the van, we were able to talk freely. *The funny thing is,* said Leslie, *he's the only one that ever sees him. I'm bloody sure he's making it up because he's always complaining about his eyes — he even squints when he's rolling a fag. I don't doubt Julie did see a prowler, but that was weeks ago. He's just keeping the story alive to scare the hell out of everyone. Olivia, I'm really worried about you. Please be careful.*

On our way to town, Leslie told me when he was a little boy, he remembers Collin doing some home improvements. He tiled the bathroom and ran an electrical cable from the chrome soap dish around the bathroom and into the bedroom next door. Then he connected the wire to the radio, so when his wife took a bath, he turned on the radio. When she touched the soap dish, she got a shock. One morning, after he left for work, she broke down and went next door in tears. Her neighbour was suspicious when the incidents only happened when he was at home. She called an electrician who smashed the tiles and found the wire with 230 volts. He checked other appliances and found everyone had been tampered with... the police were waiting for him that night.

Then he stole a uniform and charmed a 15-year-old girl into believing he was an officer. When he got the girl pregnant, her brothers threatened to kill him unless he married the girl. So he used a false name and married the 15-year-old, failing to mention he had a wife at home with three children… he served an additional nine months for bigamy. The story of bigamy surfaced when he was arrested for murder. Perhaps he wanted to get rid of his wife so he could play happy families with the schoolgirl.

I was reeling from shock… our next stop was the library. Leslie pulled out the newspaper and printed them off for me to read at leisure. Of course, keeping them from my husband could be a problem. Taken from the newspapers — it was May 1951 when, at the age of 30, Collin was found guilty of premeditated murder. The Judge said it was a cold-blooded and deliberate murder attempt. His mother and family were in court when he was given a 10-year prison sentence. But sending someone to jail can often be futile… they become better criminals.

After an eventful day, Leslie dropped me at the corner of our street. *Don't forget to have a good look for the pick handle, Olivia, because he is definitely up to something. And don't turn your back on him for a minute, okay? Be careful, love. See you tomorrow.*

I arrived home the same time as my girls. Being empty-handed, he wanted to know where I had been. I avoided confrontation but discreetly searched the house and garden for the pick. I checked the sideway and peered over fences. The more I thought about it, the more I suspected Collin had it safely hidden because the only place I did not look was his bedroom. He hounded me all evening and continued to pass snide comments until I lost my temper. *Okay, so you want to know where I have been… well, I've been to see Inspector Gibson… I told him of your plan to kill me with the pick handle that you've safely hidden, and when I least expect it, you're going to bash me over the head and the innocent prowler will be blamed for my murder… oh, by the way… the inspector is going to call in a couple of days, he wants to speak to you.* I have no doubt that lying about my day with Leslie and the inspector saved my life.

He stomped upstairs and began dragging things about in his bedroom. I thought he was trashing the place. Then he came racing back, cussing and swearing. *There's your bloody pick!* he snarled, throwing it across the floor... it spun round and landed at my feet... I went cold. Leslie was right — he was waiting for an opportunity, like bringing the washing in before bed... and it would all be over. I was pretty shaken knowing I was weeks — possibly days — from being murdered. It would be a waste of time to phone the inspector. Besides, I don't suppose he would have been on duty, and I could prove nothing — it would be my word against his.

Collin was always one step ahead of everyone. He never left anything to chance, but it was his careful, calculating, waiting for the right moment that, for once, went in my favour.

I ran from the house over to Julie's, then noticed her lights out... damn. Then I saw Doreen and Cyril were up, so I knocked. When Cyril answered, I asked to speak in private. He led me into their sitting room where he was watching TV with the family, so he pulled up a dining chair for me to sit. I stared at the screen until whatever they were watching had finished. Doreen turned off the TV, and Cyril walked me to the door. As I stepped outside, he asked what I wanted to speak about. I told him Collin was planning to kill me. He patted me on the back and quickly closed the door. I did not know what to do next or where to go. I was cold and scared but did not want to go home. But with nowhere else to go... I crossed the road to the house of horrors. I opened the door and heard my girls crying hysterically. They were almost screaming. I slammed the door and raced along the hall. They fell silent when they heard my footsteps and peered over the banisters. I saw the look of surprise on their tear-stained faces as they raced to greet me. I fell to my knees as my twins threw themselves into my arms. I asked what was wrong. *Daddy said you had left home and you wasn't coming back anymore.* Morgan was clinging to my neck, begging me not to leave, and Allison was sobbing and stroking my hair. I prised myself away and raced to where he was standing in the corner of the second staircase. I punched him in the chest a few times, then continued to the next level with my twins close behind, to where Tiffany was sobbing in her sleep. Dear God, what must she have felt, thinking her mummy had gone and would never return?

I touched her face to gently wake her. She opened her eyes, then threw her arms around my neck and began to sob uncontrollably. Everything the twins had told me — she confirmed it all. I told them to climb into one bed so I could hold them, kiss their little hands and tearstained cheeks all at once. I needed that connection. I couldn't imagine the fear they'd felt, the pain they'd been made to carry. What kind of pleasure did he get from breaking their hearts like that?

All I could do was reassure them — pour my love into every word.

"I promise you, my darlings, I would never leave you. Not in a million years. I love you far too much. You're the reason I wake up every morning. Without you and the boys, I'd have nothing to live for. Yes, I get cross sometimes, but I would *never* leave you. Don't believe anything he says — he's a spiteful, wicked old man. If I ever decide to go anywhere, I promise with all my heart I'll take you with me. Do you understand? So please, don't listen to him. He's evil."

I held their tiny hands, kissed their faces again and again, and spoke softly until they calmed down. Once they were settled, I tucked them into bed and read them a story. I kissed them goodnight and promised I would be the one to wake them in the morning, and as I left the room, I turned to see their little faces smiling at me from their pillows. I blew them a kiss, whispered, "I love you," and gently closed the door.

Tears are streaming down my face even now as I relive that night. Just remembering the fear my girls endured — it rips me apart. What kind of monster takes pleasure in hurting children? What kind of man would make them believe their mother had abandoned them?

But now, it was time to face him.

I found him waiting in the lounge — sitting there like the beast he was, anticipating the storm he knew was coming. I didn't think twice about my safety or the neighbors sleeping on either side of our terrace. I marched right up to him and got so close I could smell his foul breath. And I let it all out — every bit of rage, grief, and terror that had built up inside me.

"You fucking evil monster!" I screamed, my lungs nearly bursting. "You've already driven my sons away — and now you want to break my girls too? Is *that* what gets you off, you sick piece of shit?"

I was shaking with fury.

"What made you do that? What's going on in that twisted, diseased mind of yours? And you've got the nerve to accuse *me* of turning the children against you? You've done that all by yourself, you clever bastard."

I jabbed my finger into his chest, trembling with rage.

"You don't deserve to live. You don't even deserve to breathe God's air. You should be strung up. You're going to die a lonely old man because you've turned everyone against you. The kids hate you.

I hate you. Oh, and by the way — I've restarted the divorce. I'm done living with your sick games. Now there's something to chew on, you pathetic excuse for a man."

I kept shouting, kept swinging. He didn't try to restrain me — just cowered like the coward he was. He wasn't a man. He was a shell filled with evil.

I believe now that he told the girls I was gone to test their reaction — to see how they'd take it if I was actually dead. Because that had been his plan. But I ruined it when I told him I'd spoken to the inspector. I think that lie saved my life.

Tiffany used to wake at night sobbing, saying she dreamt I was dying. I see it now — those weren't just dreams. They were premonitions.

That night, I crawled into bed and wept. For all of us.

I couldn't stop thinking about the pain my daughters had endured. I wanted my boys home too, but first — I had to get rid of the monster. And that was proving harder than I ever imagined. The divorce was dragging on. He had promised to make me fight for my freedom. And he was keeping that promise.

Thank God for Leslie. He called that morning. He warned me. He saved me. I never saw him again after Hazel stormed over, flinging accusations about an affair. She had no idea what she'd done — or what she'd cost me.

Later, I called to speak to my son. Howard answered.

"No — he's not your son, is he really?"

His words stung. I still don't understand what he meant or what he was implying. But it broke something in me. I wasn't to blame for all this. None of us were. We were all victims. Collin made sure of that. Not a week passed without some kind of incident. I had no control.

If being scared of living with a murderer makes me a bad person — then I'm guilty as charged.

When I tried once more to explain Collin's prison sentence to Mrs. Lamb, she cut me off again. So I reached into my bag and pulled out the old newspapers. I placed them on her desk.

She gasped when she saw the headlines and immediately called her secretary to bring us coffee. As she read, her face changed. She looked up at me and said the words I'd waited so long to hear.

"This changes everything."

She began conducting interviews with my family — at their homes, after hours, which she said was highly unusual. She told them mine was the most horrific case she had ever encountered. The divorce, she said, would be heard in the High Court in London.

And it would be a three-day battle.

Chapter Thirty-Six

Let's Party

Uncle Howard had his own car repair business. He was great with anything practical but always got himself in a muddle when it came to the paperwork. Joan was relieved when he gave up the garage and went into catering. Most of their work was weddings, and whenever they were short-staffed, he'd call me in to help. But that caused problems with my family. Nan had Robert, and with no other choice, my girls had to stay with Collin.

I *hated* leaving them, especially knowing how upset they'd get. One Saturday, in particular, still haunts me. The girls were begging me not to go, each taking turns to plead with me. Then I heard the car pull up outside. I kissed them goodbye and told them to be good so Daddy wouldn't get cross — but by then, all three were crying, grabbing at my arms, desperately begging me not to leave.

I made my way downstairs, my heart in pieces, and I could hear them running to the window. *I kid you not — it was heart-wrenching.* I opened the car door and looked back. All three were at the window, shaking their heads, tears streaming, and little Allison was banging on the glass with her fists.

Howard, watching this, had the audacity to say, "They need a bloody good hiding, carrying on like that. Bloody well spoilt, that's their trouble."

I could kick myself for not slamming that car door and going straight back inside.

Christ, they weren't spoilt. They were terrified. They didn't want to be left with that beast, knowing he'd make their day hell. He was either nagging at them or poisoning their minds with cruel words about me — and it always left them distraught. They never cried when I left them with Nan. In fact, they used to wave me off, smiling.

They weren't spoilt. They didn't have nice clothes, barely had any toys, and rarely got their own way. *How dare he imply otherwise?*

The contrast between my cousins and my children was like chalk and cheese. My cousins *loved* being with their dad. He hardly ever scolded them, and if he did, it was brief and fair. They had everything they wanted. That was typical of Howard — always ready to put the boot in when it came to us, especially me.

Even the neighbours used to refer to my kids as *"those poor little kids."* Everyone knew they had a rough time — *and so did Howard.* Craig being suicidal was a prime example of just how deep the damage went.

Howard would pay everyone else at the end of the night, but I always had to wait until Sunday. Then he'd drive round and hand me a crumpled £5 note — which worked out to about 42p an hour. I should've refused, but I needed the money. Besides, they were family.

One Sunday, he went a step too far. He pulled out a fat wad of notes, fanned them out in his hand, and suggestively flicked them in my face. I turned and walked out of the room.

It was July when Collin got the letter confirming his surgery for Friday. I was *thrilled.* He'd be gone for two nights. I ran straight over to tell my neighbour, Beryl, who immediately suggested a celebration.

"You ought to let your hair down, girl. Have a party! I reckon you need it."

With no money, I scoffed at the idea. But Beryl offered to bring food and drink and started naming neighbours who, having seen through Collin's façade, would jump at the chance to celebrate his absence.

Once the word got out, Flo and Mick offered to bring food and drink. Julie was up for a party at the drop of a hat. I invited Mary — she lived a few doors down. A single parent like me, and loads of fun. We'd hit it off the first day we met. Same sense of humour. Always found something — or someone — to laugh at. Fiona and Dennis, from across the street, knew money was tight and offered to bring food before I even mentioned snacks.

All I had to do was provide the music.

Flo and Mick were the first to arrive, arms full of party dishes. Julie turned up with her favourite drink in hand. Fiona and Dennis came bearing snacks and wine. The only men there were Dennis and Mick. Julie and Mary were divorced. Beryl had just separated from her husband. And *my* other half was tucked up safely in the hospital.

As the night wore on, the house filled with laughter and music. It felt like *freedom*. Before everyone left, I told them we'd party again the next time Collin had surgery — and promised I'd be better prepared.

About a month later, he got another appointment. I told Beryl to spread the word. She asked if she could bring friends — I agreed, as long as they brought drinks.

At 7 PM, people began to trickle in. The music started, and the house came alive. My girls were excited, picking at the rare treats our lovely neighbours had brought. Robert was with Nan, so he missed out.

Beryl answered the door to the friends she'd invited. Ken showed up alone — his wife was unwell. Owen came solo too — his wife was on holiday. At least they brought drinks. But of course, just my luck — *I finally get rid of my husband for a night, and Owen spends the evening following me around, trying to talk about his marriage problems.*

Blast him for putting a damper on my party.

The following day, I skipped cooking and had a picnic with the leftovers our neighbours had generously donated. Treats were rare, so my girls were more than happy to enjoy cold party food in the garden — giggling and munching without a care in the world.

Then Beryl called down from her window. "Owen's phoned — he wants to see you."

I rolled my eyes and told her I wasn't interested. I reminded her of some of the awful things he'd said about his wife. "He's full of bull," I said. "I've heard it all before."

She looked genuinely surprised. "Well, if that's what he told you, it must be true. He's the most genuine person I know."

I was taken aback. *Could he really be decent?* Maybe I'd misjudged him — which wouldn't be hard, given the circumstances. *After all, what kind of woman trusts easily when she's already survived a monster?*

Still, I thought it might be interesting to see what he was like sober. If he was truly as unhappy in his marriage as he claimed, then maybe we had something in common. I agreed to a coffee at Beryl's that evening.

I let Owen do most of the talking. And to my surprise, he didn't seem so bad after all. We kept things light — no discussion of his marriage or mine in front of Beryl. The next evening, he visited me at home but didn't stay long.

Apparently, when he left Beryl's the night before, the police had stopped him. There'd been a local burglary, and the suspect was seen driving a white van. Owen, being a builder, drove a white van — unlucky timing.

Then he said something strange.

He told me, "My biggest fear is going to prison."

What an odd thing to say. I brushed it off at the time... *but years later, I'd understand why.*

Owen and I began meeting during the day. Being self-employed, it was easy for him to lose time here and there, but it was much harder for me. Collin watched my every move like a hawk, his suspicions never far from the surface.

Owen said he wanted a divorce — claimed his wife was unstable and capable of anything. She'd threatened suicide before and blackmailed him every time he tried to leave. I was still waiting on a date for my hearing, so I took everything he said *with a pinch of salt.*

Owen was rough and ready — not polished, but strong. He had a bold character, a far cry from Collin's manipulative control. If someone crossed him, he wouldn't think twice about swinging a fist.

He told me, "If Collin ever hurts you again, I'll sort him out."

How gallant.

Chapter Thirty-Seven

Time To Celebrate

It was October 1975 when I travelled to London for my divorce, there were eight of us in the carriage including my dear friend Pat.

Mrs Lamb was waiting inside the main door when we arrived; then I noticed Collin with his solicitor grinning at me. Mrs Lamb went and spoke with one of the clerks, then our names were called. Collin quickly whispered to his attorney, who promptly walked over to the clerk and spoke out of earshot. Mrs Lamb looked puzzled and went to find out what was going on. She returned with a smile and said Collin had decided not to contest the divorce after all. Perhaps, seeing me with my entourage, knew he didn't stand a cat in hell's chance. Collin went into the Courtroom with his solicitor and mine. Ten minutes later, Mrs Lamb reappeared. She walked over to me smiling – took my hands and told me I was a free woman. Collin made me squirm unnecessarily but he promised to drag the divorce and make things as difficult as possible. That must have been the only promise he ever kept.

My journey home was one I will never forget, I brought wine and paper cups and got tipsy, our train was standing at Romford station, the guard blew his whistle and we began to slowly pull away. Then I leaned out the window and called how long before we reach Fenchurch street? The guard came running over, *Madam you're on the wrong line and you're going in the opposite direction.* Laughing, I collapsed into my seat. The guard, trying to keep up with the fast-moving train, shouted to my fellow passengers, *Did she just get married?* They all shouted, *No, she just got divorced!* The guard disappeared as the train gathered speed.

Goodness knows where Collin was but I didn't much care, nothing could possibly dampen my spirits that afternoon. When I walked through the door Nan greeted me with a huge bunch of flowers and a congratulation card from her and my children – *relieved he was out of our lives but bad news is never far away,* the divorce would not be absolute for six weeks during which time he was allowed to stay in the matrimonial home, under the circumstances he should have been escorted off the premises for all our safety.

His six weeks was finally up and he still had no place to live so Owen found him a flat and dumped his belongings, but Collin was not going down without a fight. About a week after he left I took my washing from the machine and noticed everything had a brown tinge. I put it back to wash again but it came out worse than before. I checked the kitchen tap and brown water gushed out. I waited for Owen who climbed in the loft and found handfuls of rusty wire rammed in the pipe of the tank – *which Collin did before leaving... it didn't bother him the children would be ingesting contaminated water.*

Conclusion

1 – The day Collin received the solicitor's letter about a divorce was the day he decided to kill me, but it was after his heart attack when he began to put his plan into action. But first, he had to isolate me.

2 – He convinced me to give our marriage another chance by using a four-bedroom house as bait. He needed to get me away from Nan who lived too close and called in too frequently.

3 – Simon's visits came to an end when he told Emma about our affair.

4 – He put a stop to Leslie's visits by telling Hazel we were having an affair.

5 – He convinced our neighbours I was unbalanced, disturbed and neurotic, so I would have no-one to turn to. Collin spent hours in the garage with the door open chatting to passing neighbours. Everyone knew him as Mr. Nice Guy, Mr. Friendly who couldn't do enough, so obliging and considerate, always with a smile, always with a compliment and ready for a joke. He was never short of something to say. It didn't take him long to build their trust and convince them of my mental state so I would have no one to turn to, which is why Cyril shut the door on me.

Little did I realise when Julie told us about the prowler that my days were numbered, with murder in mind he took the pick out of hiding and left it for Robert and neighbouring boys to play with, my final hour would be when I brought in washing which would co-inside with Mick collecting Flo from her evening job the attack would be quick and there would be no witnesses because everyone lived upstairs and our gardens were hidden by trees…it was pitch black…menacing. Collin had the strength of a bull I would have gone down with one blow I would not have seen it coming, he would have had plenty of time to clean himself undisturbed with the children sleeping two flights up, as we were not sleeping together I would not be missed until morning, all he had to do was be patient and that is something Collin had plenty of…patients…he was like a black widow and just as dangerous, time was of little consequence but his plans were foiled with Leslie's warning and my threat of the Inspector, the innocent prowler never knew how close he came to being framed for murder and I lived to tell my story. The pick was what he used to smash my twin pram, he brought from our old house.

I later discovered that Collin was under a psychiatrist; if he got caught, what better way to ensure a lighter sentence than having a psychoanalyst on your side.

It had taken my cunning husband six years from declaring his undying love and sterility to planning my murder. He was evil to the core. If he had put as much effort into our marriage as he did his scheming games, we could have had a happy home. But a blissful marriage was not what he wanted. He had murder in mind.

Sociopaths can be dangerous, they feel no guilt or remorse and can be hungry for power. They are habitual liars with no empathy and are excellent performers. They can't imagine what other people are feeling neither do they care, but contrary to popular beliefs sociopaths are not all evil, many live normal and productive lives never revealing their true nature. Sociopaths have excellent social skills they can be charming productive and magnetic – drawing people in but they can also be cool calculating and patient, taking all the time they need to lay the ground work for a situation that will be beneficial to them.

Chapter Thirty-Eight

From Frying Pan To Fire

I introduced Owen to the family who took to him immediately, especially Howard. Once he realised, they shared the same interest in sport, they started going to the local football match every Saturday but rather than travel in two cars, Owen offered to pick Howard up and drop him off after the game. They had been going to football a few weeks when Howard told Owen I had an abortion when I was 17 years old. I was so stunned I did not know how to respond. Christ, haven't I been through enough with the bastard husband without him telling blatant lies about me? I couldn't wait to tell Nan who advised me not to say anything that may cause Joan to act on impulse. Perhaps I should not have taken her advice and risked the inevitable, whatever punishment Joan imposed would be no more than he deserved.

Many years ago, it was rumoured within the family that Joan paid him an unexpected visit at his workplace. She found the garage locked and her husband in the café across the street playing cards, aware the woman that owned the place was a little too familiar; it aroused her suspicion but when he got caught, he'd get angry, attack being the best form defence which is admission in itself.

When Nan and I were in Canada, Joan wrote with exciting news to say Canada House had accepted them and they would be joining us soon then she discovered Howard had gambled most of their savings from the sale of their home with her dreams shattered, she was inconsolable so she packed her bags and walked away from her children and the husband that betrayed her. Howard pleaded for her to return but she refused. Not until social services threatened to take the boys into care did she return. 12 months later, she gave birth to Charlotte. I don't think Joan ever trusted him again but she was a good woman and stayed loyal until he passed away, just as her Mother had done many years ago. It was for this reason Nan told me never to say anything that may cause them to separate. She turned a blind eye to his faults to protect her family and asked me to do the same. *We mustn't say anything;* she used to say *we can't risk upsetting Joan then there's the children to think of. If anything should happen between them I would never forgive myself.* I respected her wishes but shielding the family gave him freedom of speech so now it is time for me to let go of the past.

There will be some that will be disturbed by my story but those that live in glass houses should never throw stones because he was far from perfect.

Whenever company was expected, Howard called on me to help, leaving my boys with Nan. I'd help Joan in the house then prepare and arrange food which was something I enjoyed. I remember standing by the dining room door when their guests arrived. They complimented him on the fine spread and asked him to stand by the table to have his picture taken...my name was not mentioned and he avoided eye contact. He certainly wasn't shy about taking the credit. Don't get me wrong, I did not expect a drum roll but a mention for my efforts would have been appreciated. Joan often needed help and I was pleased to oblige but eventually stopped because I never got any recognition from him and God forbid if anyone paid me a compliment, he couldn't bear anyone to think or speak highly of me, as slander and gossip spread like wildfire people selectively believe what they chose and scandal is so much more interesting.

I could go on and on about Howard but this book is not about him but as he's contributed to a lot of my problems, he is going to be mentioned. I have lived in the shadow of his lies long enough. I should have spoken up sooner if Joan walked out...or better still kicked him out. It would be no more than he deserved but he took every precaution to shield his immediate family. I know my cousins will be upset by my writing and may want to silence me to protect his image but I am the victim here, not him; fare is fare and right should be righted.

Nan loved and protected all her family although Charlotte believes otherwise, Charlotte was aware of Nan's reprimanding glare assuming she was not liked but we have all experienced that glare when we were out of line, Howard worshiped his daughter she could do no wrong, she has never forgotten the time Nan called her a little bitch, Christ when I was a child she often called me as a little bitch or little cat with a piercing look to boot - she did the same with my children which they probably deserved, Nan had little patience for tantrums, despised laziness and could see through crocodile tears and did not welcome back chat but she loved all her grandchildren and was protective towards every member of her family (staying silent was proof enough) Nan had a strict upbringing and raised her family the same me included but I was never rude or cheeky I knew better, she could flash one of her looks and bring me down to size if I was out of line, but something I learned from an early age was never to cross her, she was a strict parent and grandmother she was not generous with hugs and kisses but if you were good you were rewarded with kindness which meant a lot to me and my children, she was an amazing woman.

Nan was especially close to my boys but it didn't mean she loved her other grandchildren any less she just wasn't as close, she had been part of their lives since birth and she helped me raise them which has nothing to do with favouritism, my cousins had two parents for guidance and so did my boys.

They say you should never pass judgment on anyone until you have walked a mile in their shoes, yet I have been criticised and judged for all the bad things my children have been through but no one should draw conclusions without being in possession of the facts I think the venom from the past still trickles through the family so now it is time to clear my name although I'm not sure it will clear the air.

With my writing, I often jot little reminders to myself and leave them lying around. One was (do not want Auntie to read book) most of what I have written she will remember anyway but I did not want to open wounds she may have forgotten…allow me to explain…

As a youngster, I spent hours with Joan, she cared for me while Nan worked and she treated me like a daughter which – with no mother I happily accepted and we became close.

I was living in Canada when Joan and Howard separated but when they reconciled Nan told me not to upset the applecart. She did not want to say or do anything that may cause them to separate again.

As time passed, Joan did not have age on her side and I did not want to open wounds or events from the past she may have forgotten. It would have been too upsetting, hence (do not want Auntie to read book). I always study the feelings of others but it is rarely reciprocated.

Chapter Thirty-Nine

The Night Stalker

Owen confessed to Judy that he'd found someone else. She refused to accept their marriage was over and got a flat, hoping he would ditch me and return home. When that didn't work, she threatened suicide but that didn't work either so she left the children and moved in with friends - that also failed. Judy was an attractive woman, she was slim, good looking and had a nice figure but she also had dark hair…was this the dark-haired woman the gypsy warned me about, I wondered.

I looked forward to the weekend when Owen stayed over, knowing Judy's kitchen skills were not up to my standard. I enjoyed cooking for him but I was too proud to say my budget was being stretched and I was struggling. It niggled me when he said he gave Judy £60 a week. Goodness knows what she did with the money because Owen paid for everything apart from groceries. One evening, I was about to serve dinner when Craig said *Oh, mincemeat, that's three times this week and it's only Wednesday* I laughed at his wit then realised it wasn't funny.

I was at the street door waiting for my girls when my neighbour Mable came over to speak. *I saw your hubby the other night* she said, pointing across the road; *my hubby and I kept peering through the curtains, wondering what he was up to because he was there a long time looking up at your windows.* She went on to say she had seen him the previous week at the end of the close watching the house *only. I thought you ought to know, being as he doesn't live here anymore.* Thank goodness I was at the door and grateful to Mable for the information; with no car on the drive, Collin would have known I was alone. I would like to thank my kind and elderly neighbour who came to my rescue for the second time.

I recently watched a documentary about the behaviour of coercive husbands after divorce. Their unpredictability can be dangerous, having lost the power they once used to control their victim which made me wonder how much time he spent lurking about at night. We had no bolts on our external doors and they were glass top and bottom with glass side panels so breaking in would have been easy…it was time to move.

As soon as the children left for school I caught the bus into town and hoped I would see someone right away and not have to make an appointment, I made my way to housing and asked to speak to whoever was in charge of exchanges because my case was urgent, I was taken to a room where a gentleman was seated behind a desk I told him about my X being a murderer and stalking me, he allowed me to ramble on for a few moments before easing me out of the chair he guided me to the main desk to collect the relevant forms to take home, I was still rambling on about being stalked when the elevator doors opened and out stepped my old rent collector Pete who greeted me with a smile, I quickly turned to the none believing officer and said *why don't you ask this gentleman he'll tell you all about my husband he knows him* I quickly told Pete about my divorce - Collin's threats and being stalked - Pete's smile quickly faded he told me to take a seat then they disappeared into a side room, 10 minutes later they reappeared, Pete touched my arm and assured me everything would be fine, the officer apologised and guided me back to his office and asked if I had any preferences as to where I would like to live and promised to be in touch soon. I was more than grateful to have bumped into Pete that morning.

Within a week, I received a letter offering me an exchange in Bowman Boulevard. They asked if I would like to view the property but I declined. It was 16 houses away from Joan and Howard.

It was 1976 when Judy and Owen officially separated - Owen suggested we move in together as a family. I was downsizing so it was a bit of a squeeze with no garage to stash anything although we did have a shed but Owen claimed that, as a builder, he wanted it for his materials. The move was a straight swap so Owen moved my stuff into our new home and brought their belongings to the property I was leaving. I could see Owen getting angrier by the minute because Giles (the woman's husband) was not pulling his weight. I watched Owen load their washing machine in the van but did not secure it properly; as he pulled away, the van doors flew open and the machine landed on the road. I pretended not to notice and closed the door.

It was midnight before the children were settled. Owen and I were in the kitchen drinking tea and munching biscuits. After the problems I had endured with Collin, I told Owen I wanted honesty in our relationship and if either one of us was unhappy, we must talk things over, to which he agreed. It was a couple of weeks before we got the children settled in their new schools. My boys had further to travel with his daughter Cathy who at the last minute decided she wanted to live with us. Not wanting to start off on the wrong side of the law, we spent the afternoon at DHSS to inform them we were living together. Owen told the guy that he was prepared to support me if they would continue to provide maintenance for my children. The officer appeared uninterested so we left without advice.

Collin phoned every couple of weeks and arranged to see the girls. Owen refused to let him in, so he took the girls off for the day. Collin had a lady friend. I have reason to believe she was on the scene long before we were divorced…water under the bridge…I liked to think he was not alone in spite of what he had put us through but I will never understand why he chose to destroy any future he had with me and the children. What a stupid man to have thrown everything away. I did not love him but I was prepared to live in a loveless marriage. All I wanted was stability with a little respect and kindness. I wondered if this new lady would show the same tolerance if he played her up or should I say when he played her up, she could leave at any time because there were no children involved. It was only a matter of time before the evil monster reared its ugly head because leopards never changed their spots.

It was the week before Christmas when Leslie phoned to say Collin had been found dead in the home of his lady friend. She came downstairs and found him on the settee; she was naturally upset to think their wedding would not be taking place as planned but what a lucky escape she had, who knows what he had in store for her. Leslie said he would keep me informed as to when the funeral would be but I had no wish to attend then realised it was my duty to represent our twins.

Snow lay on the ground on the day of the funeral. Owen went to start his taxi but was unsuccessful. I watched as he fiddled under the bonnet. I was anxious and time was getting on. 20 minutes later, he came in, rubbing his hands and said he would try later. Needless to say, I never made the funeral. He tried an hour later and the car sprang into action…how strange.

I suspected his unsuccessful attempt earlier was deliberate.

219

The twins were upset and annoyed with me for not attending but by the time Owen had finished messing around, it was too late to make alternative arrangements. Owen, a self-employed builder/decorator, drove a cab in the winter so he could have got another driver to take me - or at least given him a jump start.

It was spring when Judy was banging on the door, causing trouble. Owen was a bundle of nerves; he over-exaggerated when blinking and started chain-smoking. One night, he hid his taxi a few streets away so she couldn't find him.

Judy had been in and out of mental hospitals for years. She'd had ECT treatment in the past and survived on tranquilisers and all sorts. Owen didn't think she was ill now but said she was using past experiences to control him. After weeks of causing havoc, she'd disappear like a speck of dust and life returned to normal.

We spent a peaceful summer before she showed up again, causing us to bicker. Owen became moody and kept picking on the children. He told me they were lazy and I needed to be tougher. Robert was a lively lad with an abundance of energy, thundering up and down the stairs two at a time then he'd disappear in the shed which infuriated Owen who said the boy needed more discipline. Our arguments where about Judy, my children or money. I was still trying to come to terms with how generous he had been with Judy while I continued to struggle.

One evening, Judy phoned from her neighbours to say she'd locked herself out and wanted him to let her in with his spare key as soon as he left. I called her house and she answered, *Oh, I'm glad you found your way in then* I hung up before she had a chance to speak but she called me back and gave me a mouthful when I questioned him about having a spare key he said he liked to check on the children to make sure they had sufficient food, what about our food cupboard I thought, but I didn't say anything he had enough on his plate with her.

Another time, she called and spoke softly in a husky voice. I can't imagine who she was trying to impress but as I answered, she said *I'm sorry to bother you* I replied 'that's okay. I wasn't busy and hung up and walked away laughing; she called back and swore at me.

Owen came home one day looking agitated and told me never to open the door because Judy was threatening to throw acid over me. I was furious and ready for battle should she come knocking but he went mad and dared me to open the door. How gallant! I thought Collin never showed protectiveness towards any of us; in fact, we needed protection from him. I was concerned that in one of Judy's outbursts, she would start a fire by shoving something through the letterbox. The street door was at the bottom of the stairs so a fire would have prevented our escape. I hated the dreaded woman; she caused all sorts of mayhem; her doctor could vouch she was a troubled sole and on medication but that gave her licence to do as she pleased, her get-out-of-jail card so to speak…she had the whole pack.

The trouble she created continued for weeks then she'd disappear. Nan said, *She's got something on him* but I wouldn't hear of it. *Don't be daft; what on earth could she have on him?* I said in his defence but I must admit he was scared.

Someone once told me Judy had a manipulative mind. She could make you believe anything she wanted which was funny, really - I had not long escaped from Collin who was guilty of the same.

I answered the door one morning and was confronted by a couple of men from Social Security. Someone had tipped them off.

I had a man living with me whilst claiming benefits. I explained that we had already spoken to one of their officers but did not know his name. With raised eyebrows, they took my payment book and left.

Having read about women being slapped in prison for less, I worried what lay in store for me; who could have tipped them off? I wondered, the only person wanting to come between us was Judy. Once the children left for school, I headed for the job centre. The agency sent me for an interview at a local company where I was hired as a receptionist, telex and switchboard operator. My hours were 8.15 am until 5 pm with a weekly wage of £43.

My job did not require skill but it was essential. The company could not have functioned without the efficiency of the receptionist whose job it was to receive clients, sort incoming mail, collect incoming telexes and man a busy switchboard, all of which I was responsible for. I loved it. I'd arrive home about 6 pm, kick my shoes off and get straight on with dinner which Owen said the girls should have prepared and waited but I did not want them handling saucepans of boiling water which could easily turn into an accident, knowing how they used to tease and mess about when I was not around I told him they could prepare vegetables and that is all.

I had been working about 3 months when Owen called into the office and said he'd booked our wedding although thrilled, I was more relieved to think Judy would be out of our lives because she was behind most of our problems but airing on the side of caution Owen told me not to tell the family just in-case word got back.

Our wedding took place without family so I told my children when they came home but they did not look thrilled to have him as a permanent fixture. Perhaps they thought he would pack his bags and take his troublesome X with him.

Two weeks ago, we were at the registry office and now my husband thinks he's made a mistake, just what every new bride wants to hear, he was chain smoking and squinting more than usual…it was her…she was back Cathy told her we were married, I was wary of this woman she had proved just how controlling she could be.

But life wasn't always bad; we trudged along with a few hiccups like most, although I must admit we seemed to have more than most. I have highlighted some of the bad times which Judy seemed to be the main cause.

I had been working for 6 months when my alarm went off, I climbed out of bed and my legs turned to jelly. I climbed back and buried myself under the covers. I slept for another hour then phoned the office to apologise for my absence. The following morning, I handed my notice in. I was exhausted and knew I could not continue full-time employment, run a home for a family of 7, sometimes 8 and two dogs; if I had neglected the house, things may have been different but I kept the house immaculate often working till midnight, surprisingly Owen did not seem to mind I think he could see I was struggling.

My family was getting older and wanting snacks before bed, Owen said they were greedy, to which I disagreed so he'd get his own back by turning the volume up on TV when I was trying to sleep or he'd throw the bed covers off leaving my back exposed, one night he kicked me out of bed another time he made me jump by throwing the door open hard so it banged against the bed to wake me…what a bastard.

I made friends with a neighbour 5 houses away. Elaine had two boys about the same age as my girls. When I got fed up with him bitching I'd escape into hers but she was never alone. It was an open house where everyone used to congregate. I'd return home and he'd be soaking in the bath or watching TV in bed, no apology, no regrets, nothing.

He often accused me of being lazy and sitting on my arse all day. I cannot imagine why he thought I sat on my arse because preparing meals for a family of 7 was a chore in itself, not to mention laundry but to avoid the ever-increasing rows, I applied to the local school as a cleaner, they were always looking for casual workers.

I had been working a few months when Elaine told me about a factory in Rochford that was looking for casual workers from 6 pm until 10 pm. I applied and was hired with an immediate start. The factory had its own bus service for those that with no transport. I was pleased Owen offered to drop me off in time for the bus so I didn't have to walk which was quiet away from the house. It was tiring keeping two jobs on the go but shopping was a lot easier and I was saving for home improvements as well as buying new appliances to transform our kitchen. Owen was unprepared to help financially but would do the work if I purchased the materials but what annoyed me - he was never at the designated spot to pick me up after work. I used to hang around in the dark then a car would slow down or circle the block and make gestures. It was intimidating and a little scary eventually, hubby would turn up looking irritated which made me feel like a nuisance. I wondered if he kept me waiting deliberately; none of the other women were left hanging as they got off the company bus and into the car of whoever was meeting them.

I kept the job until Christmas. I decided if he was unprepared to meet me at the agreed time then I was not prepared to keep two jobs and run a house for a large family. The factory was dam hard work. They moved workers each night so you were never on the same machine twice, some of which were heavy and difficult to use. I used to go home hurting like mad and Owen was unsupportive so I handed in my notice.

I had just finished watching a show with the girls when Robert called *quick, get some water; there's a fire;* seconds later, he called *don't worry, it's out.* I shook my head - what was he going to do next then he called again *quick, there's a fire; get some water.* I was about to walk up the stairs when I saw smoke bellowing from his room. I called the fire brigade who arrived in minutes but the damage done in a short space of time was phenomenal; my boys lost everything. Owen arrived at the same time as the firemen - he surveyed the damage and left.

I was not angry or scared in fact I was incredibly calm. All I remember was asking the firemen if they would like a cup of tea (I was told that my calmness was due to shock); my children must have gone to Joan's because I don't recall them being with me all I remember was walking downstairs the following day and seeing Nan and Joan in my kitchen. Apparently, I had taken something which – to this day I do not remember, Howard prescribed a bloody good shaking; perhaps those unsympathetic words should not have been repeated, blessed if I can remember who told me it could have been my girls. I wonder if he would have prescribed a bloody good shaking if his daughter or wife had experienced similar…I think not; surely someone must have realised I needed help. It's time like this when family/friends or neighbours rally around…I should be so lucky. I was in shock, for Christ's sake and certainly did not need bloody shaking but Howard was good at dishing out verbal advice when it involved me, bloody good shaking being the favourite or having my bloody brains tested and those were just two that I got to hear about.

I pulled myself together but it took weeks before I was able to function properly. Perhaps a visit to the doctor would have been sensible but no one offered advice and I was not in the frame of mind to recognise I needed help. It's surprising how long it takes to get over these situations. You don't wake one morning and everything is back to normal or wait for things to pass. The constant problems and situations I have had to deal with knock the stuffing out of you and can take weeks or months to recover from. Each time you get knocked back, recovery takes a little longer, leaving scars that never heal.

Some may say I was weak to take pills but I consider myself strong, having pulled myself together with no help…that makes me a survivor.

We were drifting apart and had been for a while. Owen was spending more time with Judy sorting out the many problems she created, the dreaded woman was not going to give up until she had succeeded in coming between us. Sunday evening, I phoned Mathew and asked if he fancied coming to the spiritual church; with a bit of luck, the medium might give me some news to uplift me, Mathew agreed but it was a split-second decision so he asked his dad to drop us off - Joan had my girls until I returned. Unfortunately, I did not receive a message from spirit but I did get a message from my children when Howard dropped us at the church. He told Charlotte (who came for the ride) *she wants her bloody brains tested, leaving these girls to go gallivanting, she doesn't deserve to have children. It's about time someone gave her a bloody good telling-off.* My girls were disturbed by the harshness of his words and upset about having to wait for me in his presence.

We arrived home and I thanked Joan for looking after my girls, then we left. We were almost home when Allison burst into tears and repeated what Howard had said. Then Morgan and Tiffany started crying too and confirmed everything Allison had said. I'm surprised he spoke so openly about me in the presence of my children. Anyway, I was not gallivanting; for Christ's sake, I was at church with his son. It amazes me how far he was prepared to go to discredit me. I divorced two husbands for their misconduct, but as Howard was family, contact was unavoidable, and having been advised to say nothing, I kept my mouth shut. *I could write some interesting stories about him but as they don't involve me they are not mine to tell.*

Harsh words and discipline resulted in Robert moving out to live with Nan. The family held me responsible even though it was Owen that drove him away. We sometimes took the girls to visit them on Saturdays, but my name was strictly taboo. Any pictures of me were either hidden or destroyed. Speaking of which – Nan had a tiny picture of me when I was in hospital covered in plaster. All that was visible were my eyes and puffed cheeks. Nan showed me the photo when I was about 18, but I found it disturbing, so I handed it back without really looking. *But I could kick myself for not taking more interest in that chapter of my life.* My girls were always in good spirits when we picked them up, having spent valuable time with Nan and Robert, who always made them laugh.

I walked into the bedroom to see Owen shoving cloths in a bag. He was going to Norwich to visit his nephew for a few days... *but isn't that something you discuss with the wife,* this is not how newly-weds were supposed to behave. These unexpected visits continued until December when he said he'd bought a house and we were moving the first week in January. The news came as a shock and gave me little time to collect boxes, pack, inform the school and cancel work. I did not know which way to turn. Owen decided we would continue renting where we were living and Craig could have a couple friends (house share). They would be responsible for the rent and utility bills. The girls and I were not happy with the arrangements. None of us wanted to move away, although Craig didn't seem to mind. *In fact, he was glad to see the back of Owen.* I didn't have to worry about informing the family since none of them were talking to me. I did not realise how much Owen dictated everyone's lives without discussing his plans with those concerned. *Maybe Craig did not want to house share but he had little choice and no-one stood up to Owen.*

January 1st, we loaded the van ready to leave at first light for a life in a house we had yet to see. Kevin and Clarissa (Owen's nephew and wife) greeted us on our arrival with a hot meal then helped us unload. It did not take long to get straight, as we only brought what we needed. *The rest of our home we left for Craig and his friends.*

Chapter Forty

Norwich

The girls and I hated the house; it was cold and gloomy unlike what we had left behind. I was unsure about Kevin too; he was loud and self-opinionated who - like my husband wore trousers. Keven became a regular visitor and was delighted to have someone to go drinking with which they did most evenings.

The girls' school was a 15-minute bus ride away, I worried how they would adjust to new teachers, different lessons and a bus route in unfamiliar surroundings and Owen refused to take them - he could be such an arsehole at times, my only consolation was they were together but I met them off the bus each night until they became adjusted but they were smart kids so it didn't take them long to find their way around.

I didn't waste time looking for work. Owen made it very clear if I didn't bring money home we didn't eat. I don't suppose he went hungry he'd have eaten in some cafe. I scoured the paper each night looking for office work but there was very little so checked the column for domestic work within the month. I had six. The toughest of them all was the Red Lion Pub. Every morning before opening, I'd start by scrubbing the carpet with a yard broom where cigarettes had been trampled then I cleaned the toilets where I'd find needles and all sorts of unmentionables. From the pub, I cleaned private houses. They were a lot easier and I was paid before leaving so I could shop on my way home then I did chores before starting dinner.

Owen had a tantrum if his meal was not ready, especially if he'd arranged to go drinking. One evening, he was showing off and accused me of not having a proper job. I was surprised when Kevin intervened; *for goodness sake, give the girl a break; she works bloody hard, she probably brings more money home than if she had a full-time job*…no more was said about me having a 'proper job.'

My last job of the day was at the Chamber of Commerce; they gave me a master key so I could clean the place when the building was empty which suited me and the girls because I took them with me - having knowledge or switchboards, I took it off night extension and phoned Nan I connected the call to three phones in the main office so they could chat at the same time I always knew when Robert was on the line they never stopped giggling.

We had been in Norwich less than six months when Owen kept disappearing to Essex for days at a time; the girls and I enjoyed having the place to ourselves. I had got used to the City and knew all the back streets and shortcuts to all my jobs.

I had just got the girls off to school when the phone rang. It was Owen to say he'd hired a removal van and he would be down at midnight and told me to be packed ready, was there no end to his impulsive decisions? I hurried to local shops, collecting boxes before racing back for more. When the girls came home, they stared in disbelief at the boxes stacked in the lounge, ready for a hasty retreat in the morning.

True to his word, he arrived with Craig and a couple of his friends to help with the move; by midnight, the van was stacked, ready to leave at first light. The sun was rising when I climbed in the van and headed home with my girls, Craig and his friends, the kestrel and our two dogs.

Chapter Forty-One

Back Home

The sun was shining by the time we reached Essex. I could hardly wait to see my house; it had been months since we left for a life that had been thrown at us and now we were on our way home. As soon as we arrived on, went the kettle then we unloaded the van. There was much excitement as we unpacked boxes, made beds and drank numerous mugs of tea. It wasn't easy getting straight because of the unorganised way I had packed, not to mention working around everything Craig's friends had left. The girls couldn't wait to visit the family but Owen insisted they unpack and sort out their room.

It had been a long day; tired and exhausted. We ordered a Chinese meal and retired early.

We had been back a week when I looked out of the landing window and saw Craig talking to Robert. I called the girls from their room and told them their brother was outside. *Robert's here, Robert's here!* They shouted as they flew past me on the stairs. I watched their smiling faces from the window as they took it in turns hugging him. I would love to have joined them but knew my son wasn't ready. I remained behind my nets and hoped one day, the gap between us would recede. I watched him drive off then the girls came racing in beaming with excitement. Robert put the sparkle back in their eyes that afternoon. I had not seen them that happy in ages.

The move seemed to have done Owen good because he made inquiries about buying the house and doing home improvements. I had been a council tenant for many years, so we were entitled to a decent discount. The following day, he came home with the forms that needed both signatures but there was still an issue with money so I got an afternoon job above an electrical store which fitted in nicely with my household chores.

It was September 1982 when Craig celebrated his 21st birthday; it was an open house for his friends and our family; laughter could be heard above the music as the lads reminisced over school days, gigs and funny stories and whatever else they got up to, the following morning I went downstairs and found Craig and some remaining friends crashed out in the lounge with the empty biscuit tin in the middle of the floor and empty mugs dotted about but that's when you know the party was a success.

We were on our way home when I saw Joan's next-door neighbour waiting for a bus. I asked Owen to stop so we could give her a lift. Dot was grateful and asked us not to drop her outside her house in case Joan saw her because they were not speaking so we dropped her at ours. Eager to show her the changes we'd made, I invited her in. Over coffee, she volunteered information involving my uncle then she apologised for speaking out of turn. I laughed and told her there was no apology needed. When she realised he was not flavour of the month. She told me he'd made a pass at her. I shook my head in disbelief then she dropped another bombshell. Howard told her I'd had an abortion when I was 17…I was furious…he told Owen the same shortly after we started dating. Dot and Owen had not met until today. Jesus Christ, how many other people has he told these lies to what in God's name must people think? How would he like it if someone spoke about his wife and daughter the way he spoke of me?

I shudder to think of all the slander he's spread over the years because people always believe the worst. Perhaps Howard was the reason the two women were not speaking…he was never sure if Dot would keep her promise not to tell Joan that he'd made a pass. He would have done whatever it took to keep his wife from knowing. Perhaps that is why Joan lost her neighbour/friend. Anyway, so what…even if I did have an abortion so bloody what…it had nothing to do with him or anyone else for that matter but why was he so hell-bent on turning people against me? I was innocent until my night with Johnny which was two months before my 21st and there's not many that can confess to that, perhaps I should have taken the matter further and not bothered about the outcome.

I was made redundant when the family-run business closed down as if things couldn't get any worse, Owen stopped my £20 housekeeping then his foul moods returned. Was he deliberately trying to make life difficult? Craig was giving me housekeeping which I added to my family allowance but it wasn't his place to provide for us.

The girls were getting older and stretching their wings. Allison used to dig her heels in more so than her siblings. One Friday, I refused to let her go to a party. I locked the back door and stood guard by the street door as soon as my back was turned, she slipped past me and disappeared. My mind was all over the place, wondering where she was and was she safe when she would return. I hardly slept. When I wasn't worrying about one thing, I was angry about something else. Owen reminded me I was too soft and she needed the belt but I disagreed so he stormed out in a huff. Saturday morning, Allison had still not returned and I needed to shop. I took Tiffany and Morgan into town but with limited funds, I had to economise which was nothing new. I was dropping food in the trolley, keeping tag of how much I was spending then I saw the half leg of lamb, I stood admiring the meat and imagined carving the joint surrounded with roast potatoes I could almost hear them sizzling, I pondered for a moment then glanced around, no one was paying attention so I dropped the lamb in my shopping bag…no one screamed so I added pork chops for him (purely so he wouldn't bitch) I added chocolate biscuits then deodorant, Owen told me deodorant was an unnecessary expense, soap and water was all you need which was funny because Collin said the same…two of a kind, I paid for my goods and was about to leave when a hand touched my shoulder and this woman asked me to come with her, I gingerly walked to where I was being led with my head down, embarrassment prevented me from looking my girls wondering what they must be going through, the police were called and I was carted off to the station where my finger prints were taken and forms were filled in, someone made a note of everything I had not paid for then it hit me suppose they search the house, Owen had turned the meters back to front so he could get free gas and electric, why I cannot imagine because he had money stashed although I did not realise it at the time. I was locked in a cell for what seemed ages before being taken to a small office where a plainclothes officer was waiting to question me. I told him about my daughter skipping out the night before and not returning, I told him about Owen and my limited housekeeping and Judy's threat with acid. I told him about the house fire and my overdose. Once I started, I continued to ramble and went as far back as Collin, relieved to get everything off my chest and pleased someone was interested enough to listen. The officer did not take his eyes off me for a moment then he pushed back his chair and left the room. When he returned, he spoke quietly…*you shouldn't be here, you know. I have tried to stop your papers from being sent to court but they have already been submitted. I am sorry but it is too late and there is nothing I can do.* He rose from his seat and took me to where my shopping was waiting, minus the items that had been returned to the store then he drove me home in an unmarked car.

My girls had been driven home ahead of me and were upstairs when I arrived. The officer was in the kitchen with Owen and spoke quietly: *this girl does not need punishing; she needs help – I want you to take her to the doctor first thing Monday and here is the number of a good solicitor that will get her off, make sure she sees him as soon as possible* I kept my head down like a naughty child then once the officer left I shut myself away for the remainder of the night just as I had years ago, the following day I confessed to Elaine what I had done, she was easy to speak to about such matters because these incidents did not faze her, she had mates that got up to all sorts and went out regularly, to them it was no big deal but a way of life. We drove Morgan to the hospital on Sunday without the support of Allison and she was released within the week. When Nan heard about Morgan's surgery, she paid us a visit. The atmosphere was a little strained but I knew she was pleased to see us determined to close the distance between us. I invited her for dinner the following week. She looked uneasy about accepting my invitation until I said *well, you think about it and let me know...unless you're worried about what Howard will say* I saw her stiffen as she realised the gap between us was being fuelled by her expression changed and she accepted, the gap between Robert and I slowly improved when he visited his sister too.

I did as the inspector advised and made an appointment to see Doctor Warburton. He was a lovely man who used to swing his chair around to discuss the purpose of my visit, knowing I would not be fobbed off with 'take these twice a day.' It was difficult confessing to what I had done but he was gentle and asked the name of the solicitor that was handling my case.

My next appointment was with the solicitor recommended by the officer. He also showed empathy and asked me to write a list of the items I had purchased and a separate list of those I had stolen. I was writing everything down then stopped when I realised everything I had stolen were things Owen would not allow me to buy, items that if I purchased, I would have been at the mercy of his tongue. The solicitor seated opposite noticed the change in my expression as the penny dropped…yes, I was guilty of having stolen the goods but Owen was responsible for my actions. He called it financial abuse.

The day of my hearing was frightening, to say the least. I worried in case there were reporters present with cameras, Elaine told me not to be daft. She said my case was not worth leaving the office for. My solicitor met me at the entrance and ushered me into court. I was asked to give my name then the solicitor walked to the bench and spoke quietly on my behalf. I watched as the Judge flicked through his papers. You could have heard a pin drop then he looked over his glasses and gave me a ticking off and told me no action would be taken.

I walked out on a high, relieved to be going home without punishment - although being dragged off in a police car - locked in a cell then having to face my family and worrying about the outcome was punishment enough. I am not trying to justify my actions but I would not have stolen the food if I had sufficient funds in my purse.

It was a couple of weeks before I saw Dr. Warburton who asked about the hearing. The Dr said he'd written to the solicitor and explained the problems in our home. The inspector also put in a good word for me when he realised things were not as they should be. I walked away a free woman because they said my actions were a cry for help, a situation my husband had created.

My girls often called in to see Joan on their way home from school. One afternoon, they came home in tears so I asked what was wrong. *Uncle Howard said some horrible things about you so we left.* I asked what did Auntie Joan say; they told me she was in the garden and never heard. I was fuming so I advised them accordingly, *okay, now listen to me, don't go down there when he's around, do you understand - if you want to see Auntie Joan then you'll have to wait till he's out - you know when it's safe to visit because his car will be gone* as his car was there most of the time they stopped calling in but they also stopped waving when they passed by. It was a few weeks later when Joan approached Nan. *I don't know what's the matter with the girls they used to call in on their way home from school - now they walk right past they don't even wave* Howard, never one to miss an opportunity - *Well, it's that bloody bitch down there isn't it, she's stopped them from calling in.* If Nan had not repeated that conversation I would have been none the wiser so I explained how the girls came home upset because Howard had something unpleasant about me. She looked disturbed and reminded me not to say anything for fear of repercussions. She was concerned about how Joan would react if she knew the problems her husband continually created but he was careful how far to take the aspersions in the company of Nan who would have defended me. I presume he was miffed to think we were on speaking terms and was doing his best to drive another wedge. I never did ask my girls what he'd said but it must have been hurtful to have upset them, having been advised not to say anything I did not want to know. What a pity I never had a decent man to protect me and stand up to Howard.

One evening, I invited my Aunt down for a cup of tea, hoping to build bridges. I went against Nan's advice and told her a few things that disturbed me which proved unsuccessful - she stayed silent and left without comment.

When living in Canada, I addressed my letters to Mum and Dad and she referred to me as her daughter and called me poppet. She ended her letters with 'Mom and Pops.' I kept them for years because they meant a lot to me. When I returned to England, we spent hours talking over nothing in particular but everything in general. She was grateful for my company as I was hers but as time passed, I was aware of her slowly turning away. I have made mistakes like everyone but most of mine have been created by lies to which I had no control without lighting the blue touch paper.

Chapter Forty-Two

The Attack

Owen accused me of mollycoddling, then it was my lack of discipline, but everything I did was wrong. He was pulling me in one direction, and the children were tugging in the opposite. Sometimes, I did not know which way to turn.

I arrived home one afternoon and noticed Owen's writing desk was gone from the hall. I checked the wardrobe, and his clothes were also gone. A week later, he returned. There were brief spells of silence followed by more rows. I did everything possible to keep the peace, but the more I tried, the more he found fault. I could not shake the feeling that something bad was about to happen. I needed to talk to someone. I thought perhaps a therapist, but they were expensive, so I decided to meditate. I have always been able to put myself in another place, so I wrote a list of everything I thought could be the cause:

House – children – husband – money.

I closed the blinds, turned on soft music, made myself comfortable, and concentrated on House. I closed my eyes and sat for a while. I saw myself in a beautiful house with everything a woman could desire. The house, although beautiful, was very quiet, and I was lonely… *House* was not my problem.

The second on the list was *Children*.

I sat once again and obliterated them from my life. They did not exist. I looked around, but there were no tell-tale signs of children ever having been here. I walked from room to room, and everything was neat and tidy. I did not like what I felt, so I pulled away. *Children* were not the problem either.

The next word on my list was *husband*.

In meditation, I saw my children playing happily, music was playing, and laughter could be heard. Everyone was relaxed in our carefree home. There was no man around, nor was one due. Aware of the change, I knew '*husband*' was the problem. He was the fly in the ointment, and that secured his fate. Perhaps I knew all along. I just needed confirmation. But getting rid of him was not going to be easy. He would probably make me look at fault, even though he had no reason. I kept a clean house, although not always tidy. I was a good wife and worked hard to bring money home, so I decided to gather as many charges on him as possible. I searched the house and found the book where he logged his earnings from the two taxis he had working night and day. I made notes of all his movements, the rows, and what they were about. Keeping a journal was sensible – it would be my protection and our ticket to freedom.

One night, he came home stinking of beer and woke me as he climbed into bed. I should have known better than to reject his advances while he was tanked up. He told me unless I reciprocated, he would go into my girls. I pushed him out of my face, grabbed my pillow, and went downstairs. Then I heard him stomping across the landing. He was angry at being snubbed. He stuck his chin out and continued with his previous threat. Unsure how far he was prepared to go, I climbed the stairs and returned to my bed.

When I spoke to Nan about his appalling behavior, she told me to get shot of him, but I could not afford to walk away with nothing.

I had my children to consider. I needed funds to start a new life for my family. Besides, I needed proof he had two taxis on the road as well as his building work and was earning good money. I told Nan not to worry. I would get shot of him when the time was right. Meanwhile, I had to stick it out.

I was cooking dinner when I saw him getting out of his taxi with a face like thunder. He stormed into the kitchen, pushed past me, and marched into the hall where Craig was talking to his lady friend on the phone. I heard Owen shouting, then I heard a thud. Seconds later, I saw the glass door bowing, then it shattered, and Craig was lying on the floor, rolling in shards of glass, with the beast leaning over him. My girls and I were screaming, then we ran from the house in a panic. I raced back, and so did my girls, who were running in circles like headless chickens, screaming uncontrollably. Then I realized I was screaming, too. Craig ran past and shot out the door with me and the girls close behind. We followed him to Elaine's, where she gave him a shot of whisky because he was shaking. She said he looked like he was about to pass out. Craig left Elaine's and made his way to the family, who took him to the hospital. He was stitched for a deep cut in his back. Howard came to survey the damage, by which time the angry beast had scurried off like a stinking rat to report the incident and to build a case against my son.

There are no words that can describe my distraught at the ferocity of the violence that swept through the house that afternoon. It was like a shockwave. My gentle, kind-hearted son would not have fought back other than shielding himself from his attacker because he was not aggressive and did not deserve the brutality from the beast, who was in a foul mood and took his anger out on my son. I have deep regrets about not fighting the monster off, but everything happened so quickly. All I can remember was screaming.

Why didn't I defend my son? I could have thrown the pot of potatoes boiling on the stove or grabbed the knife I had been using, but then – I would have been arrested.

The following day, Craig phoned and asked if it was safe to collect his belongings. My poor darling had been driven out once again, only this time it was Owen.

The day of the hearing, Owen was ready to leave. Realizing I would not be defending him, he lost his temper and smashed the portrait of me and my family. Then he grabbed me around the throat and held me over the kitchen table. I could barely breathe and tried fighting him off, but was unable to move. So, I brought my knee to his groin. Only then did he release me. His actions were to keep me from the hearing. When I told him I would not be speaking on his behalf by not attending, I let Craig down. The bastard was bound over to keep the peace for 12 months. I cannot imagine how my son felt not seeing me there or how he coped in the weeks that followed because it is not the scars you see that cause the most damage, but those buried beneath the surface… they penetrate to the core and leave you mentally scarred.

Owen could be more violent than Collin. Owen was impulsive and didn't care what people thought or who witnessed his outbursts, whereas Collin was calculating and spent months planning his moves to avoid detection. He was cleverer than Owen and far more dangerous.

This is another chapter that has been extremely hard to write. I cannot shake the pain from my heart, but I am angry for not pouncing on the bastard with something instead of screaming. I let my son down when he needed me most. I look back and wish I could relive these times. I would love the opportunity to stand up to those responsible for hurting my son, even though it would mean serving prison time because there is no justice for self-defense. I am angry having missed opportunities from the past.

Now, the monster had forced my hand; it was time for action. I had hoped to gather more charges on him, but attacking my son was the final straw, and I wanted him out. I took the journal out of hiding and headed for the nearest solicitor. My appointment was in three weeks.

All hell broke loose the day he received his papers. He threatened to smash everything in the house rather than leave me anything, although most of what we had was mine to begin with, not to mention everything I brought out of my earnings. That night, he packed his bags and left. It was a relief having the place to ourselves. I cleaned and shifted furniture to wipe away all traces of him.

I was working in a popular little café in town. Peggy was the proprietor who worked alongside her husband, Doug. It was a small café but clean and very popular. It was hard work with little time for a break, especially on Saturdays when the market was open. You couldn't move with people looking for bargains. I arrived home after another busy day and saw a padlock on the door of the master bedroom, with my furniture shoved inside the box room. My wardrobe was in front of the window, blocking out daylight, and the dressing table was just inside the door, blocking my entrance. Beyond that was a single bed. I had to get help in moving everything. Otherwise, I would have no place to sleep... *bastard*. His solicitor had told him to move back in case I added desertion to my list of complaints. She said he had as much right to be here as anyone because he was paying the mortgage.

Tiffany left school and was doing work experience. When she wasn't at her job, she was dating Darren, a young lad from school who was either round ours or she was with him at his parents.

Tiffany and Darren were both quietly spoken and shy. In fact, they hardly spoke, but when they were alone, they never stopped talking. I could hear them in the sitting room twittering like little birds. Darren's parents were respectable people, so I had no worries when she spent more time in their home than in ours. When the couple announced their engagement, his parents arranged their party.

Robert was still living with Nan, who had come to depend on him. She was suffering from the early stages of dementia. Robert, now 16, was working at an electrical company and dating Karen. She was a real scatterbrain. Craig also had a lady friend, but because of Owen, it was some time before we were introduced. I loved Melody; she was gentle and quiet, like Craig – unlike Karen, who was loud and boisterous but a lot of fun to be around.

It had been weeks since Owen received the divorce papers. I used to dread the unpleasantness each time a letter arrived, so I suggested we work together. After all, he wanted to be free of me as much as I wanted to be shot of him. So why bitch and fight through solicitors when we can discuss the letters between ourselves first? Our attorneys did not like the idea, but we were their clients, and they were working for us. Then I suggested he become my lodger. He could pay me to cook his meals and do his washing, and he could keep the master bedroom on the condition he did not bring women into my home while I was living there. Perhaps we should have done that sooner. He had his freedom, and I was better off financially.

Owen was eating breakfast when another letter arrived. He was livid to read I had told my solicitor about the night he threatened to go into my girls. He insisted I withdraw the allegation and said he would accept everything else on condition, I erase the threat. This made no sense whatsoever. Threatening to go into my girls (as far as I was concerned) was just an idle threat brought on by drink, but

I agreed to his terms, pleased he was not going to make a fuss about everything else.

It was just before Christmas when Tiffany told me she was pregnant. Not wanting her to make the same mistakes as me, I was disappointed when Darren told his parents. They insisted they marry before the baby arrived. Within a matter of weeks, they'd arranged a visit with the Pastor and booked the church. They found the youngsters a flat, decorated and furnished it – they were amazing, but I was not entirely happy about these arrangements. I thought it was too much too soon, but went along with their plans. Had Tiffany or Darren shown signs of not wanting to settle down, I would have said something.

With a forthcoming wedding and a baby on the way, Owen suggested putting the divorce on hold. But that was the last thing I wanted. The wedding was booked for April, and I needed his help. I was more than grateful when a relative through marriage offered to make Tiffany's wedding dress and dresses for the twins at a reasonable price. Tiffany and I selected the patterns and material, but my budget was tight, so I made their bouquets and headdresses out of silk flowers. I bought lace and made elbow-length gloves for the bride.

Doreen – Melody's mother – made their wedding cake, and the family helped with food while Owen supplied the drink.

It was bitterly cold on the day of the wedding. Dad and Camilla were the first to arrive. Craig, who had not been in the house since the attack, arrived with Melody and her parents. Poor kid must have felt uncomfortable.

Tiffany and Darren settled into married life. Three months later, Darren phoned to say the baby was on the way. I raced to the hospital and arrived minutes after my granddaughter made an appearance. I cradled the little one while Darren's father took photos. Tiffany and baby were discharged a few days later. I offered to have them stay with me, but Vicky did not approve, so I stood back. A couple of days later, mother and baby were readmitted with complications. They were discharged a week later and accepted my invitation to care for them all so Darren could continue working while Tiffany recuperated at home with the baby.

Once life returned to normal, I continued with my divorce. I was keen to draw the relationship to an end, so I began looking for two-bedroom flats to rent but could find nothing suitable. Joan could not understand why I was so blasé, but I told her something would turn up when the time was right.

My solicitor wanted to pressure Owen into giving me half of the value of our property, but over dinner, he said he was unable to raise that sort of money. Had we not been living under one roof, I would have allowed my attorney to fight for what I was entitled to. But not wanting to rattle my soon-to-be husband, I settled on a figure far less than I should have. Then Owen asked me to sign a document releasing him from giving me any monies in the future. I wasn't very smart and signed the papers. Once the divorce had been finalized, it came to light he could have given me half the value of our property. I was stupid not to have listened to my counselor, who wanted me to take him to the cleaners. But Owen could be real nasty, as I had experienced in the past. He knew how much pressure was needed to get his own way – it's a pity he never used it on Judy.

It was March when I answered the phone to Tiffany, who said things were not working out and they were separating. She was coming home the following day with 8-month-old Coral, and Darren was going back to his parents. I wondered if the pressure of married life caused them to separate so soon. Perhaps they should have taken things slower.

When they first announced the pregnancy, I would have preferred Tiffany to live with me and Darren to stay home with his parents. Then, the lovebirds could continue dating and allow their future to unfold in their own time.

The day after they separated, Vicky phoned and asked Tiffany if she could see Coral on Saturday. Tiffany replied, "Our separating has nothing to do with you or Coral. I would never stop you from seeing your granddaughter. You're welcome to see her any time." Vicky burst into tears. She feared Tiffany would prevent her from having contact with Coral. Very often, there is bitterness when parents part and use the children as weapons without the slightest consideration for the child's feelings or needs.

Coral celebrated her 1st birthday in the marital home. Darren and Vicky came laden with gifts. It was a wonderful afternoon. We watched the little one, who could barely stand, putting on a performance for her audience. She took center stage, dancing to the music we taped for the occasion. The more we laughed, the more she chuckled. The more she chuckled, the more she fell. Then she was up again, waving her arms and shaking her bottom until she fell once more. The falls did not deter her in the least – it would take more than landing with a thud to keep this little lady down. She wasn't the type of girl to give up easily, but it was her determination that would see her through some difficult times in years to come.

Ashley was a friend of Craig's who was celebrating his 21st birthday, and I was invited. I recognized some familiar faces but felt out of my depth, surrounded by so many youngsters and their music. I mingled for what I thought was a polite period before thanking his parents for a lovely evening and telling them I was heading home.

They were about to leave and offered me a lift. Knowing of my pending divorce, Tony asked whether I planned on staying at the house. I explained that Tiffany and the baby had returned home, so I needed to rent a three-bed house. Tony told me to put my feelers out and find someone who could get me a mortgage that was... perhaps a little 'tarnished.' That gave me something to think about.

Having made inquiries, I was given the name and number of someone that could be of help. The following day, I hurried home and called Wilson. Even though buying a house seemed totally out of my league, Wilson told me to look for a property and get back to him with the price once I had found something. Although excited, I did not want to build my hopes up for fear of disappointment.

Wednesday was a half-day closing at the café, so I called into the nearest agent and said I was interested in buying a three-bedroom house. The guy pulled out four properties that were on the market. I liked the look of the first house, situated in a tree-lined street with a driveway. Being empty, he took me to view the property that afternoon. I set one foot in the door and knew this was the one. It had a wonderful feeling and looked amazing. I could not believe this beautiful house had not been snapped up sooner, but it had been waiting there for me. I was anxious for the agent to drop me home so I could call Wilson... this house was going to change our lives.

I dialed his number and held my breath. Once I had given him the information he needed, he said he'd be in touch. Was this really happening? Could this be our future?

It was a few days later when Wilson phoned to say I had been granted a mortgage. I wanted to rush outside and tell everyone – shout from the rooftops – but I sat on the stairs grinning. I could hardly believe my luck was about to change and we were going to be free to start a new life in a new house with no man to spoil our happiness. What could possibly go wrong? But little did I know, there was a shock looming in the shadows. A shock so unexpected it would knock me off my feet. What a fool to believe everything bad was behind me. Then Craig asked to come home because he and Melody were separating. My son was devastated.

Chapter Forty-Three
Willow Chase

We moved into Willow Chase in October 1986. Craig and his friends helped carry furniture boxes and bags while I supervised as to what went where midday. I brought everyone fish and chips which we ate at my new oval glass dining table with padded swivel chairs, with not enough seating. Some sat on the wide window ledge of the bay overlooking the garden. Everyone was in good spirits; there was plenty of laughter and leg-pulling, I took a few days from work to organise the house while Tiffany (who also worked at the café) took my shift and Coral, the happy toddler with a house full of women to care for her needs spent most of her time following Morgan who used to sing to the little chatterbox but she was a real fuss pot and only ate bolognese that Mummy cooked which was heavily laced with garlic, she may have been tiny but she knew what she liked.

Our first Christmas in Willow, we watched Coral open her gifts from Santa. Life revolved around the little one then it was a fight for the bathroom as I had organized Christmas dinner at the Concord restaurant by the airport. The meal was originally for Nan and my children but as months passed, friends and other family members joined us. Nan was a little confused but coped well.

With the meal over, we returned home to pick up the tree. I watched from the extension, trying to capture this moment for when my family where no longer around. What a wonderful atmosphere, with everyone laughing and being silly. Christmas music played and fairy lights twinkled. The only one oblivious to her surroundings was Coral who was busy with her Santa gifts; it was magical...this is what we had missed...this is what Christmas was all about.

It was Boxing Day when we cooked our first Christmas dinner at Willow. There's nothing quite like home-cooked turkey roast, plenty of treats and an abundance of laughter. Tiffany took control of the cassette in the kitchen and played her favourite Christmas tapes whilst basting turkey and potatoes. The aroma that wafted through the house brought members of the family drifting in to check on dinner. I feel quite nostalgic remembering our first Christmas at Willow in 1986 - if only we could go back, I would give anything to re-live those days.

I do not remember New Year's Eve who went where or who did what but it was time to put away the tree for another year. Tiffany enjoyed decorating the tree, the house, the ceilings and anything else she could hang tinsel and lights on. She enjoyed packing everything away as much as she did decorating then it was time to settle into our daily lives: Tiffany and myself at the café, Morgan and Allison looking for work and everyone taking turns caring for Coral.

We woke one morning to a four-foot blanket of snow. I had never seen this much since Canada. The car across the street had almost disappeared, there was a small portion of our fence visible in our back garden. It looked beautiful and very peaceful, there was an eerie silence everywhere. Coral had never seen snow before so Tiffany put on her coat so she could stand by the door. Tiffany gave her a handful but it quickly melted - she stared in amazement, oblivious to our laughter. You can't beat the face of a toddler trying to rationalize nature.

We eventually admitted Nan to a care home 10 minutes from where we lived. The poor darling was depressed and did not take kindly to her new surroundings which was upsetting. She used to watch the door patiently waiting for her loved ones to appear but we did not visit as often as we should....me being one of them, I don't mean to make excuses but I was working full time and those visits were hard never knowing what to say and I hated saying goodbye. I have tortured myself for years when I think of the hours she spent traveling in all weathers to visit me in the hospital and I leave her in a care home just around the corner. I can never forgive myself. My guilt will stay with me until we meet again.

Tiffany was sensible in not depriving Coral of Darren's family which she has benefited from. She has grown up with their children, attended BBQs and parties, and been a flower girl and bridesmaid; in fact, she has never missed out on any of their celebrations.

Jumping ahead - Coral was about 8 when Vicky phoned to thank me for making her welcome and treating her like one of the family she said our house was a happy home then she thanked me again for all I had done for our Granddaughter which at the time I did not understand, I told Vicky she had done so much more, every Saturday she'd arrive and take Coral off for the day then bring her home at 6 o'clock exhausted and in time for bed, Vicky was a working woman with a good job, what-ever Coral needed Tiffany was unable to afford Vicky was there to help, after I brought this to her attention she told me I had done much more than she herself had done, Vicky said our home had a wonderful atmosphere and Coral had grown into a beautiful child being surround with love laughter and music, she was always laughing, singing and dancing she was a happy little girl, Vicky said I had given our Granddaughter roots which was far more important, not until then did I realise our home was indeed a happy stable environment in which our Granddaughter flourished so I would like to thank Vicky for bringing this to my attention.

Coral is a woman now and often remarks on the house we once shared. She says it was the happiest time of her life so I am proud to have given our Grandchild her roots.

Chapter Forty-Four

A Trauma Unfolds

Morgan was in love, at first I thought he was a little old but he adored her and treated her well. He was the sort of person I wanted to see her with and knew she would be well looked after when I was not longer around. Vince said the bond we shared as Mother and Daughter was very special which said a lot about him, so I accepted the relationship. To have shown disapproval would have been futile anyway. Morgan could be stubborn at times and would have continued to see him regardless of anything I said. Morgan and I had always been close. She depended on me more so than the rest of my children and needed someone who was going to take care of her. I don't mean to sound intimidating in any way, shape or form but Morgan was not as strong or confident as Allison so when Vince came into her life, I accepted him.

I was waiting for a bus when Don pulled up. I had not seen him since Collin and I shared our evenings at the Flair Path. I accepted the offer of a lift home and a drink in my local on the way. I asked whether he knew Collin had passed away. Most of our conversation was about Collin; he was the one person we both knew well.

Don told me how - many years ago and concerned for my safety, he used to drive past our house most evenings or walk past until he saw me through our open blinds. He was disturbed to hear all I had tolerated during the marriage then said *you know blossom - we didn't expect you to survive that marriage, how you managed to escape is a miracle, Biscuit and I thought you were gonna* then he explained why he suspected Collin of being responsible for the death of his common-law-wife, Don had evidence that could have put Collin behind bars for a very long time it revolved drink, drugs and a devious mind, unfortunately, he kept the information to himself.

The day in question…Collin borrowed the airport ambulance to check on his common-law wife who had been drinking heavily the night before. He was gone all morning - used a lot of fuel and clocked up mileage. Don catalogued every vehicle and suspected Collin of applying the woman with more alcohol and barbiturates. Being inebriated, she would not have been able to resist. Don suspected he drove her around until she could no longer be helped – the verdict was accidental death through drink and drugs, but if Collin wanted to check on his wife, why take the ambulance when his car was outside? The police suspected foul play but could prove nothing. They would have had a field day had Don given them the valuable information that could have put Collin away for a long time so I understand why he had reservations as to whether I would survive and why he felt the need to drive past each night the same as Pat phoning every morning not to mention Leslie's daily visits.

It was 1988 when Morgan came home in tears because Vince had ended their relationship, I held her in my arms and assured her it was nothing serious *tomorrow he will call and things will be back to normal* I soothed but she assured me he was not prepared to resume their relationship until she had spoken to me about something he thought I should know, puzzled I held her at arms-length and asked *what could possibly be so bad that he doesn't want to see you until you have spoken to me* I cannot recall how the conversation started…neither do I remember how she broke the news in fact I never heard all she said…reeling from shock I ran from the room and called Allison to verify what Morgan had told me then I went into Tiffany and got her side of the story too, all three girls confirmed the devastating truth that Owen had abused them, I ran downstairs and phoned Peggy to say I was on my way then phoned a cab, by the time I arrived Peggy had one of her famous cocktails ready as I fell through the door in tears, the rest of the evening is a blur, all I remember is Doug driving me home once I had calmed down having drank more than a few cocktails and smoked them out of their 'no smoking zone home' what little sleep I had that night was due to Peggy's cocktails.

The following morning, I worked like a zombie, cooking meals for hungry customers. I told Peggy I wanted to stick a knife in him but she told me not to talk silly and advised me to speak to the Samaritans which I did but got angry when the creep accused me of wanting revenge which I strongly denied. I wanted justice.

My next call was to the child protection team at Rayleigh police station but was told there was nothing I could do. The only ones who could take this matter further were the victims because they were adults. Angry at their casual reaction, I told them I was going to confront Owen but they advised me against doing so; they told me criminals could often turn violent if they feel threatened so they instructed me not to approach him under any circumstances (leave him to us they advised) meanwhile my inside was screaming, I was frustrated with my girls for refusing to take the matter further I paced the floor wondering if I would ever feel normal again knowing I had failed to keep my family safe from the husband who had betrayed my trust, it's true I was not always around but I was not aware they were in any danger.

When I next saw Vince, he was beside himself with anger and wanted revenge, he was prepared to pay someone to break his legs and beat him to a pulp but I advised him not to do anything that would make Owen the victim because it would only be a matter of time before the truth surfaced and Vince would find himself behind bars instead of the real criminal because people talk, I had to go through the proper channels because I wanted the monster put away, I wanted him shamed and locked up it was time the fiend took responsibilities for his actions, then the night he attacked Craig returned to haunt me I was too numb to shed tears I felt totally screwed, I did not know how to cope with the torture that had taken over my life, I found it impossible to concentrate at work, my doctor gave me something to help me deal with the blow but the pills made me feel like a zombie and fear of taking an overdose in a moment of despair scared me so I flushed them away. I tried time and again to convince my girls to take the crime to the police but the more I pleaded, the more they refused. It was all in the past, they said. They were also worried they would not be believed, I encouragingly told them that whatever lies he told it would be three against one but it made no difference - they were not going to be swayed and the subject always ended with heated words, stomping up-stairs and the slamming of doors but I was not giving up until he was behind bars where he belonged.

A few weeks later, nature took over and I shut down, weeks passed and everything seemed normal. I went about my day without a care in the world then I would see something on TV or hear something on the radio and the nightmare surfaced. I questioned whether I had dreamt the whole thing or perhaps I had misinterpreted what my girls had said or maybe they exaggerated because this stuff was what you read about in the papers, so I questioned them only to cause another row but they did not want to discuss the matter because it was all in the past...but how could it be in the past when I have only just discovered the truth, I wanted to lash out at every man that came in the café even though they were strangers but they were men and they needed to be punished – all of them.

The battle with my family continued. I'd approach them again and again carefully and delicately but no matter how gently it always ended the same. I'd take a deep breath and back away until the next time, and yes, there would be a next time…and a next because I was not going to give up until justice had been served…months would pass before I brought the subject up only to cause another row but I was sure my patients would pay off one day.

I don't know how I survived knowing what the bastard had done and even more frustrated knowing there was nothing I could do…it was all in the hands of my girls. There were three daughters but there were four victims and it was killing me now I understand why he refused me housekeeping - it was to get me out of the house.

I suffered 22 years with two coercive husbands who kept me short of money for devious reasons. Collin's was to stop me from leaving and Owen wanted me out of the way.

Very often, when Owen was in the area, he had the audacity to call in with the excuse of using the loo or in need of a drink. As difficult as it was, I did as the police instructed and acted normal but it appeared I could not have cared less. I ignored his request to make tea until his tone became arrogant. He may have suspected I knew something by my cool reception. On the other hand, he may have been testing the waters to see how much I did - or didn't know, what is the old cliché…keep your friends close and your enemies closer.

Allison left home and went to live with my aunt where she had more freedom. She was always rebelling against my ground rules that her siblings willingly accepted. One night whilst out clubbing, she met Jake. When she moved in with him, she seemed less rebellious.

Whilst working at the café I met workmen of every trade that were involved in the building of the royals shopping centre, every morning the men used to pile in for breakfast and again for afternoon tea, it was where I met Chris who was head of plumbing, Chris lived in Kent but travelled to Southend early Monday and stayed in B&B until Friday, Chris was a happy guy and was never without a smile, he had a great sense of humour and had everyone laughing so I began to enjoy seeing him walk through the door every day, Peggy encouraged me to take him up on the offer of a date she said he seemed genuine and reminded me that I needed a distraction from the problems that were suffocating me *go* she said *it will do you good, you might even enjoy yourself* but I always had an excuse ready however Chris was not about to give up neither was Peggy, between them and weeks of gentle persuasion and teasing I agreed to go for a meal at my local Chinese restaurant, not having been on a date for some years I was a little nervous but it didn't take him long to put me at ease, he was the same jolly person all evening that he was during the day and behaved like a gentleman, after our date he visited me at home until his contract finished.

Chris's next contract was at Docklands. Living in Orpington, he was able to travel from his home then he'd visit me at weekends. I looked forward to Fridays when he'd arrive by cab in his grubby clothes, take a bath and change then order a Chinese meal for me and my girls. He was generous and did not begrudge them whatever they wanted then Monday at 5, he'd call a cab and head off to the station.

Chris played an important role in my life but it was some time before I realised. I laughed constantly when in his company which helped me through the impossible situation that was destroying me; then, over time, we became more than just friends.

Chris talked me into leaving the café and seeking work in London. He said I could stay with him during the week and travel home at the weekend. Peggy was none too pleased when I handed in my notice but with a mortgage and family commitments, she understood I needed to increase my income. I found work in a law firm in North London. It was tiring having to rise early but I loved the job and looked forward to Fridays when I'd catch my train home to be with my family.

Chapter Forty-Five
My Grandson 1989

Morgan gave birth to a son she absolutely adored... as did I; she had always been maternal and couldn't wait to become a mother. As a child, she went to every school jumble sale and arrived home with baby clothes, then she'd wash, iron, and store them away.

I remember the day her pregnancy was confirmed; being single, she burst into tears. The *Dr* was about to comfort her when Morgan assured her they were tears of joy.

What a privilege when Morgan asked me to be present at the birth. I was overwhelmed when the nurse placed this beautiful creature in my arms. I gazed into his adorable face—reluctant to let him go—but it was time to hand him over to Mummy, who was waiting to nurse him. I have heard that being present at the birth builds a special bond that can never be broken. Having experienced the arrival of my grandson, I can confirm this to be true. He is very special to me as if I had borne him myself. This does not mean I love my other grandchildren any less—because I love them all—but there will always be that special something I have with Brendon.

Vince passed away with a massive heart attack when Brendon was two weeks old. I was working in London, and the company would not allow me to leave because Vince and I were not related, so Tiffany helped Morgan through her grief until I came home. But there was nothing we could say or do to relieve her sadness—all we could do was be there.

Chris brought me a camera one Christmas, which I put to good use snapping away at the two little people in my life. Ninety percent of the films were Coral and Brendon. The closeness I shared with my two grandchildren was due to them having spent their early years with me. Coral was eight months old, and Brendon was with me from birth. My grandchildren enjoyed family life at Willow until they moved away. I had a framed picture of my family on my desk at work for everyone to admire—I was a proud mum.

Eighteen months after losing Vince, Morgan met and married Alex.

It was February when I phoned my father to wish him a happy birthday. Camilla answered and told me Dad was very ill and he was disgusted with me. This came as a shock and made no sense. Then she made a lot of fuss getting him to the phone—or the phone to him—which sounded very baffling. Then I heard this husky voice that was barely a whisper. Surely, that was not my Dad. The husky voice said he had been in hospital most of the day and he was a sick man. Then Camilla took the phone before he could say any more. She reminded me how disgusted he was, then hung up. Alarmed, I replaced the handset, wondering what tests he'd had done and why he had not told me he was ill—and why he was disgusted with me. With questions that needed answers, I booked the following day off work and paid them a visit.

Allison had recently passed her test and drove Morgan and myself to Romford. Camilla was surprised to see us and tried slamming the door, but Allison came prepared. She had Jake's cosh hidden in a Sainsbury's bag and rammed it through the door. The woman demanded she remove the device, which Allison refused—until I had seen my father. She reluctantly opened the door for me to squeeze through and pointed to the sitting room, which had been converted into a bedroom. Once inside, I opened the door for my girls. We entered the dark room and walked round to his side of the bed, but I barely recognised the frail figure lying in the dimly lit room. I reached to take his hand and asked what was going on and why he hadn't told me he was ill. Then the 'wife' began to shout, *Keep calling here all the time, trying to cause trouble.* I don't know what else passed her lips because I was trying to hear what Dad was saying, but his voice was barely a whisper and could not be heard above the phantom standing guard by the door. Dad was shaking his head. *I don't want no trouble, I don't want no trouble.* Bless him, he thought we had come to cause trouble. Perhaps each time the phone rang, she told him it was me causing trouble. But not wanting to cause him further distress, we left. I hope by turning up unannounced—and my shock at seeing his declining health—was proof enough that I knew nothing of his condition. I pray to God he was able to piece two and two together. Cancer may have eaten away at his body but had not damaged his mind. Aware he did not have long, he wanted to see and speak to his daughter. Alas, he was helpless and depended on this woman who claimed to love him— but how can you hurt the person you supposedly love in their final days? I've often wondered what he wanted to tell me that afternoon, but nothing could be heard with Camilla on guard, shouting like a fishwife to drown any form of conversation between us. But leaving before he could speak was the result she wanted. *The bitch needs to rot in hell.* She deprived me of a father and him a daughter.

A few days later, I received a letter from Camilla's son Duncan, which reads as follows:—

I would be obliged if you would have no further contact with Mr. and Mrs. Hawkins as your last visit offended them both. Any further correspondence will be conducted through our solicitors.

My father would not have known of this letter, and the only person that was offended was Camilla.

Sunday, 22nd March, I got the call to say Dad had passed away. My informer had been instructed not to say where he was lying, but I was given details of the funeral and advised to stay away as I would not be welcome… so I went to the funeral with Tiffany and Allison. I wore the silk scarf my mother embroidered with his initials. I carried one lily to represent the love they once shared—Mum's bouquet was mostly lilies. We sat at the back of the church. Then, the organ played a familiar hymn Dad would have chosen. I sang loud, and my voice carried through the church. Heads turned as I sang my farewell to the father I barely knew. *Farewell till we meet again—give my love to Mum.*

The bitch told everyone prior to the funeral that Dad had been asking for me but I never acknowledged him. But she failed to tell them she had not passed on his messages. She did not have the decency to honour my father his dying wish, and he was too ill to call me himself. As for the phone calls, she probably told him I was causing trouble, which would explain why he was supposedly *'disgusted'* with me (*disgusted* would have been her choice of words). I also got the cold shoulder from Dad's side of the family I had known since a little girl.

I always thought the bitch would die first. I imagined us sitting together catching up on father/daughter stuff. I never considered for one moment she would outlive him. But she was too obstinate to kick the bucket and leave him behind so we could pick up from where we left off forty years ago. I felt cheated because he had been taken from me before we got to know each other—the same as I felt cheated not knowing my mother. There are no words to describe the bitterness I felt towards Camilla. Then, as time passed, I blamed my father for not standing up to her. So I put his pictures away and banished him from my mind. It was easier to blame him… but by doing so, I was hurting myself.

I hated my journey to London every day. As the train approached Romford, I closed my eyes. When the brewery came into sight, I couldn't bear to look, so I studied the passenger sitting opposite or examined my nails—anything rather than look at the platform where I had stood as a little girl, waving him off to Aden with my lace hanky… times before Camilla, when we used to leave Nan at home and catch the bus into Romford and pick a treat for our tea, sitting in Lyons Corner House for our mid-morning snack and giggle like a couple of teenagers. Romford was where he started married life with his first love, and now he was gone. I refused to look at the platform as we sped through the station.

I was made redundant after five years—it was about that time Chris and I parted too. Chris came into my life when I needed help. He rescued me from the trauma that was killing me. He made me laugh till tears rolled down my face. We laughed every day over everything but nothing. He was an idiot and a lot of fun to be with, but we drifted apart. We used to talk on the phone from time to time, but that came to an end, too. There were no harsh words—no arguments—it was simply time for him to move on and rescue someone else. I missed the laughter, but I loved being home with my family more. Chris was an angel sent to rescue me through another difficult time of my life.

It was the summer of 1993 when my neighbour invited me to a psychic tea at a friend's house. Being interested in the spirit world, she did not need to apply pressure before I accepted.

The first thing the clairvoyant said was *I have your father here. He tells me he's been trying to contact you but you are blocking him...* well, well, well. She said more, but the message from my Dad was all I recall—or needed to hear. I couldn't wait to get home and take his pictures from the drawer and place them about.

Not only did I find solace from my reading, I was thrilled knowing he was with Mum. So I decided to share the information with Camilla... after all, she had a right to know he was doing okay. I looked for an excuse to call. Then I dialled... she told me how Dad pleaded *let me go, let me go, please let me go.* It was time to put her out of her misery. *You have no need to worry over my father. He has arrived home safely and is free from pain. My mother was waiting for him... you do remember Elizabeth, don't you... well... they are together again and will be for all eternity, so there's no need to worry. He's doing fine. Bye-bye.* I replaced the receiver and went to bed contented. Although I am not sure peace was with *her* that night, thankfully, I will never have to see her face again. I hope when her time comes to leave this world, her departure will not be trivial.

Chapter Forty-Six

Triumph

Since being made redundant, I returned to the café as cook/waitress. I loved the atmosphere and enjoyed talking with the regulars I had missed. I'd see them approaching and have the bacon on the griddle before they opened the door. One customer we called *BT*—he always ate beans on toast—another we called *Poison* because he wore that particular perfume. I knew everyone's name and what they ate.

I was getting ready for another busy day when the door opened and Owen walked in. Peggy half turned and muttered, *Shush, don't you say anything.* In spite of the cool reception, he gave his order and sat reading his paper. I don't know how I cooked his breakfast without spitting in it. The following morning, he returned for another one of my breakfasts. I placed the meal in front of him while Peggy observed me closely. He had almost finished when he asked for another tea—without looking up from his paper, he asked whether I had heard about Maureen and Adam, to which I curtly replied *no.* He went on to say that Adam had been arrested for raping Maureen's daughter. I walked over and placed his tea in front of him. Leaning close, I whispered, *Well, I guess that's where I was lucky then. I always trusted you with my daughters. I knew you would never do such a thing.* I stood for a moment, allowing my words to penetrate. Then I picked up his empty plate. Without raising his head, he began to blink uncontrollably. For the first time, he was lost for words. I watched him squirm as he melted into the chair. Regrettably, I had gone against the advice of the police, but the opportunity had presented itself and I was unable to resist the temptation.

It was a beautiful spring morning in 1995. My girls and I had planned to eat fish and chips in the garden. Allison arrived early, having been to the market where she had seen Owen's stepdaughter. She gave Diane a drop-dead look and muttered something equally nasty, which made me cross. *Why are you taking your anger out on her? She hasn't done anything. In fact, she's probably a victim too. If you want to blame anyone, then blame him. He is the guilty one, not Diane.* I was surprised when she agreed to contact the police, but Tiffany and Morgan were holding back. She offered to help me work on them—*YES! One down, two to go.*

It had taken from 1988 to 1995 before my girls agreed to take the matter to the authorities. I could hardly wait to be interviewed, with much to tell. I was one step closer to reaching my goal. I hardly slept with excitement.

Apparently, when the police knocked at his door, a young woman answered. She was his fourth wife and young enough to be his daughter. Furthermore, she had a little girl the same age as my children when their abuse began.

I concluded—it was the night of my party when Beryl brought Owen into my home. He saw my girls having fun, and their fate was sealed. But first, he had to groom me—my knight in shining armour offered to knock Collin into next week if he ever laid a finger on me again.

Sex offenders can spend years grooming their unsuspecting victims to gain trust before moving on to their prey. Every move they make is premeditated. They have a certain charm they use to deceive everyone they come in contact with—there was only one way the creep was going to be part of my girls' lives, and that was through me, which would account for his on/off affection in the relationship… because it was not *me* he was interested in … it was *my girls.*

The reason he told me (*never to open the door to Judy*) wasn't because she was threatening to throw acid—she was threatening to expose him. Judy also had a daughter who (I am convinced) was a victim because the girl had some medical issues at night. Judy should have done the decent thing and reported him, but instead chose to blackmail him. The £60 a week he gave her was to keep her quiet. Judy could get anything she wanted out of him, which would explain why he was so scared. He was never sure if or when she was going to say something—but using her knowledge to gain financially made her no better than him.

It was because of her endless threats and tantrums that he moved us to Norwich. Nan was right when she said Judy had something on him—it's a pity I never listened.

The reason he moved back home during the divorce was to make sure I never mentioned the abuse—which, at the time, I was unaware of. He wanted me to believe he was being amicable by discussing our statements before returning them, when, in fact, by living under my roof, he could continue intimidating my girls… *devious bastard.*

Something else which did not make sense at the time—the day after we met, he told me his biggest fear was going to prison. *How odd.* Only someone that had something to hide would say such a thing. But it was his fear of prison that made me determined to have him put away in the very place he feared more than anything—and only by serving justice was this ever going to happen.

I asked my daughters why they had not confided in me sooner. I cannot remember which of them spoke:—but the night he attacked Craig, one of them was about to tell me, but her siblings refused to back her up. My God, if I had known, I would have had him arrested immediately, and it would have strengthened Craig's case and exposed Owen as a paedophile as well as a violent bully. His sentence would have been a hell of a lot tougher because my girls were juveniles at the time. Alas, their silence allowed him to walk free and continue his reign of terror.

I will never forget the day Morgan returned from one of the court hearings. She came over to where I was sitting and shouted, *You don't know how close you have come to getting a smack in the mouth.* There was more said, but I cannot remember. Goodness knows what had transpired for that outburst—she knew I had no knowledge of the abuse... assuming that's what it was about.

I don't know how I survived those frightful years until the police became involved in the summer of 1995, but it was February 1996 when the creep was sent away for three years—but would be released after 18 months—which (to me) was a crime in itself. It should have been three years for each of my daughters. But at least he was off the streets and behind bars where his inmates would give him a hard time—one can only hope.

The day of his sentencing, I went to bed contented. It had taken seven long years of heated discussions, disagreements, and rows, and now his picture was on the front of our local paper. I slept well, knowing the misogynist creep was behind bars in a cold cell. The only thing that puzzles me is why the two officers dealing with the case treated me with contempt. On every visit to my home and throughout the trial, they ignored me. Any fool could see they had reservations about my involvement in the case—almost as though I was perhaps an offender too.

I wonder who put such thoughts into their heads. Someone must have said something for them to treat me with contempt. Christ, they only had to look at their records from seven years ago to know it was *me* that reported the incident—they even warned me not to approach him when I said I was going to confront the bastard. When questioning my family, they were warm and friendly but were abrupt each time I spoke. When I offered refreshments, their reply was curt to the point of rudeness. I am more than a little ambiguous as to why my family did not speak in my defence—because clearly, the police saw me as a villain. Furthermore, they did not want to interview me. They were not interested in anything I had to say. Very weird.

I was furious, having recently discovered that Allison confided to a family member about the abuse at the time it was happening—but what I don't understand is why they kept the information to themselves. If they had spoken to me, I could have dealt with the matter. But their silence allowed the fiend to take advantage of his position. There are numbers to call if they want to remain anonymous also—when a child confides in someone, it is a cry for help, secretly hoping someone will speak for them. If this family member had spoken up, they would have been called as a witness, and their testimony would have got the beast a tougher sentence…

I have been blamed for what the abuser put my family through, but there is only one person responsible—and that is the offender who kept his cards close to his chest. The guilt and blame belong to him alone. People should not be so critical; neither should they pass judgment without being in possession of the facts. We all carry scars but have learnt to hold our heads high—and that is something we can be proud of. My children have been through hell but have survived the abyss and managed to stay on the right side of the law.

Morgan still had the bit between her teeth and was not about to let the abuse be brushed under the carpet. On the eve of his release, she had flyers printed and distributed them on telegraph poles, trees, and anywhere she could nail them. His picture was on the flyer with a warning to every parent. In spite of her anger towards me, I couldn't help smiling at her bold attempt to punish him further. Unfortunately, we were visited by his social worker, who told her unless she took the flyers down, she could find herself in serious trouble because he had served his sentence and had rights. *I beg to differ—what about my daughters' rights? They were the victims, not him.*

I admired Morgan when she and Alex made two appearances on the TV programme *'Kilroy'*. She was joined by other women who had experienced similar. Strangely enough, my name was not mentioned on either of the shows, which made me look—and feel— like an offender. I wonder how many viewers questioned the whereabouts of the *'mother'* and *could she have been involved in any way.* Morgan knew how much the crime had eaten away over the years—it almost destroyed me. I can forgive the bastards for what they put *me* through, but I can never forgive them for what they did to *my children.*

Brendon was in his teens when he told me he'd seen a picture of me on the noticeboard at his school alongside the paedophile— *WHAT*—I was never a threat to any of my grandchildren, for God's sake. I have been called on for childminding and sleepovers every weekend and short breaks. It was no secret that they often slept with me. Perhaps my grandson was mistaken. Otherwise, *may God forgive those responsible* for sticking a picture of me on the noticeboard beside a paedophile—that was cruel and nasty. Their actions are inexcusable. *Words fail me.*

Morgan told me that her counsellor said *I must have known about the abuse because the writing was on the wall.* After that enlightening bit of information, I chose to have counselling myself from two independent therapists, who both assured me that the advice given was unprofessional. *The wife/mother is always the last to find out* because perpetrators spend years concealing their fixation on children and cleverly disguise the monster that lies beneath. My therapist said Morgan's counsellor was *not very wise— unprofessional—spoke out of turn—and needs reporting.*

For the sceptical-minded:—

Firstly *– Vince could not have forced Morgan into telling me if I already knew.*

Secondly *– How could the beast blackmail my girls if I 'supposedly' knew?*

Thirdly *– Let's not forget—it was me that reported the crime to the police seven years before they became involved.*

Fourthly *– If I had known of the abuse, my daughter would not have told a member of family not to say anything to me.*

And what about the night the beast attacked Craig… one of my girls wanted to confide in me but without the support of her siblings, stayed silent.

Last but not least *– if I was guilty or involved in any way, why didn't the beast report me when he was arrested? He could have had me locked up.*

Having recently read my medical records, I was treated with depression in 1970 when I was married to Collin and again in 1979 when married to Owen. That speaks volumes.

Chapter Forty-Seven

Mind Games

Over the years, we have had our ups and downs, but no family life runs smooth—least of all mine. I decided to sell my house when it became impossible to stay. All sorts of strange things were going on which I could not account for. Someone was playing games and wanted me to think I was crazy—or perhaps they were trying to drive me crazy—but I was of sound mind and knew these incidents were not my imagination. I spoke to my family about the events but could not understand why they paid little attention… *but first, let me take you back to 1986 when we moved into Willow Chase.*

Up until buying Willow, we had been council tenants. In fact, my twins were very nearly born in one. We didn't have a lot in the way of furniture, but our home was clean. Some may look with contempt at living in-in a council property, but it is not *where* you live that is important, but *how* you live. I have met some charming people who live in-in council property, and I have met some undesirables from private dwellings that make life unpleasant. It is not where you live but how you live that depicts who you are—and I was a decent person living in a council house. My home was suitable in which to raise my family. Cleaning was something I enjoyed, but as far as tidy—well, that was another matter, especially when my children had their toys out. But they had very little, so tidy was never a real problem. My kitchen seemed to be upside down most of the time with a sink full of dishes. I was either preparing a meal or clearing one away.

I remember the day we moved into Willow Chase. Everyone was in high spirits. The days that followed were just as wonderful with music and laughter—most of which my granddaughter was responsible. Not yet two, I used to record her chatting to her dolls and picture books with a few swear words thrown in. Years later, Robert transferred the cassette onto a disc which we played at her 21st for all to hear. Give her the telephone and she'd talk in a language that only she could understand, then throw her head back and laugh at the jokes and local gossip she shared with her invisible friends. She surprised me one day when I realised her conversation was not with an invisible friend but someone from Scotland. The bemused woman was anxious to know who her caller was and how they got her number. She accepted my apology and had plenty to share with her family that evening. Coral's next call was to the police. Visions of flashing lights and squad cars wailing down the street caused me concern, so I put my phone out of reach and brought her a spare so she could talk to her heart's content.

When alone, I'd dream of coming events at Willow and sit on the couch and look towards the stairs through the open door and imagine one of my striking daughters descending in a beautiful gown. I never dreamt for one moment I would be in a position to buy my own house, but at the age of 46—I had achieved what I thought impossible. There were times that we struggled, but with discipline, we coped.

I had great plans for the future. This house would eventually be my children's inheritance, but for now, we enjoyed being together, happy and free.

As treasurer, I was responsible for our finances. I collected a year's utility bills and totalled them. Then I divided the total into 52, then divided 52 between us so I knew how much each of us needed to put in the jar. I labelled them *BANK* for standing orders and mortgage, *BILL* was utility bills, and the third was *FOOD*. If we were going to survive, this was the only way forward.

We had been in our house six months when our neighbour Sybil from two doors away lost her husband. Understandably, she was upset and lonely. We used to talk over the picket fence whilst hanging out laundry and invite her in for coffee or afternoon tea—which became the odd meal. As time passed, she became part of our family and was never left out of anything we had planned. We enjoyed her company as she did ours. She told me how she used to watch my girls walking down the street with their long hair blowing in the breeze. She envied the relationship I had with my children and told me I was lucky—but I did not need reminding.

I arrived home from work and realised I had forgotten my keys and Tiffany was out, so I sat with Sybil until she returned. Sybil suggested leaving a spare key with her in case it should happen again, which seemed sensible.

A few years later, the company made me redundant when they relocated to their head office in Norwich. Now that Chris was no longer in my life, I enjoyed spending time with my family and pottering in the garden. It was about this time Sybil introduced me to second-hand shops and boot sales, and I began collecting stuff to display in my display cabinets to accompany the memorabilia my family brought me—not forgetting what I had of my Nan's. I loved re-arranging my latest treasure of lamps, ornaments, and furniture. Someone once told me I was like a little girl playing house—they were not far wrong, actually. Playing house was something I always enjoyed. As a child, I spent a lot of time with Auntie Joan. I was in my element when on my knees with a tin of lavender floor polish—until Howard, in stocking feet, slipped and flew down the hall at speed. I was not allowed to polish the floor again—and definitely not under rugs.

I have always been a home person, so it is unlikely I will ever change. I have never been house-proud, but I do like to see things looking nice. There is no point in having something nice if you don't look after it. Although it was suggested to me once that my well-kept, organised home was because I had a domestic—which made me cross—it is *myself* that is responsible for the way my home and garden look. Any domestic I have had in the past would have been temporary due to injuring myself (which I do frequently). It is *myself* that takes credit for my home and garden—no one else.

I was never cut out to be a businesswoman but a homemaker ~~that~~ who got pleasure in turning my house into a comfortable home where I and others could relax. Pottering in the house and garden was something I enjoyed. Some of my collectables are what have been rescued from skips. I could never resist picking something up that someone had discarded. If I saw its potential, I would clean, paint, or repair my latest treasure—but this is something we can all do. My family frowns as I stoop to pick something up on my travels but have been happy to relieve me of my latest treasure once I have brought it back to life. Collecting things I have no use for, I take them to the charity shop for someone else to reap the benefit.

My next daughter to move away was Morgan with two-year-old Brendon when she met Alex. It put pressure on Tiffany and myself, but we coped. Tiffany was running the local chippy and often brought home a fish supper. If we shopped with care, we could indulge in a takeaway at the weekend and hire a video for £1—a treat we looked forward to. Life was simple, but life was good.

Allison and Jake parted company when she met Stefan, who was decent, kind, and generous. Everyone liked him. I was thrilled when they made the relationship permanent and began planning their future. Stefan applied for a mortgage and purchased a house close to his family. Then, to everyone's delight, they became parents to a beautiful daughter. Shelby had huge eyes with long lashes, but she was a mummy's girl who got upset if she could not see either one of her parents—especially when I was around—then she'd scream. She was fine with Stefan's parents, who saw her every day, but if I was around, she'd snuggle into the neck of whoever was holding her and observe me from a distance. I rarely saw Shelby, so she did not take kindly to my presents—which does little to build a relationship that every grandmother needs in order to become popular. Within two years, Shelby had a little brother to care for. Taylor was a gem who did not mind being in my company. He was a happy little guy with the most amazing smile and smart enough to recognise that being generous with smiles guaranteed cuddles and attention.

Morgan, anxious to increase her family, gave birth to Kym, who was very different to Shelby. Kym did not mind who she was with—which could be worrying. As a toddler, she would look for any escape and wander off to make new friends, always looking for adventure or something in which to dabble that was usually none of her business. *Lively* is an understatement—she was an accident waiting to happen. Dress her up, and she'd fall in a puddle. Tie her hair in ribbons, and she'd end up with a sweet buried in her curls. Her drinks ended up on the floor or whoever happened to be nearby. If she didn't have a drink to spill, she'd knock someone else's over. If you left anything around that took her fancy, she'd be off with her latest treasure. The incidents she created were laughable—although I am not sure her parents would agree. Now in her 20s, her parents can look back with some amusing stories.

Taylor was a darling and was at peace with the world. Shelby was shy—she'd silently observe everything and everyone, whereas Kym liked to be heard. She would join in everyone's conversation because her opinion was of the utmost importance—or so she thought.

The weather was on the turn, so I decided to put my electric blanket on my bed but was surprised when it wasn't *where* I left it. I asked Tiffany and the family, but no one knew of its whereabouts. The blanket had been a Christmas present from Vince and had only been used for the remainder of that season—now it was gone. The next thing to disappear was Tiffany's new blouse. She searched her wardrobe and laundry basket and in unlikely places like Coral's drawers, but the elusive blouse was never seen again. Eventually, one stops looking and erases the item from their mind.

I was upset when Tiffany said she was moving out. I enjoyed her company on the nights she wasn't working, and I was going to miss her—she was the last to leave the nest. I wondered if I would be able to cope financially or would I lose my dream home. It was going to be a challenge, so I decided to look for casual work.

The horrible smell in my kitchen was getting worse. I could not understand where it was coming from. I sniffed in the most unlikely places, then discovered a rotten Brussels sprout at the back of the cutlery drawer. It was barely recognisable, which I thought strange, as I only bought sprouts at Christmas—and this was spring. It could not have survived in the drawer for all those months.

It didn't take me long to find casual work at the local taxi company. I was hired to escort underprivileged children to and from special needs schools. It was upsetting to see the children with severe disabilities lashing out through no fault of their own. I could see the exasperation in on their faces when trying to tell me something, but it was equally frustrating for me not being able to help or understand what they were trying to say. Thankfully, they were not my regular children—I was only called upon when their escort was away. Then, there were those from dysfunctional families who were difficult to control.

My regular run was mornings and afternoons, Monday to Friday. After a few months, I was given a distant run—Monday mornings and picking up Friday afternoons—to a boarding school in Ipswich, so the office had to do a bit of juggling.

I answered the door one afternoon to Sybil, who walked past me in tears. I followed her into my sitting room, where she plonked herself in the armchair. When I asked what was wrong, she said, *It's him,* referring to her son Neil. She said he'd been drinking and was being abusive. Apparently, he pushed past her on the landing and was slurring insults. I poured her a sherry and made myself comfortable as she got everything off her chest.

Fifteen minutes later, I answered another knock, and Neil walked past into the sitting room. He paced the floor, then turned and said, *You don't know what she's like, really you don't. You haven't got a clue.* He continued pacing back and forth, then repeated, *You don't know what she's like.* I stayed silent, as did Sybil. Neil continued to pace, then left without another word. I topped up Sybil's empty glass and reassured her she was a kind and generous mother who should not have to deal with Neil and his drinking problem—which, as a mother, she was concerned about.

I was horrified when I opened the drawer and saw the tablecloth my Mother embroidered had been damaged. The scene was of a crinoline lady by a stream with wildflowers and bulrushes. Unfortunately, the bulrushes had been cut. I have done a lot of embroidery over the years but have never seen bulrushes before—

they looked real. I have made enquiries hoping to find someone who knows this particular stitch but have not been successful. I have nothing of my Mother's, so the tablecloth is very special.

Before Tiffany left home, we paid for a water filter to be fitted in the kitchen. The smooth-talking salesman was filling in forms and asked about my occupation. I innocently told him I was an escort. A year later, I was lying on the settee recovering from a chest infection when the doorbell rang. Rolling off the settee, I wrapped the blanket tighter around my housecoat, wondering who could be calling at this hour, and headed for the door—I glanced at my reflection as I passed the mirror in the hall and cringed, but with no hairbrush in sight I ran my fingers through my hair, by which time my impatient caller was using the knocker. I opened the door and was amazed to see the salesman... wondering if he had come to the right house. His smile quickly faded as the woman standing before him resembled one of the homeless. *I am sorry to bother you at this time of night, my dear, but a friend of mine—how are you, by the way?* Before I could reply, he continued, *I have a friend who is looking for a nice young lady to accompany him to a dinner/dance in London and asked if I knew of anyone.*

I immediately thought of your good self. When I told him about this lovely lady I know, he said he would like to meet you. He glanced around, hoping no one was within earshot. *Anyway, my dear, you do understand that there are no strings attached... by the way, you still do escorting, don't you?* Finally, the penny dropped. *Yes, of course,* I replied with a grin, *but I escort underprivileged children to and from special needs schools.* The guy did not know where to put his face and almost fell over, escaping off my drive. I wonder what he really thought when I opened the door that evening... *lovely lady* does not spring to mind as I glanced once again in the mirror. A letter of apology arrived three days later.

I returned from my Ipswich run about 5 p.m. and was greeted by Maxi and Ruffles anxiously waiting for their dinner. Once fed, I took my mouth-watering casserole from the fridge and popped it in the microwave. I managed a couple of mouthfuls then felt something sharp. I removed it gently and rinsed it under the tap—to my horror; I was holding a shard of glass approximately one inch long and pointed at each end. I wondered where it had come from, having stirred the meal frequently during cooking, but then… my dish was circular and brown, but the shard was straight and clear. Bewildered, I showed Sybil but was surprised when she passed no comment—in fact, she didn't look up from what she was doing. I returned home and tipped my dinner and the remainder of the casserole down the toilet.

I showed the glass to the family but cannot remember their reaction, but when I showed my two regular drivers, they told me if I had swallowed the shard, it would have done serious damage or even killed me. Still trying to come to terms with how close I had come to harming myself, I kept the shard in a matchbox on top of the microwave. A few weeks later, I opened the box and saw the shard in two pieces. Who broke the shard? Where had it come from? And who hates me enough to want to harm me? Terrifying memories of Collin began to surface.

Neil phoned and asked if I would record something on my tape-to-tape recorder. When I agreed, he brought in the cassette and told me what tracks he wanted. I was setting up the recorder when he wandered into my extension and looked down the garden with a slight grin, which I thought strange. Months later, I noticed the 7ft conifer by the summer house turning brown. Then, the miniature conifer in the brick-built tub died. Within months, my trees and shrubs were beyond help. I wondered if the fox was responsible and using my garden as a toilet. I showed Sybil where my nightly visitor

trampled the earth by the gap in next door's fence to gain entry—
she passed no comment.

Sybil hated trees. She told me they were menacing. She also
spoke about her days as a child, but that story belongs to Sybil and
is not mine to tell.

Sybil drove to the supermarket most Saturdays and often invited
me along. On this particular day, whilst applying lipstick, she
pointed to the pen and asked me to add sausages to her shopping list.
I admired the pen and told her Tiffany bought me the identical pen
last Christmas with the same logo, but as of yet, I had not used it…
I got no response. A few weeks later, I opened the drawer of my
desk and saw everything upside down, as though someone had
tipped the lot on the floor then shovelled it back. I thought one of
my girls had been searching for something and not said anything,
but on questioning them, no one had touched my desk. I straightened
the drawer and found my designer pen loose and the box in two
halves. I put the box together but was mystified when the pen would
not fit. The pen was too big and did not have a logo on the side. Then
I remembered the pen at Sybil's but pushed the thought to one
side—after all, she was my friend.

Another time, I was about to do some filing when I noticed my
papers in complete disarray, as though they had been shuffled.
Nothing in the file was where it should have been… was this
something I had carelessly done, or was someone letting me know
they had been through my files? I pondered over other incidents,
then realised these things had been going on for some time, but I had
brushed them aside—*"When did I do that?"* or *"How did that
happen?"* I went to bed that night mystified and slept restlessly.

Sybil invited me for dinner one evening and introduced me to
her friend Molly. She was gentle and sweet-natured—I thought she

was lovely. Molly worked as a cleaner in a private school, was a back sufferer, and complained bitterly about having to stoop to retrieve rubbers, pencils, and sharpeners, and anything else the kids left on the floor. I suggested over our meal that she throw everything in the bin—then the kids would think twice about leaving everything on the floor. As an afterthought, I asked her to pop a pencil sharpener in her bag for me. Then Sybil asked if she could have one too. Knowing how lazy the kids were, I knew I would not have to wait long for my sharpener. The following week, Tiffany, Molly, Sybil, and I had tickets for the theatre. It was during intermission when Molly opened her bag and took out two sharpeners and handed one to me and one to Sybil. I thanked her and dropped the sharpener in my bag without looking.

A few days later, I opened my wardrobe and saw a psychedelic green pencil sharpener on the shelf beside my face cream. I stood for a moment, then realised I had not been to my bag since the night of the show. I raced downstairs and tipped my bag onto the dining table—and out dropped a psychedelic yellow sharpener.

Whilst working in London, Tiffany brought me a black poncho with the *tie rack* label sewn in the corner above the fringe. It was after I was made redundant that Sybil and I started going to boot sales and second-hand markets. I loved mooching through stalls, looking for bargains. One morning, she pulled me to one side and pointed to a blanket lying on the floor with—what looked like—rags, with a sign *everything 50 pence.* I left Sybil rummaging through and wandered off. When we arrived home, she showed me all she had purchased: a blouse, two scarves, a brooch, and a worn-out poncho with bobbles from being repeatedly washed.

It must have been a year later when sorting through drawers in my bedroom, I took my poncho from the bag where I kept it for protection and special occasions and noticed it was old, shabby, and covered in bobbles—and there was no *tie rack* label on the corner. I tried to outsmart my neighbour and asked if I could borrow her poncho, as I had lent mine to Elaine. She returned with a shawl that belonged to her mother… how could I accuse the woman? I had no proof.

When Craig moved out, he left a carrier bag full of little notelets in the shape of bottles—there was tomato ketchup, wine, Daddies sauce, beer, martini, tonic water, and others. I showed them to Sybil and gave her those of *Daddies sauce* because that was her son's favourite. A few weeks later, I discovered the bag almost empty… we had just returned from the market, and I went into hers so we could sort out our bags. Then I noticed quite a few beside her phone, but none were *Daddies sauce.* When I approached her, she shrieked and said I had given them to her. I grabbed the notelets and left.

The next thing was Craig's green shark he made at school—it was repeatedly being damaged. I wondered who had accidentally broken it and not said anything, so I glued it back together, only to find it broken again. In all fairness, some breaks may have happened years ago when my family were around, but not now I'm alone. I realised the damage was no accident when part of the fin disappeared. The poor shark was under constant attack, so I wrapped Craig's 12-inch masterpiece in bubble paper and put it away. Over the years, the shark had many scars from where I had made a lousy attempt at gluing it back together.

It's strange how everything Craig brought was damaged—just like the gold pear-drop earrings he bought for my birthday. One of the earrings was buckled as though it had been stamped on. I took them to a jeweller but was told there was nothing they could do. Another gift was a glass table lighter—it looked like a giant ice cube.

Within weeks, it was in two halves. Then, there was the delicate glass ornament he brought from Cornwall. The latest to disappear were my two heavy brass mice from the display cabinet... that was recent.

I loved the bazaar at the church hall. Parking was easy, and we were under-cover. We paid our fee and went to the first stall, when my friend picked up an unglazed ornament of two little children. The little girl was holding a bucket for the little boy to pump water—but his hand was missing. Sybil tried persuading me to buy the ornament, but I refused, so she opened her purse and bought it herself, which surprised me because Sybil looked for perfection. She turned everything upside down, making sure there were no chips or cracks.

A week later, I was dusting my cabinet, then stared in disbelief—the broken ornament was in my cabinet in place of the skunk Craig brought when he was a boy. I took the ornament and smashed it in anger, but I should have returned it to my *friend*. Goodness knows what happened to my skunk.

One morning, I noticed about six inches of rubber seal in the window of my spare room had been pulled out. My first reaction was to push it back with scissors, then realised I should have left it to show the family... I had not long had them installed.

Next time Sybil invited me for coffee, I noticed my grandmother's doily on her little table. When I approached her, she told me she'd bought it from the market. I finished my drink and went home to check on those of my Nan's, and there were hardly any left. So I hurried back, but she'd replaced it with one of a different colour and design. When I approached the woman, her manner was alarming—she was warning me off.

I began to wonder if… when she invited me for coffee, she was taunting, otherwise; why put something of mine on display then hide it? Like the designer pen, the little notelets, and now the doily. Perhaps she was goading me into some sort of confrontation, but I could prove nothing, and I was not strong enough to confront her on my own.

When I told the family, they offered no comment. In fact, they didn't seem interested. But having been married to the master of devious games, I know only too well that when *one* chooses to play mind games, the perpetrator covers their tracks so the unsuspecting victim is unable to prove what they are saying—and people think the helpless victim is either stupid or seeking attention.

The more my family ignored me, the more frustrated I became—the more frustrated I became, the more I pounced on the first one that walked through my door. But their silence and lack of support spoke a thousand words. Maybe they did not believe me, or perhaps they were unsure what to do with the information because they would look for any excuse to leave.

But when I spoke to Craig, his reply was encouraging: *Sounds like someone's playing mind games with you.* Hallelujah—I was relieved he took me seriously when others appeared detached. My boss from the taxi office also warned me to be on my guard, the same as my neighbour/friend John. I go to great lengths to avoid a row, the same as I trust people—but that makes me a target.

I had stopped encouraging Sybil into my home and taken my key back, but out of curiosity, I still went into hers. I walked in one afternoon and commented on the lovely smell, which I recognised but could not place. She nodded towards the stairs. *That's him up there getting ready to go out.* It was months later when I opened my new box of men's Lagerfeld deodorant and was shocked to see the bottle scratched, dented, and almost empty—that's when I recognised the smell. So I paid her a visit. I sat with my coffee then asked if I could use the loo. Once inside the bathroom, I peeked inside her cabinet, and there was my full bottle of Lagerfeld. But with nowhere to hide it, I left empty-handed. I was not brave enough to confront the woman—besides, what proof did I have it was mine? Then I remembered how she used to hunt through boxes in the market where stallholders sold unwanted colognes, lipsticks, and cosmetics. I am 100% sure that's where the damaged bottle came from. You'd think after Collin, I would have been on top of these situations, but how was I to know my trusted neighbour/friend also played these games? Perhaps I put the idea in her head when I spoke of Collin and his devious tricks.

Long before these problems surfaced, Allison asked Sybil if she would be Godmother to Shelby. At the time, I was pleased my friend was going to take part in another family event—until I realised the problems she created. So I asked Allison to reconsider, but she refused.

On the day of the christening, Sybil could not find her christening card and was running from room to room in a panic. So I offered to help hunt for the elusive card and followed her upstairs. She disappeared into her bedroom and I headed for the box room where she dumped everything. Within seconds, she was behind me and screamed, *Don't go in there, wait downstairs!* Hearing the alarm in her voice, I stopped dead—I was two steps short of entering the room when she rushed past me and closed the door.

Molly had also been invited to the christening and was pacing up and down, very agitated. She opened the car door and asked why we were late. Sybil cocked her head towards the back and blamed me. I angrily replied, *No—you made us late looking for the damn card!* Molly never heard me above Sybil's overpowering voice, ranting about her son. I have often wondered what was in that spare room I was not meant to see.

Because of our late arrival, we were trapped at the back of the church along with my cousin Sonia and her husband Brian, who were also late. After the service, Brian asked if I would travel with them so I could show them the way to Allison's. I agreed but asked if they could take me home first so I could turn on some lights and feed my dogs. Unable to reach my family, I told Sybil of my plans and asked her to pass the message on. I should have known better than to trust her with a simple message.

It was Molly who answered the door when we arrived. *Where have you been? We've been everywhere looking for you—we walked round the grounds and tried to get into the church but the minister said there was no one inside and refused to let us in. Robert was worried, thinking you may have had an accident.* I was understandably shocked and told her Sybil knew exactly where we were—by which time she had walked away. Then I noticed my *'friend'* eyeing me from a distance, sipping tea and making small talk with both sides of the family. Then Robert tore me off a strip for disappearing. I cannot imagine what game Sybil was playing but realised she was quite the manipulator—rising above every situation like the cat's whiskers. And I was not about to approach her, having witnessed how overpowering she could be. Besides, this was a family event, and it was not my home. Sybil had proved she was not a woman to mess with, although I did stand my ground once—but she beat me down with her shrill voice. She was too quick for me and razor sharp.

I was telling a member of the family about the latest episode when I overheard, *(She's off again)*. I was upset to think no one believed me. I used to think I was indestructible, but there are no shortcuts in life. Shocks can upset the balance of the body, which you may not be aware of until later in life. I have had my share of shocks, and this episode was so unexpected it knocked me off my feet—which was probably the impact intended. But then—all my shocks have caught me off guard and arrived out of the blue. I began to struggle with mundane things, but not being taken seriously was soul-destroying. Then came the panic attacks. Living alone and unable to control the trembling was frightening. Tiffany let me stay with her for a while, but she was a working mum with a teenager, and I was in the way.

I reported these incidents to the policeman who lived a short distance away. I followed his advice and changed the locks, but the incidents continued.

I opened the cupboard in the hall when my hand lightly touched the wall mirror. Thankfully, I caught it before it smashed to the floor. Then I noticed the string hanging, with the eyelet still attached. I turned the mirror over and was about to screw the eyelet in place and was shocked. At the back of the dusty frame were three deep fingerprints where someone had held the mirror to unscrew the eyelet—leaving it to balance. When I purchased the mirror a few years ago, I watched the chap screw the eyelet tight with pliers.

The couple separating me from Sybil had two carp ponds. Unfortunately, the fish kept dying. The guy cleaned his filters and emptied the pond more than once, but it made no difference to the health of his fish. After months of work and frustration, the chap called in a specialist. I had just arrived home from my school run when a white van came and parked outside my house. The guy went next door carrying a large case that looked rather like what the doctors carried their medicines in years ago. An hour later, I heard voices, so I went to my window—but shrunk back when the guy kept looking at my house. He put his bag in the van and sat writing on his clipboard, occasionally turning to my windows.

The following week, a fencing company installed a seven-foot fence from top to bottom, cutting out a lot of sunlight. My garden had been my sanctuary where I loved to potter until dark but it was now shaded and gloomy. When leaving the house, I felt I was being watched, so I kept my head down—which made me look at fault. I could not go on living this way… *I had to escape.*

I could go on and on about my neighbour/friend but have decided to end it here. Everything that happened was approximately over 8 months, but it could have been more. Some may be in the wrong order, and there are some I have not mentioned.

Regarding my uncle… *I am not out for revenge—I just want to clear my name he destroyed.* I did seek legal advice, and everything I have said is true. But why would I lie?—*I would have nothing to gain.*

If I have given the impression I am *Mrs. Perfect* that is not my intention. I have never claimed to be someone that I am not. I am no better or worse than the next. Over the years, I have made many mistakes but did what I thought best at the time. I have given advice and guidance where it was not appreciated—which is what Nan would have done. Any advice given was to help where I felt (at the time) it could have been beneficial. Unfortunately, diplomacy was never my strong point—neither was it Nan's.

When I was young, advice was something you accepted with gratitude, but today, it is taken as an insult when youngsters do not appreciate the wisdom or advice that is handed down. But knowledge from the past *can* be valuable. I continue to annoy family when I say something out of place, but no harm is meant—*until someone takes offence where none is intended.*

Having recently read my medical records, I was treated for depression in 1970 when married to Collin and again in 1979 whilst married to Owen. *That speaks volumes.*

Chapter Forty-Eight

The Sale Of Willow Chase

1999

Before I put the house on the market, I told the family of my decision, hoping someone would step forward and offer support. God knows I needed them to believe in me. When it failed to raise a response, I went to an agent and asked for a valuation on the property.

This house had been my dream home that, in the past, had enveloped me with love and security but had now turned cold and menacing. I could not get away quick enough—away from the neighbour that I no longer trusted, the neighbour we welcomed into our home within weeks of losing her husband. She attended our christenings, weddings, parties and meals out, and we never left her alone at Christmas, so much for offering support and companionship at the time of her loss—what a kick in the teeth that turned out.

I called the building society and asked if they could transfer my mortgage over to another property... how difficult could it be to transfer a mortgage from one property to the next? I was relieved when they said they would do everything to help and would get back to me once they had spoken to head office, but selling my house with no advice or experience was not my wisest of choices.

When the building society returned my call, they said I had to put the collateral from the sale of my house on my next property, and they were only prepared to lend me £58 thousand. But Willow was worth a lot more—Willow had integrated cooker/hob, all three bedrooms had fitted wardrobes which I would need to replace, not to mention legal fees and removals. I viewed properties within the price I was allowed, but they were not up to the standards of Willow and none had the fittings I was leaving behind. So my lenders were making things really difficult. They said they would help but were making my escape impossible, and I was in no fit state to challenge their decision.

Never having sold before, I did not have the slightest inclination what I was doing. Every property I viewed was in undesirable areas, but I continued my search and collected boxes on my travels and hoped something would turn up soon.

I sold Willow with no trouble—well, it was rather special and I kept it immaculate inside and out. My buyer worked at the bank and, being first-time buyers, things went through quicker than expected, but her parents were dealing with everything. It was probably a month after they viewed it when her mother phoned to say they were ready to exchange contracts. They were not in the least bit concerned I had nowhere to live—they just wanted me out.

What a fool I was not to have contacted Wilson, who would have taken control of the sale and advised me accordingly. He certainly would not have allowed my buyers to bulldoze me into moving before I found something to my liking. He would have told them to bugger off. In fact, they had no right to keep phoning me. Robert found a three-bedroom property in Byrne Drive. I loved the look of the semi-detached with a long drive. The surrounding properties were neat, which is always a good sign; plus, it was close enough for me to cycle into town and not far from the park should I fancy walking Maxi and Ruffles. We looked through the windows and letterbox and saw it was in a terrible state. Undeterred, I phoned the agent who said—it was cheap because it had been trashed and I would need roughly 10 thousand to make it liveable.

Robert, bless him, offered to do the work, but I was not in the position to buy what was needed—i.e. boiler, sink, carpets and whatever else had been destroyed that was not visible through the letterbox. So, I let that go by the wayside.

I cycled for weeks, but with my impatient buyer nipping at my heels and running out of time, I looked at properties to rent as well as those to buy. Then, I saw a two-bedroom terrace for rent. The place had been on the market for ages because it was in a deplorable state. The only thing appealing was—Tiffany lived three minutes down the road and cousin Charlotte lived a few houses in the opposite direction, plus it was ten minutes from town. I returned to look at the place time and again before deciding to rent *Southern Chase... I should have had my brains tested.* The agent organised block viewings, so everyone arrived at the same time. They looked no further than the kitchen and walked out, but I decided to take the rundown terrace and put my mark on the place with money from my sale.

The owner of the terrace called at Willow with the excuse of needing papers to be signed. He could not understand why I was leaving such a beautiful house. Without going into detail, I told him it was too big now that my family had flown the nest. It could not have been further from the truth—I had been driven out.

Chapter Forty-Nine

Southern Chase

The day before I moved, Elaine offered to help with last-minute packing. By midnight, the video and recorder were packed along with the sky box and cables. That night, I crawled into bed and spent the last night in what used to be my dream home.

June 22nd, the removal men arrived and loaded the van while Elaine vacuumed through, then it was time to leave. Elaine wondered if I was going to shed tears, but I couldn't wait to slam the door on my past and start a new life in a dumpy two-bedroom terrace with Maxi and Ruffles. I refused to look at the windows of any hostile neighbours who might be gloating behind nets. I told her to drive and looked straight ahead.

It took months getting straight because the place was small. Angie, my school driver, offered to lend me her husband to assemble a new kitchen because what represented a kitchen at the moment was nothing more than an uninhabitable scullery with one free-standing cupboard and one wall cupboard, neither of which matched. The sink had no front except for the broken drawer, and God knows how many creatures lived under the unit. The floor was concrete with no floor covering, and the flex hanging from the ceiling had a 25-watt bulb and made the place look like a torture chamber. There was an outside toilet that backed into the kitchen and took up quite a bit of floor space... so work began... with the landlord's permission, I had the toilet taken out and the wall knocked down to square the kitchen off—I had the small pantry window removed and replaced with a three-foot window to bring in more light so I could admire the broken fence and overgrown garden and rubbish left by the previous tenants. Russ, my son's friend, arrived with his truck and dumped the broken wall cupboards and units along with the dirty sink. I couldn't wait to have my new sink fitted. I replaced the two broken wall units with six new and six free-standing cupboards and a carousel for extra storage. I had matching worktops that surrounded the entire kitchen. I had never had so many cupboards. The job took six weeks because the chap could only work weekends. Meanwhile, I survived on take-away, microwave meals and an electric frying pan. Tiffany invited me for the occasional roast, but with money dwindling at an alarming rate, there was little hope of buying anywhere, so I made *Southern Chase* my home for my faithful pets and me.

By the time I decorated and added decent flooring, the terrace looked a lot different to when I first arrived. My chandelier that had taken pride of place in my hall was now in my sitting room with a dimmer. Robert put dimmers in every room, just as he did at Willow. It took time before the house adopted the ambience that made the house my comfortable home.

Good morning – my neighbour called from across the road as I was leaving one morning. *Don't be alone now,* she added. Ruby was tall and elderly with white hair – smartly dressed and spoke well. I knew she was respectable by the way she took pride in her appearance and the condition of her property. She was out every morning wiping window ledges inside and out, sweeping the footpath and plucking dead heads from her hanging baskets, while her husband observed from the doorway. Standing safely out of reach, I'd watch him point to those she missed before walking away with a grin. I was pleased to think I had a decent couple living opposite that offered some much-needed friendship.

I had been in the terrace for a couple of months when I realised my tormentor was still with me. I turned a blind eye, hoping whoever was playing cruel tricks would eventually become bored because I refused to accept what was happening. It would be pointless talking to family when, in the past, they ignored me. Besides, I did not want them to think I was paranoid—which, of course, I had every right, living with treachery. Then I began to wonder how much of what happened at Willow my neighbour was actually responsible for. I know she was accountable for quite a lot because of what I witnessed, not to mention the situations she created. Perhaps someone decided to join in with her cruel game and torture me further, or perhaps someone was trying to destroy me like Collin threatened—as my nightmare continues, I feel him reaching from beyond the grave. I was suspicious of everyone who walked through my door and tolerated the odd comment, like when Robert was putting up my large wall mirror. Having used the drill, he asked for the hammer. I glanced around, wondering where I had left it, then he said, *perhaps Sybil's got it* and laughed. The remark amused him, but it cut into me.

I have been accused of having a suspicious mind, but can you blame me? One cannot go through what I have and not come away without reservations. I do not have a suspicious nature until someone gives me cause—the same as I trust everyone until they give me cause not to.

It was a year or so later when speaking to Wilson about my policy, he asked why I had not called him sooner. His mother passed away the same time I was house hunting and said I could have bought their property. Wilson had seen Willow more than once and knew his childhood home would have been well looked after. When I told him about the under-priced property that had been trashed, he said I could have got a grant to have the work done... *I could kick myself... if only I had phoned him sooner.* But *'one' does not think clearly when 'one's mind has been tampered with.* I shredded my *'Will'* which I had not divided equally, but allow me to explain:-

In order to purchase the house, Wilson would not have got a mortgage on my low income from the café, so he conjured up a fictitious place of employment with a handsome wage. But it was still insufficient, so he included Tiffany—not yet divorced, she had a different surname. Wilson gave her a fancy job with an equally handsome title.

In the 13 years we occupied the property, Robert did everything electrical and more besides. He put dimmers and wall lights in the lounge, dining room, hall, landing and three bedrooms. He put subtle overhead lighting above the bathroom sink. One of his customers gave him a beautiful cut-glass chandelier, which he put in the hall. Robert did all the maintenance—he fixed the roof to the large summer house, replaced the damaged wood and repainted, then added a dusk-till-dawn light. He replaced fencing, ripped up floorboards for rewiring, and more besides. I never paid him for the materials or the work. I can't thank my son enough for turning my house into a beautiful home, and without Tiffany's fictitious job, it would not have been possible to purchase Willow. So I thought it only fair they have a larger portion of my estate. But selling the house was unfortunate because my children lost their inheritance— so whoever was responsible for driving me out not only deprived their siblings of inheritance but themselves too.

I had been in my terrace for 3 months when Ruby invited me for dinner on Saturday. *Joyce will be joining us,* she said, *arrive at six so we can enjoy sherry before we eat*—Joyce was Eric's sister. Since losing her husband, they invited her for dinner once a month. I made my way to 54 promptly at six. When Ruby gestured me into the sitting room, I came face to face with Joyce—the lovely lady that had cared for me when I had my twins. We hugged briefly, then she asked after my children. I raced home to gather pictures and spent the next hour bragging about my family, leaving out the problems and pain I kept hidden from the world. Only Nan could see the pain and sadness behind my endless smiles and chatter—she could read me like a book, as she did my mother.

Leading up to Christmas, there was always room for unexpected guests—we drank sherry while waiting for coffee to percolate, we ate miniature mince pies dusted with icing sugar with a sprig of holly, served on dainty square plates with festive serviettes. Everything looked impeccable and tasted amazing. It was New Year's Eve 1999 when my friends invited me to join them for drinks. As the clock struck midnight, we stood outside waving our glasses before going inside to warm up. My next-door neighbour and others drifted in from the cold and were made welcome. Eric kept me topped up—champagne in one hand and wine in the other. Everyone was engrossed in conversation and appeared not to notice me sitting in the comfortable leather armchair talking to the person nearby. Then, I felt myself sliding gracefully down. I tried to make it appear that I preferred the floor to the comfortable armchair and hoped no one noticed, but it was too late... silence fell and everyone watched as I slid elegantly onto the carpet. I said *was whoops* and carried on talking without spilling a drop. That night—or should I say morning—I staggered home and woke with one humdinger. Ruby must polish those *dam* chairs daily for them to be so slippery—nothing to do with being drunk of course.

Chapter Fifty

Family Tensions

It was March 2000 when Morgan phoned and said we need to talk. I asked what it was we needed to talk about. *YOU,* she snapped. *You are the worst mother in the world, no-one deserves a mother like you. You're the mother from hell. Everything bad that has happened to me you are responsible for – you don't know how close you have come to having a smack in the mouth. As of now, you only have two daughters, not three, because I disown you.* I calmly replied, as long as you remember it is you that have disowned me and not the other round. *Now, my dear, you must excuse me,. I am busy.* I gently replaced the receiver and burst into tears. There was more said that morning, but I was too upset to remember. I wondered what or who was responsible to have fuelled her anger. It's true we had not spoken for ages, but there were no harsh words. I had been aware that a problem had been brewing for some time, but I avoided confrontation because I did not want to lose touch with my grandchildren. But it was not easy acting nonchalant when she used to tell everyone she had the best mother in the world. I can only apologise to my family for the pain they endured over the years, but I did not set out to marry a murderer or a paedophile—they groomed and tricked me with deceit, and George only wanted revenge.

July was my twins' birthday. A family meal had been arranged along the sea-front. In spite of Morgan's outburst four months ago, I gave both girls crystal. If my daughter chooses not to recognise the unconditional love of her mother, then that is a problem she is going to have to deal with.

It was Christmas, and all the family were invited to Tiffany's to pick the tree. With ill feeling, I was not looking forward to the event, but Tiffany had put a lot of effort into the preparations, so I put my feelings to one side. I arrived with gifts and did not leave anyone out. I watched Morgan open the joint gift I brought for her and Alex. Then we were interrupted by a crash and the youngsters shouting. Everyone hurried into the dining room. The commotion was centred around Kym, who dropped the hamster ball with the hamster still inside. Tiffany soon had the problem under control. I turned to walk away and collided with my estranged daughter, standing close behind. Before I could squeeze past, she pulled me into her and thanked me again for the gift and said she loved me. I can't tell you how thrilled I was to have my daughter back—that was the best gift I could have received.

Two months later was my birthday. Morgan, Alex and the children treated me to a meal along the sea-front. When they drove me home, Alex stayed in the car while Morgan carried my cake in the house. She placed it on the dining table—gave me a hug and said she loved me. I told her I loved her too, but having been down this road before, wondered how long it would last. Within a month, the atmosphere had cooled and the distance between us widened, which I could not understand. I am her mother and want only the best for my daughter. When I think of the times I used to worry when she was young—wondering who would be there for her when I am no longer around—and now she believes the worst of me, it's unbelievable and difficult to comprehend.

With the sale from Willow, Elaine and I began taking coach trips. Finding a dog sitter was not a problem. My friend John was always obliging—he'd make himself coffee and eat in my garden or in front of the TV.

Elaine and I visited some lovely places and got to know a lot of regulars. One in particular was a little Jewish lady. Helena was always alone and asked to join us—then she asked for my phone number. I didn't have long to wait before she put it to use. In fact, she phoned that same evening. She advised me what trips were worth doing and those to avoid. This was the start of our friendship. Finding a dog sitter was not a problem—John, a kind neighbour/friend, was always obliging. He'd make himself coffee and eat in my garden or in front of the TV.

I was in the market when I bumped into Albert, who I had not seen in years. He had recently divorced and wanted to talk about his marriage. I politely listened, then suggested he pay me a visit where we could talk in the comfort of my home instead of the draftee market. I wasn't sure he'd remember, but he arrived at 6 in time to watch *Coronation Street*. He left at 10 and said he would call again the following Monday. Albert, like Helena, was grieving... not for his wife, I might add, but grieving with loneliness. Every morning he'd leave home and jump on the first bus to pull up and arrive home late evening. He certainly put his bus pass to good use. Poor guy used to wander through towns and markets, parks and shops throughout the country purely out of boredom. He knew where to buy a good bacon sandwich, where to get a decent cup of tea, and who served the best fry-ups. Helena happened to be with me one Monday. She didn't waste time dropping hints about 5-day holiday's and dog sitters. Albert jumped at the opportunity to care for Ruffles and Maxi so I could holiday with Helena.

I closed my eyes to incidents in my home when I realised the problem was here to stay and one I have to live with, as I chose not to be drawn into a row so that *(one)* can say *you'll never guess what I have been accused of* – guess I am in a 'no win' situation. But I have listed some items that went missing – well, those I'm aware of anyway.

The large salt crystal tea light holder from Craig. A large glass cube from Venice with a picture of my two grandchildren inside. Numerous DVDs including the complete series one and two of *Faulty Towers*. An expensive leather wallet and my collectable Lilliput Lane cottage still in the box. Nan's watch she brought from Canada. Ornamental ballerina Aunty Joan brought from Canada. A welcome baby card for my 1st great grandson due in 2011. A red beaded evening stole with beaded fringe, never worn. Vintage black velvet evening bag with tortoiseshell clasp. Long black velvet evening gloves. Long black satin evening gloves with diamante trim. White fur stole made by a relative in the 70s. USB lead to my camera, used once. Coffee-scented candle with leather strap and tag (brought as a gift). Mother of pearl pendant from Aunt Katherine in 1949. Two large brass mice from Craig. Scarab watch on a chain. Unglazed ornamental skunk from Craig. Electric blanket from Vince. My gold cross and chain. Designer pen never used, and my Buckingham Palace pen in a velvet case. Tiffany's floral blouse. Items were missing from my sewing box, some of which were Nan's. Whilst working in London, someone made me a press to use on correspondence—disappeared from my bedside cabinet. Nan's boxed set of 6 decorative brass spoons—only 3 are left. My miniature pliers and my designer glasses.

I have a passion for perfume. Whilst working in London, I brought colognes from a distributor at a low cost. There was *Lagerfeld* deodorant for men, *Jazz* for men, *Eternity,* boxed set of *L'Air du Temps* cologne and body lotion, unopened. *Knowing. Red Door. Lou-Lou. Paris. Beautiful. Opium. Anaïs Anaïs. Red* and *Obsession.*

I kept my colognes on the overcrowded shelf in my wardrobe with cosmetics and everything else that women collect, so it was a while before I noticed the odd one missing because they disappeared so gradually—it is not until you go to use something you realise it's not there.

When on coach trips and holidays, I brought myself useful souvenir wax-coated shopping bags for the supermarket. Those I collected were *Woburn Abbey, Hastings, Windsor, Tower of London, Bournemouth, London Bridge, Wales, Rochester, St Albans, Hever Castle* and *Stratford-upon-Avon.* I think there were more. Regrettably, every bag disappeared, but it was months before I noticed. I support and contribute to many animal charities, including IFAW, who show their appreciation by sending me wax-coated shopping bags with pictures of wildlife on both sides. Because I had been using those from IFAW, it was ages before I missed those that I purchased.

Tiffany gave me a boxed set of 6 decorative coffee cups and saucers from Italy. The inside of the cups were painted gold. The coffee set was in the original box and never used. I brought 6 coloured Coca glasses. They were in use when I had the family round for lunch. After everyone had gone, I was clearing away and noticed one missing. I searched for days, but the elusive glass was never seen again. About three months later, I went to my cabinet and noticed it was back—but it wasn't alone. I started with 6, then I had 5, now I have 7 – so someone has a real problem.

Items broken – my Grandmother's 3-row grey pearl necklace; as most of the beads disappeared, there's not enough to string one row. The glass case containing a mother-of-pearl ship I brought Nan in 1961. Someone cut the cord to my brass doorbell—I had it fixed, and then it was cut again. And not forgetting the killer casserole with the glass shard. I know it sounds bizarre, but I am no fool.

I would never say anything to deliberately hurt or upset anyone, the same as I would not repeat anything if I thought it would cause trouble. But I am guilty of ranting about something that may be troubling me—but who else can I confide in if not my family? I have defended my children in the past and lost friends in doing so, but my loyalty has not been reciprocated. It wasn't so long ago that Allison told me of her recent coffee morning with Sybil, who wanted to know why I sold my house. Allison told her it was because I did not *'like'* my neighbour. Then, they discussed my odd behaviour.

I spent many hours with Allison when she first had the children. I enjoyed pottering in their easy-to-clean modern house. I'd return home and mull over our conversation of the day and recall something I had said that could have upset or offended her—so I'd call her. *I bet that's Mum,* she'd say to Stefan on her way to the phone. She knew an explanation was guaranteed.

I do have the occasional senior moment—but am I not allowed that privilege at my age? Thank goodness they did away with hanging. I would like to be loved for who I am and hope someday I will be forgiven for my mistakes—after all, none of us are perfect. Tiffany is the only person I can bitch to now when things go wrong because what I say goes no further. I have an excellent memory, but I am unable to retain everything I'm told—but that proves my age and not stupidity.

Everyone was upset when Allison and Stefan parted. A few years later, she met her future husband. Jason was a successful businessman who provided Allison and the children with a stable home and everything they desired, so she did not need anything from Stefan—however, when he fell behind with maintenance, she refused him access. I am unsure if that included his parents, but what my daughter didn't realise—she was hurting the kids, who were innocent victims caught up in their dispute. My concern was, if anything should happen to any one of the Grandparents before they became reunited, Shelby and Taylor would never forgive their Mother for the distance created, especially as their Nan was not in the best of health. So when the kids stayed with me, I allowed them to use my phone. I'd make myself scarce but could hear them laughing in the dining room. Then they'd come running in full of excitement where Grandad had made them laugh. I was not trying to cause trouble, neither was I turning them against their Mother, but having witnessed their sadness, I knew their little hearts were breaking. It brought back memories of how distraught my children were the night Collin told them I was never coming home. I get upset when I think of it now.

I remember when Allison and Jason flew to Spain for a week and left the children in my care. Knowing the kids were pining for their Grandparents, I arranged to *'accidentally'* bump into them. We were walking past a popular restaurant in town and there they were, sitting in the window, drinking coffee. The children screeched with delight and ran to greet, kiss, and hug their Grandparents. I left them to catch up while I crossed the road to make a purchase. The children were delighted to have spent valuable time with the Grandparents they adored. They chatted excitedly all the way home and went to bed happy and very contented. The elderly folk phoned later that evening and thanked me for the short time they spent together.

When Allison found out, there was a showdown—but we always clashed horns. My daughter's principles were different to mine. When two people separate, the children should never be made to suffer. I don't believe in depriving any child from having contact with their Father unless there is cause. I could understand if Stefan was anything like Collin, but Stefan and his parents were decent people. If there was anything amiss, the children would have spoken to their Mother—anyway, Allison trusted me with her children, and I would never do anything to put them in danger. My job was to keep them safe—*my house, my rules.* I wonder how she would have felt had I prevented her from seeing her Father—the Father that was planning to murder her mother. Now, there was genuine cause in preventing visitation rights, but I allowed my girls to spend time with him. If, for any reason, they came home distressed, I would have put a stop to the visits.

Allison was about 10 when I was talking to Elaine about some of the things Collin got up to. She went sulking out, so I followed and asked what was wrong. *That's my Dad you're talking about,* she said tearfully. For her to have such a high regard for him proves I did a good job covering the abuse I went through to protect them. Perhaps it's a blessing she doesn't remember.

Chapter Fifty-One

Moving On

It was 2012 when Tiffany showed me a bungalow that was up for rent from the estate agent where she worked. I have always wanted to live in a bungalow and couldn't wait to put my mark on the place and make it my forever home. Within a few weeks, I discovered I was living next door to a woman who was known as the troublemaker of Hillside... how did I get that lucky? She made my life hell.

Brendon called and asked if I could take a rescue dog. Missing the company of Maxi and Ruffles, I was more than interested—until he said it was a boy... but I only do females. Then he told me it was a long-haired Chihuahua... I don't do designer dogs, either. Apparently, Jasper had been bought for breeding, but he was the size of a Jack Russell, so he was up for grabs. When Jasper and I were introduced, he blanked me... not interested, as he turned and cocked his leg... thankfully we were in the garden. Our first night together, he howled and barked, so I allowed him in my bedroom where he made himself comfortable at the foot of my bed. It took time for Jasper and me to get acquainted, but once we gelled, he would not let me out of his sight. Some mornings, I would wake to find his head on the pillow next to mine. How he managed to get under the covers without disturbing me is a mystery, but I loved to wake and see his little head on the pillow, watching me sleep. I didn't need a man for protection—not when I had Jasper.

I stood by the runway as my twins flew to Spain for a week. I jumped up and down, waving frantically, hoping they would see me as they flew overhead. The roar of the engines made the ground vibrate; I had a sharp intake of breath—then they were gone. At the time, feeling sorry for Alex at home caring for Kym and the animals, I invited him for dinner. He would not have had time to cook and probably snacked on whatever was available or indulged in a takeaway. After our meal, we sat in the garden with our coffee and talked like never before until he realised it was late and the animals needed feeding, too. *This was how families should be.* I mused as I cleared away our empty plates. I was pleased we had moved forward and all the bad stuff was behind us. Unfortunately, when my girls returned, things were not the same. The atmosphere had shifted and there was a coolness in the air as that *'all too familiar'* distance returned. I would like to think the bond we once shared will return one day, but I won't hold my breath as we drift further apart.

Allison phoned one morning to say Jason had booked a 5-day holiday for herself, the children, and me to an exclusive resort at Potters. As holidays go, it went far too quickly. To show my appreciation, I bought Jason a large cut-glass tankard and I bought Allison sparkly place mats. I was delighted when, the following year, he paid for us to return to the same resort. I bought Jason another cut-glass tankard after Allison confessed she'd broken the first one.

In August 2014, Allison and Jason tied the knot. On the eve of the wedding, Allison booked the children and me into a country hotel. After breakfast, we travelled to the venue where her hairdresser was waiting. At 3 p.m., with guests seated, Allison made an appearance. She looked beautiful. I watched with pride as my daughter walked in, holding Taylor's arm and led her to where Jason was waiting. That night, the children and I stayed at their hotel and travelled home the following day. It was a wonderful wedding and a weekend to remember.

In September 2015, Allison told me to pack my bags—she was taking me to their villa for five days. I rushed to update my passport, bought euros, and gave her money so Jason could book me on the same flight. I've wanted to visit Spain ever since Connie introduced me to their fiery music. I took sufficient euros for eating out and snacks for the villa, but Allison didn't tell me I had to pay a portion of the private hire car for five days plus petrol. When we landed in Alicante, the cab driver was waiting and held up a card with her name. When we arrived at the villa, the 4x4 was on the drive with the driver waiting to hand over the keys. Perhaps I'm wrong to assume, but Jason is generous to a fault—he would have paid for the private hire car when he booked our flights. I can't remember how much the cab was.

Allison ruined my holiday with her attitude and nasty comments. I was talking to her one morning when she spun around, flicked her hair over her shoulders, and quickly strode out. The insult put a damper on the entire day. One evening, we were getting ready to leave the restaurant and I was counting the euros when she snatched them out of my hands and gave them to Shelby to count. Allison and Shelby got up to leave and walked ahead of me. I saw the proprietor, so I stopped to thank her for a lovely meal. When I caught up with Allison, she accused me of asking for the tip back— I could have burst into tears. Another time, she asked if my teeth were new because they made me look goofy. Then she tucked her bottom lip in to indicate protruding teeth. There is never anyone around to witness these spiteful comments and incidents, but they ruined my holiday.

On our flight home, she suggested I join a local women's club. *You never know—you might make some more enemies,* she said, rocking with laughter. She was referring to my troublesome neighbour. Tearfully, I turned away. I have decided to say nothing more about my holiday and made a promise never to set foot in Spain again. We never spoke for months.

I had been in the bungalow five years when the landlord said he was selling the property. I was mortified to think that, at the age of 78, I had to start packing up and looking for somewhere to live. I searched for ages but could not find a bungalow suitable. Then I saw this three-bedroom house.

I had been here two days when Jason and Allison arrived unexpectedly. I had not spoken to my daughter for over a year, so the atmosphere was a little strained. Jason was shocked to see the unorganized mess I was in—wading about in bubble wrap and newspaper. He told Allison to sort out blinds for the windows and promised to call in on his way home on Tuesday to put my shrubs in the front garden, which were in tubs and starting to wilt. Then he suggested sheeting so I could have gravel. I hastily agreed. Then he told Allison she had to *look after me*—crikey, no one's ever said that before, so it came as a shock.

True to his word, he arrived on Tuesday. Within half an hour, all four shrubs and one tree were safely in the ground. The following week, he arrived with sheeting and sleepers and told Allison to order gravel of my choice. I chose gravel/shingle like I had at the bungalow and not the white stuff my neighbour had. She arrived the next day with the *white stuff...* we won't mention blinds.

It does not seem long ago we were celebrating Auntie Joan's 95th birthday. Less than 18 months later, we were attending her funeral after she slipped away peacefully in her sleep. She was a beautiful lady and missed by everyone.

October 2018 – I could hardly believe my ears when Allison said Jason wanted to *buy me a bungalow.* I was shocked and bursting with joy. A few days later she phoned to say they'd found a two-bedroom bungalow for me to view that afternoon. My mistake was not saying yes right away, but I wanted to make sure I could fit everything from three bedrooms into two. That evening, I walked from room to room measuring floor space, then I looked at the pictures and decided I could make it work—but by the following day, it had gone.

The next property was not as interesting, and there were issues—one was the garage door, which I would need for storage. After I turned it down, she said Jason was going to put electric doors in the garage and knock the wall between the toilet and bathroom and add a shower. I was *gutted.*

The next bungalow was in need of major surgery—once I turned it down, she said Jason was going to rip the kitchen out, put in an eye-level oven, and sort out the garage door. I can't remember the next property, but once I turned it down, she told me all that Jason was going to do, so I asked if I could view the next bungalow *with them*—but she said *this is the way Jason wants to do things.*

After months of being disappointed I lost heart, especially being told all that Jason was going to do *after* I turned it down.

Jason was an active, keep-fit person who needed a project. He was either knocking something down or building something beautiful. He could look at a run-down property and knew instinctively if he could turn it into something special—he had a keen eye. With me in mind, he wanted to buy something reasonable that needed some TLC so he could knock it about. Unfortunately, I was never around when they viewed these *'run-down'* bungalows.

Reading between the lines, he may have got fed up with me turning properties away because according to Allison, he left it to her to find something. Regrettably, everything we viewed was the same story... *Jason was going to do this, Jason was going to do that... Jason said, Jason said.*

My theory was—each time they viewed something, Jason told her of his intentions. Is it possible she kept the information to herself? Not until I turned it down did she reveal what Jason was going to do. *Crikey*, the guy must think I am an ungrateful time-waster playing games when, in fact, it was Allison *playing games.* No one in the family knows how to contact Jason other than through Allison.

Chapter Fifty-Two

My Son Craig - 2019

The date was 7th May and the time was 10:30 p.m. I was on my way to bed when I got a call from the hospital to say my son was in ICU. At first, I thought Robert had had an accident—then they said it was Craig who had had surgery. The nurse would not say any more and advised me to go to the hospital. I replaced the receiver then dialed Morgan, who had only just arrived home after a late shift. She picked me up, and we drove to Chelmsford.

On our arrival, we were taken to a little room in ICU no bigger than a closet. The nurse designated to care for Craig came and spoke—all I wanted was to see my son. I don't recall anything she said other than not to be alarmed because *his head was swollen and bandaged.* She led us into a dimly lit ward with about five or six other patients, all wired to machines. I almost walked past the bed in search of my son—then she touched my arm and directed me to where Craig was propped up. I walked to the side of his bed and stared in disbelief—*this was not my beautiful son* wired to the bleeping machine... surely not. Then I saw the tattoo on his hand.

I wanted to touch him but didn't want to disturb him. Being heavily sedated, he would not have known of my presence. It was about six months ago when he reached out to me and the gap between us began to close. I recall one night in particular when he pulled me into him and hugged me really tight and didn't want to let me go... was it possible he knew of his condition and toyed with the idea of how to break the news, or did he have something else on his mind?

I clung to the memory of that embrace, wondering why he had kept his operation from me—unless he'd been called in at the last minute. Now he was on life support, and I was at my wits' end. I felt helpless as I held his hand in the half-light, staring at his swollen head with his eyes taped shut. Then the fear of dread surged through me... *I was going to lose him.*

Craig had me down as next of kin, and Robert was the second if I was unavailable. *Thank God I was late to bed that night—thank God I had not switched off my phone,* as I did most nights.

I arrived home at 4 in the morning and sat on my bed until daylight. I couldn't cry—I was too numb. The twins visited him the following day, then Allison phoned to say they might have to insert a tracheostomy to help him breathe because his throat was swollen. I was tearing my hair out. When Robert visited, he broke down seeing his unconscious brother in such an unbelievable state.

I am unsure of the exact details, but Craig was admitted with the understanding he would stay for one night. But complications set in, and he wound up back in theatre with a bleed. He came out of surgery with about 50 staples down his face and neck where they opened him up like a book, resulting in damaged nerves. *Bless him*—he looked as though he'd had a stroke. My next visit was just as heart-wrenching, seeing my beautiful son unconscious.

It was a few days before he was able to breathe on his own. When they took him off life support and transferred him to a side ward, I was still in shock, so am unsure of the correct details—but his first word was *'cancer'.* I don't know if he was asking if he had cancer or telling us he had cancer because I wasn't there. Thankfully, my son was a *fighter.* The staff told him he couldn't leave hospital until he could walk unaided, so on the nights he couldn't sleep, he walked the corridors. He couldn't wait to get home to his beloved cat. He never complained. All he ever said was, *"It is what it is."*

Craig and his 50 staples were discharged five days after surgery, which I thought was far too soon. I was with the twins when they picked him up. I sat in the back and couldn't take my eyes off him beside Allison, who was driving. *It broke my heart* to see how the surgery had disfigured him. The hospital offered him reconstructive surgery because of the significant damage to his face—but first, he would need a course of radiotherapy.

We got him settled at home and made sure he had fresh milk, cat food, other provisions, and plenty of credit. Then he *shocked the hell out of me* when he said he was going to cycle to his friend Shaun's, who had been caring for Willow. I panicked and pleaded with him to change his mind. I worried in case he felt dizzy, collapsed, or had a bleed. Also, his appearance could have drawn the attention from undesirables who would stare and make fun. He wouldn't have been able to cope with such cruelty, and he was in no fit state to defend himself should anyone challenge him... *thank goodness he had a change of heart.*

I phoned the following morning to see what sort of night he had, then made an appointment for him to see his doctor. I was so grateful when my girls visited him each day—they were *amazing.*

The hospital told Craig they would start radiotherapy once his staples had been removed. I counted the days, eager for them to kill whatever cancer may have been overlooked. As any mother, I wanted to be with him throughout, but my twins said they would keep me informed, so I stayed by the phone, *willing it to ring.* I asked many questions and often repeated myself—which I know annoyed them—but I was still trying to come to terms with *'cancer'* so most of what they said went over my head.

Allison was taking Craig and myself to the supermarket every week. She'd drop me off, then take him home and settle him in. A few weeks later, she was taking Craig shopping, dropping him home, then taking me to the same store. So I asked if we could go together. She replied, *"This is the way Craig wants to do things."* *(Where have I heard that before?)*

I wanted to be involved with his treatments too, but the twins said there wasn't enough room in the hospital—but they would keep me informed. Never having been to the oncology department, I can't argue with that, but I couldn't help feeling *pushed aside.* I wanted to be close to my son. I was *scared of losing him* and hurting beyond belief.

It was late Sunday morning when I looked up and saw Craig with Alex and Morgan—I can't remember if there was anyone else—but they were on the other side of the road heading to the airport. I later discovered they went to the airport hotel for Sunday lunch. *I would love to have gone too,* but I had no idea a meal had been arranged.

Allison repeatedly told me, *"Don't fuss—Craig hates it when you fuss. And don't keep asking questions; it's difficult for him to talk."* I must admit it was difficult understanding him, with one side of his face paralyzed, and he always got cross if I asked him to repeat himself—so we hardly spoke. But it was hard being told *not to fuss* when all I wanted was to help and hug him, sit close and hold onto him. He was *still my boy*—but where was this word *"fuss"* coming from? I am his mother, so understandably, I was anxious. As parents themselves, they must realise what I was going through.

Allison told me Craig didn't want anyone interfering—he was fine on his own. A few days later, she told me she'd changed his bed, vacuumed, cleaned the fridge, and done his washing. I cannot describe how hurt I felt to think he did not want *me* around.

When Craig finished his radiotherapy, he rang the *(all-clear)* bell. Pictures were taken—presumably by one or both girls or maybe the hospital—but it was *ages* before I was told, so Craig texted me the picture on my pay-as-you-go phone.

December 17th, 2019, was Alex's 60th birthday—that was one birthday no one will forget. He was admitted to hospital for exploratory surgery. They opened him up, then stitched him up again before sending him home and said there was *nothing* they could do. The cancer was accelerating at an alarming rate. Morgan began making plans to renew their wedding vows, but Alex was in and out of hospital and going downhill rapidly. We hoped he would make it for the celebrations.

I went to a jeweller in town and bought an exclusive figurine from the collection *"More Than Words."* The figurine was of two lovers standing face-on—the man holding the hand of his love, who was wearing a red evening gown. I bought a card for Alex to give to Morgan with the words *"I love you because…"* The verse went on to give the many reasons why he loved her, ending with: *"…but I love you because you're my wife."* I took the card to the hospital, but he was too ill to sign it.

Then I hunted high and low for a wedding renewal card but could find nothing, so I carefully (with the help of an assistant) chose a wedding card I could edit and typed and printed my words in *italics*:

To Morgan and Alex,

With love to a special daughter and husband as you celebrate the happy times you have shared over the years – a wedding is an event but a marriage as successful as yours is an achievement. As you renew your wedding vows, may the memories of your special day stay with you forever more. Congratulations to you both.

God Bless.

Love as always, Mum.

I printed and cut the verse with serrated scissors and pasted it over the original. Then, I shrunk a picture of them and the children on their wedding day and pasted it under the verse. I also bought other mementoes in Alex's memory—*because that's what mothers do.*

I was pleased with the card, so I took it back to the shop to show the assistant who helped me with my search.

On March 8th, 2020, Morgan and Alex renewed their wedding vows. Two weeks later, Morgan climbed onto the bed and cradled her husband as he passed away. Her family gathered around, which did little to ease her pain, but having the support of everyone meant a great deal—*having lost the husband she adored.* I kissed his cheek and wished him a safe journey.

Although Craig had been given the *all-clear,* the hospital wanted to see him in a few months to start chemotherapy. I was in the kitchen when he arrived with Allison. He gave me a crooked smile and said the cancer had spread to his bones and liver and there was *nothing more they could do.* The oncologist said that chemotherapy would shorten what time he had left because his body was not strong enough to cope.

I cannot imagine the horror he must have felt, knowing his days were numbered and his pain would increase. His only comfort was that he would be given strong medication. Meanwhile, the distance between us was *killing me.* I wanted to give him the *biggest hug,* but being told not to fuss, I stayed seated... there was *nothing I could do* to keep my son safe. I wondered what he must be feeling, having been handed a death sentence. The hospital didn't tell him how long he had—furthermore, he didn't want to know. I gazed at my son and silently grieved. *We had precious little time left.*

Allison and Morgan spent most of their time with Craig and had done so throughout, for which I am truly grateful. I don't know how he would have coped otherwise. But I could not come to terms with why *I* was pushed aside. I don't care what anyone says—I was *not* as involved as a mother should have been. I am not only speaking of his medical appointments but of the times Allison told me they went for drives along the seafront—*stopping for ice cream or a bag of chips,* sometimes sitting on a bench and gazing out at sea... a walk along the pier, or a drive to the garden centre for a bite to eat— not to mention the meal across the road. I was *never included* at these times, which was a *cruel and heartless* thing to do.

If it was Craig's wish—why didn't *he* say something? Because my son did not mince words and always spoke his mind. I defy any parent *not* to get upset or angry if they had experienced similar. Especially remembering when—*three days before he went into hospital*—he texted and asked if I was okay and if I needed any shopping. So, I was *confused* as to why he didn't want me around. *Someone* must have said something.

It's the little comments and innuendos that influence the mind. They may *seem* harmless, but over time can be damaging to the recipient. *I know that only too well.*

I was sitting in Craig's armchair, sick with grief, wondering how much time we had left. I couldn't take my eyes off him, sitting on the settee—aware I was watching, he turned. I whispered, *"I would give anything in the world to change places with you, my love."* He gave me a crooked smile and said, *"Yes, I know... thanks."* I went and sat with him so we could be close.

Before Craig received his death sentence, Allison told me how they enjoyed browsing through his photo albums. *Was she using the photos to remind him of the bad times they experienced as youngsters?* Nudging him into believing I was a terrible mother—which would explain his coolness towards me—or was it something else?

Monday, 2nd November, Allison phoned to say I should hurry around, as Craig did not look good. Tiffany and Robert arrived soon after, and we took it in turns to sit by his bed. My son slept on and off until the Macmillan nurse arrived and woke him... I left the room. Then I heard her speak:

"You know you're dying, don't you, Craig?"

I could not believe what she had just said—*shit,* you don't *tell* someone they're dying. Morgan thought she was brilliant—I *beg to differ.*

I was standing outside his bedroom when the nurse told Morgan the cancer was in his spine and legs, which would explain his considerable pain. *Bless him—he never complained.* The nurse said she would do her best to get him into the new hospice not far from where I lived.

A few hours later, she phoned to say Craig would be picked up the following morning. I was relieved to think he would have medical staff on hand to administer pain relief at any time—and that he was closer to my home.

Chapter Fifty-Three

A Beautiful Soul

Returns Home

I had watched the construction of the hospice for over a year but never dreamed in a million years my Son would spend his last days there. The morning he was admitted, my twins moved in so they could be near him – they never left his side, which pleased me no end. But, due to Covid, only two visitors were allowed at a time. The nurse who settled him in said we could visit any time, day or night. I asked *("me too")* "Yes," she said, "you above everyone – you're his Mother." I think those words *("me too")* made her realise I was being side-lined, but they were said innocently on my behalf...

I visited Craig every afternoon. It gave Allison the opportunity to go home, eat, shower, and spend time with Jason. My twins were brilliant – I was pleased he was not alone.

One afternoon I was leaning over Morgan in the recliner when the nurse walked in and told her to get off the chair so I could sit beside my Son because I was his Mother and had come to visit my boy. I was embarrassed but grateful. Another time, Morgan was in the bathroom with the door open – wanting to reassure my son there was nothing to fear, I began talking about the world of Spirit. Morgan told me to stop talking about Spirits because he didn't believe – *oh but he does*. He has always believed in Spirit. When Craig was a little boy, we had a lot of activity in our home. It is

325

perfectly natural for a child to be frightened of the unknown, which is when I introduced him to the world of spirit. I wanted to remove any negativity or fear he may have by explaining what little I knew. I was not surprised when, in his teens, he began reading up on the subject and collecting books of various clairvoyants and their amazing work. One such medium was Doris Stokes. A few years later, Craig introduced Tiffany to her books, who – like Craig – is an enthusiastic reader and has the complete set. So for Morgan to keep shutting me up was infuriating. Just because she was with him 24 hours a day did not give her the right to stop me from giving my Son the reassurance he needed at this moment in time. I recently spoke to Melody – Craig's lady friend from years ago – who told me how he introduced her to the Spirit world and gave her books to read on some of their amazing work.

When Craig was in his teens, we used to chat with Cousin Mathew for hours about the world beyond this one. It was a subject we never tired of discussing as we felt those from Spirit draw close. If – for any reason – Craig did not believe, it would have been because of all he had endured with two vicious stepfathers, so it was understandable for him to lose faith. I was a hair's breadth from losing my son, and I wanted to do everything possible to restore his beliefs and remove any fear and doubts he may have.

In Craig's final state of cancer, and with the help of drugs, he was in and out of consciousness. He would have been aware of his Spirit family gathered round as well as his mortal family, which can be confusing and a little frightening, so it was imperative I restore his faith. I wanted him to know that death is not just a hole in the ground but a transition to a better place where he could be with his loved ones.

I used to speak to Nan about such matters when she was elderly. She, too, was scared of the unknown, but my words of reassurance helped her when I explained that her loved ones were waiting to greet her in this beautiful place. Speaking openly can reduce any fear 'one' may have.

Over the years, I have had the pleasure of speaking to others that were not long for this world. Surprisingly enough, some have come through in my readings and thanked me for making their passing easier simply by talking to them. My Jewish friend Helena is in Spirit now and has come through to me three times. The last time was in Church when the clairvoyant said after my message that today would have been a special day for this lady. I turned and asked what day it was. Members of the congregation called out "29th June." I told them today would have been Helena's birthday. The Church was filled with ooohs and aaars and someone applauded.

It was upsetting to see my Son slipping away and even more upsetting being told not to disturb him as I smoothed the hair from his brow or covered his exposed back with his cotton sheet. Craig has always been modest and would have been embarrassed had he known he was showing flesh and I was respecting his dignity. Morgan's argument was they'd had very little sleep because he had been restless during the night, but the nurses were there to administer medication and he would have been out like a light.

When I kissed him goodbye, she told me not to touch him – *I'll tell him you said goodbye.* Each time I went near him, she watched... *Christ,* what did she think I was going to do – put a pillow over his head and finish him off? Another time I was about to kiss him when she told me not to wake him – *I'll tell him you came,* she said. I ignored her and gently kissed him goodbye.

When Craig first arrived at the hospice, he was more coherent and asked after his cat, Willow. The staff told the twins they could bring her to visit him – what a pity they did not honour his wish because Willow was all he ever asked for. He wanted to hear her purr, feel her nuzzle into him – it would have brought him a little pleasure and comfort. It broke my heart when I was told because he never asked for anything other than the cat he rescued and adored.

I noticed Craig's life was coming to an end when, each day, his appearance had slightly changed. Then, six days after being admitted, Allison phoned to say he had passed away. I was grateful to his Spirit family for taking him, knowing he was out of pain. I was upset I missed his passing and wondered if it was deliberate. By the time I arrived, Allison had left for home, so I sat with Morgan until Tiffany arrived. Things are a little blurred, but I recall two nurses asking us to leave so they could 'prepare him' – we were allowed back in once they had finished. Morgan and I were sitting either side of Craig when a nurse came and asked who wanted the T-shirt he had been wearing. I reached to take it when Morgan snatched it away and asked why I wanted an old T-shirt. She said, if you want anything, take his dressing gown, and threw it across the bed... if only she had turned, she'd have seen the look of horror on the face of the nurse who walked out in disgust. I cannot imagine what she told staff at the nurses' station. Just for the record, the T-shirt was not old – it was as white as the driven snow; any fool could see it was new. It was purchased for Craig to wear in his final days. I later discovered the T-shirt was sent away with more of his clothes for the purpose of having teddies made – they certainly kept that quiet. Allison had 4 teddies and I don't know how many Morgan had. What a pity they never included me in their plans – I would have liked one too, but at least I have his dressing gown to snuggle into.

I cannot describe how upset I was to hear that Craig woke one night and disturbed the twins in their recliners. He was sitting up, shaking his hands vigorously. When Morgan asked what was wrong, he repeatedly said, *I'm scared – I'm scared, Jesus bloody Christ...* if only she had not shut me up when I was trying to reassure my Son, he ~~may~~ might not have been so scared. She had no right – she did him wrong. I was heartbroken to hear – the day he came off life support he asked after me. He started to dial my number but became tearful, so he hung up. *My God,* why wasn't I told sooner... how bloody spiteful.

I had just finished speaking to Elaine when Coral phoned to say Brendon had been trying to contact me. Before I could respond, he texted and accused me of ignoring him and told me not to bother replying. Anxious to know what was wrong, I immediately called him, but he cut me off. I called again, and he cut me off a second time. With no other option, I had to wait until the funeral. He must have been bloody angry to reject my calls... but why? *Christ,* it was only eight months ago he buried his Father – he saw the impact it had on his Mother, so why was he miffed with me? Someone must have said something because I don't seem to be short of enemies.

Craig's landlord wanted the keys to the flat by the end of the month, so there was plenty to do in very little time. Three days after my son passed, I went to the flat with the purpose of collecting the memory box I made for his 50th birthday containing memorabilia from when he was born. There were welcome baby cards and cards from his 1st birthday and a picture he painted me in his infant years. There was his page boy outfit and letters from his Father, and the corduroy trousers he made for his teddy when he was about 7. Unfortunately, Robert and I had harsh words on the journey, so I was miffed by the time we arrived. The twins were already there, and Morgan was filling in the form to register his death and asked where Craig was born. I curtly replied, *Oh, so you want me involved now* – that was the cue she'd been waiting for – *see…I knew she'd do this…going around telling everyone she's not been involved.* I am unsure who she was referring to by *'everyone'* because no-one speaks to me apart from Connie. I have two friends – Bridget, my spiritual friend who lives over 200 miles away, and Elaine. Anyway, that's what friends are for. When Alex was ill, didn't she have the support of her family, her friends, her neighbours and colleagues before, during and after he passed? – Yes, of course, she did. So why should I be any different?

I think it was Allison who informed me they were his next of kin. She said Craig told them they could take whatever they want<u>ed</u>. To confirm this, they showed me a piece of paper with his signature, but he was ill and his writing was not good. The paper was witnessed by a friend of Morgan's – I don't think it would have stood up in court.

It was during my brief visit I told them I wanted to be involved with clearing the flat. Allison said, *perhaps we should pay another month's rent so Mum can use the flat as her holiday home – then she can come and go as she pleases* – they thought that was hilarious, but it startled me. Then Robert pointed to the rug and said it wasn't any good, *but Mum would probably find a use for it.* Then he looked at the TV and said, *perhaps Mum would like the TV too, but she doesn't have any room unless she puts it in the hall* – that also amused them. Then Morgan pointed to two candles on the fireplace and said I could take them because I brought them. There were more wisecracks, but I left the room. Thankfully, I was too upset to remember anything else. I wonder how Morgan would have felt had I taken the mickey out of her when she lost Alex – it's a pity she didn't show the same empathy towards me. Their behaviour was intolerable – they should be ashamed of themselves. I did find a home for the rug – it looks lovely in my bedroom. It's good quality, in excellent condition – it's thick heavy, and it belonged to Craig.

My next visit to the flat was just as unpleasant. Robert, Tiffany, Morgan and I were going to clean and empty the flat. I saw Craig's photo albums, so I put them in my shopping bag. Morgan took them out and said we could look through them when we were all together, reminding me that she and Allison were his next of kin. I did not want to be in the same room, so I started on the bathroom. I saw Craig's shaving brush in the cabinet, so discreetly put it in my bag... I can't imagine why I felt the need to be discreet but knew I was walking on egg shells. Having cleaned and cleared the bathroom, I poked my head round the kitchen and said the bathroom was finished.

I was shocked when Morgan checked the bathroom and even more surprised when she asked for the shaving brush because Allison brought it and wants it back. I thought it strange she noticed the shaving brush missing amongst his other personal belongings. Whilst clearing the sitting room, I saw two glass egg cups in the shape of chickens, so I put them in my bag. Morgan noticed them gone from the shelf and said Allison wants them... *crikey*, she must have eyes at the back of her bloody head to know they had gone from the shelf the same as the shaving brush in the bathroom, but if they had first pickings, they would have taken these items before I arrived. As each nasty encounter unfolded, I could almost hear Craig (*oh my God – oh my God*) – he would have been upset, hurt and disgusted. Never in my life have I heard of anyone being treated the way my girls were treating me, but be warned, no deliberate action goes un-noticed – they all have consequences.

All that was left now was the furniture... time to speak up. I told them I brought the wardrobe, the bed and chest of drawers, and the heavy curtains in the bedroom. I brought the oak coffee table and the granite coasters imbedded with fossils. I brought the bookcase and the combination microwave. I also brought the bistro set which was in use in the kitchen. They stood silently as I reeled everything off, so I continued. I brought the 18-inch bird of prey and the sparrow hawk. I gave Nan's canister set to Craig so I'm taking that. I brought the cordless vacuum, so I'm taking that too. I brought his pillows and quilt a few months ago and the two hardback illustrated books on astronomy for his birthday, but I let Morgan take the books for her grandchildren – I did not want to deprive my great grandsons of something they were interested in.

At the end of the day, I inherited Craig's expensive saucepan set with matching steamer, a mini slow cooker, a good quality chopping board and a Paddington Bear colander (*Craig loved Paddington*). I also took his standard lamp and rug.

When Craig moved into the flat some years ago, he had fallen on hard times. Typical of my Son, he never said anything, but when I found out, I took him to buy the things he needed – which is what any caring Mother would do.

We had been to the funeral directors, but grief prevented me from absorbing what had been said, so I called Nathan and asked if he could go through the arrangements again. I chose to record our conversation so I did not have to rely on the family who were tired of me asking them to repeat everything. As soon as he answered, I pressed the record button. The following day, Allison phoned – she was nasty... playing with words... tying me in knots just like Collin used to. The player was still on the unit, so I pressed record. She told me Craig wished he didn't have me as a Mother – he wanted Jeannette as his Mother. Then she mentioned my visit to the flat and said her cutting remarks were funny – I disagreed. She accused me of telling everyone I had not been involved over the last 18 months and blamed me for everything Craig had endured. But it was her Father, Collin, who destroyed my Son and made him suicidal. Then she brought Owen into the conversation... yes, he played a part in Craig's mental state, but it was her Father that moulded my Son from the day he lied his way into our home. Having lost my Son 4 days ago, I was in no fit state to deal with this crap, but I struggled to defend myself. I fumbled with words and repeated myself – which no mother should have to do or deal with at these times when normally the next of kin is surrounded by loved ones and given support.

Regarding Jeannette – she used to be a friend of mine, but she was an alcoholic. One day she was nice, the next she was patronizing, but because she was my friend, I thought she was joking so I'd laugh. After 40 years, I brought our friendship to an end. I could not take any more sarcasm, especially when she blamed Nan for my broken marriages – of course, it had nothing to do with Collin being a psychopathic murderer or the paedophile bully of a husband. As for Jeannette – I haven't seen or spoken to her for over 25 years.

The day of the funeral started with light drizzle and continued throughout the day – we were to meet outside Craig's flat at 11am for our journey to Oak Park Meadow. I was waiting for my Son to arrive when Charlotte – her husband and sister-in-law – came and hugged me and offered their commiserations. Promptly at 11, the hearse arrived with Craig in his wicker casket covered in wild flowers. It looked beautiful. His worn-out (*Doctor Who*) scarf he'd treasured as a teenager, was draped over the casket and hung over both ends.

The order of the service that I chose had eleven pictures of Craig from when he was five. The order of the service was cream with a pearl sheen and opened like a book, with pictures of poppies, wild flowers and butterflies – everything Craig loved. This was different to any I had seen.

We arrived at Oak Park, but it was bitterly cold and the rain was relentless. I paid to have the service filmed, which was just as well because I do not remember anything other than sitting alone. I had my children with me, but I was alone. When the service was nearing the end, my girls were called to give their reading *'Our Brother'*, then I was called to give mine. I was about to read, then my voice quivered. I shook my head and turned to walk away, then stopped. If I didn't do this for my Son, I would regret it always. I returned to the podium, took a deep breath and read my eulogy. When the service ended, they played a piece of music my Son chose (*Year of the Cat*). Coral walked past and hugged her Mother seated by my side. The twins wandered off, so did Robert. I went to where Morgan was talking to my cousin, but they did not acknowledge me, so I returned to my seat.

We left Oak Park and made our way to Southend Crematorium for the committal. It was about 3.30 when we arrived, and light was diminishing. We stood outside for what seemed ages, then the pall bearer spoke to Tiffany and myself. I don't know what he said – I simply nodded. I watched them take Craig from the hearse and carry him into the chapel. I started to follow when the pall bearer put out his arm to stop me. I was amazed when the twins followed arm in arm. I paid to have this service filmed also – having recently watched the video, I saw the pall-bearers enter the chapel and place the casket on the catafalque. I saw the twins and the pall-bearers pay their tribute with a bow then the twins took their seats. Then, the mourners were beckoned to follow. Although I don't remember, the video shows me walking behind Tiffany and Robert into the chapel.

I am disgusted no-one acknowledged my presence or walked with me.

With the service almost over, the girls gave their reading and took their seats. Then I was called to give mine. There was a short service, then that awful moment when the coffin disappears from view and the curtain closes. They played (*Year of the Cat*), then we were ushered discreetly outside. I left the chapel the same as I arrived – *alone*. I saw Brendon standing by himself. Anxious to sort out the problem, I walked over to him. When he saw me, he shook his head and held both arms in the air and waved them as though directing traffic, then he turned and walked away. Never in my life have I witnessed the next of kin being snubbed at the funeral of their loved one. I don't know how I got through the day. As if saying farewell to my Son wasn't bad enough, I was ignored by the family and insulted by Brendon – the little boy who confided in me about his hang-ups when he stayed at the weekend. And God forbid if anyone said anything against him. I defended him with a passion, and he didn't have the grace or decency to acknowledge me in my time of grief.

Brendon is a married man with four adorable children who will grow never knowing their great Grandmother who worshipped their daddy. I was the first to hold him when he came into the world. Ghosting is undeniably one of the most hurtful things anyone can do to someone – it conveys complete disregard for *'one's'* feelings. I doted on my family and do not deserve to be treated with segregation after everything I went through trying to protect them… unfortunately, I failed in keeping us together when my boys were driven out.

That night, I went home to an empty house. I couldn't wait to see Jasper, who I knew would be running in circles waiting to greet me. I was surprised he had not disgraced himself, but having been left for 7 hours, I had a bit of sucking up to do with cold chicken. That evening, I drank a whole bottle of wine and crawled upstairs on all fours – much to the amusement of Jasper lying at the top waiting with a wet tongue. I dropped my clothes on the floor and crawled into bed. Saying farewell to my Son was the saddest thing I have ever had to do. Jasper sensed my grief and snuggled close. It was a few weeks before Allison took me to collect Craig's ashes. The scene on the tube was that of a forest with tall trees and bluebells – Craig would have loved it. I still had Nan's ashes from 1988, so I asked the funeral director if he could put her remains in a tube with a different scene. I chose blue skies with clouds and poppies – she loved poppies, so did Craig, but he loved all wild flowers, poppies being one of his favourites. I was in no hurry to part with my Son, but the family were anxious they be scattered, so after two years I thought it was time to say goodbye. After 34 years, I thought it was time to say farewell to Nan too.

Because Craig felt safe with our Nan, I wanted them in a place where they could be together always. I decided the scattering should take place on Nan's birthday. March 24th is normally cold and wet, but we couldn't have wished for nicer weather. The skies were blue and the sun shone – it was like a summer's day and unusually warm. My girls, along with Taylor and Shelby, were already there when Robert and I arrived. Robert carried Craig to the site, and I carried Nan. I laid them side by side before placing a little soil, then whispered my farewell. Once my family laid a little soil, we left them in their peaceful surroundings.

Some brought lunch and had a picnic by the pond, which is another burial site. We had the place to ourselves – it was quiet and very peaceful. All you could hear were the birds celebrating the warmth of early spring.

Robert adopted Willow, who has settled in well. She spends a lot of time in his carport sniffing the boxes that contain some of his belongings – perhaps that is where she feels close to the master that gave her shelter when she had nowhere else to go. My son passed away in November 2020… September 2021 would have been his 60th birthday. A few weeks later, I discovered my girls went for a meal to celebrate his life. They did the same on the eve of his passing, too. I had no idea a meal had been arranged – you'd think I was a stranger instead of his mother – but not including me proves everything I have said about not being involved.

It was 18 months before Craig's photo albums were given to me. There must have been over 500 photos, but most of my Son were missing from their plastic folders, and those that were left were not very flattering because he was messing about and pulling faces.

February was my 81st birthday. Allison arrived with a card and said they had bought me a bungalow. My inside groaned—I could not do this again. The following week, they flew to Spain, leaving everything in the hands of their solicitor. When they returned, Allison and I were having coffee in town when she brought up the subject of the bungalow. As Jason was renovating the property, it would be completely stripped. I was alarmed when she told me I would be responsible for any light maintenance, which can be costly, on top of rent. Plus, I had to buy carpets, curtains and blinds, which can also be costly. Then there were the removals, so I told her I could not afford to move.

Fine, she said angrily, *I'll tell Jason not to bother—but he won't be happy after everything he's spent on searches.* Cowardly, I backed down and told her not to say anything.

A few months later, she phoned to say she needed to buy an emulsion and asked if I would like to go for the ride. We made our way to the paint section and she picked up a tub of white and placed it in the trolley. Then she pointed to the green and asked what I thought of the colour. Then she pointed to the other shades and asked my opinion on them. I told her they were much about the same—she did not respond.

It was June when she took me to see the almost-finished bungalow. It was beautiful. Then she told me how much rent I was expected to pay—it was the same as my three-bedroom house, so I told her I could not afford it. A year later, Robert asked why I chose the colour of paint if I had no intention of moving... *oh but I didn't.*

I contacted Chelmsford hospital with the purpose of obtaining Craig's medical records. It was over a year before they arrived. I am unable to understand everything that is written because doctors and surgeons have a language all of their own, but there was some interesting information that I was able to understand because it was typed, which reads:

Phoned the patient's Mother (next of kin) at 22.30 on 7/5/19 to inform her that Craig had had planned operation on his neck, then he suffered complications post-op which meant he had to return to theatre then be admitted to ICU.

I continued to read and was shocked. The twins told staff I could not visit because I did not feel well (they made my absence sound trivial). This would have been when Craig came off life support and asked to see me—they possibly told him I was not feeling well, too. That would have been beyond hurtful; in fact, it would have broken his heart after life-threatening surgery, because that's when you need your mum.

I was disturbed they told staff I married an abuser, which had nothing to do with Craig being in the hospital—it was just another nail in my coffin. Without those records I would be none the wiser as to what was being said about me. But as the gypsy once said, *"No man will ever break your heart but your children will."*

I don't see much of my twins and I miss them dearly, but how can I trust those that bear me malice? What I don't understand is— why would anyone want to hurt and destroy the love of their mother. She is the *'one'* person you can trust and rely on. She is there when things get tough. She is the person you run to for support, and she will always stand by you because her love is pure and unconditional. It doesn't make sense. I would have given anything to have my Mother around.

I do not need to avoid family gatherings because I never get invited, perhaps my absence brings a little pleasure to those that are responsible for the distance created. Perhaps it has something to do with my book—wondering what skeletons I am about to reveal— and the best way to dismantle the truth is to isolate it.

I don't mean to play the 'poor me' card but the only happiness I have known was having my children. I enjoy watching sad films, although others may weep, however I am unable to watch anything with normal family life as it makes me realise everything I and my children have missed.

I was meant to write about the bad times and the problems created. Those in Spirit that wronged me have also helped. When we pass over, we have to face up to the bad choices we made and do whatever it takes to correct them. Otherwise we would not be able to develop and move forward in the Spirit world.

This book was inspired by Spirit. If I was not meant to reveal everything, my Guides would not have encouraged or helped me with my words. They often draw close at night, making sleep impossible. I would like to thank them for their words and inspiration because this book would not have been possible without them.

I have had many readings over the years. They have helped me through some difficult times when things seemed impossible. My readings have healed my mind and uplifted me.

Ivy Furlong is a wonderful Medium who has travelled throughout the country for over 40 years, giving seminars, as well as those she does for the Church and privately from home. I have witnessed her on platform in trance as her Guides draw close and speak through Ivy—it's pretty amazing.

It was February 1999 when I had my first reading with Ivy. She mentioned a Son that was cut from a different cloth—a Son that is distant and not very close—but that will change, and there will be a tearful reunion. Having waited years, I was disappointed when that reunion never took place. Perhaps the reunion will be when I join my Son in Spirit.

The day after the funeral, I had a telephone reading with Bill Rich, who is another great Medium. I always record my readings so I can listen at a later date, which can be like hearing it for the first time. Like Ivy, Bill's Spirituality has taken him all over the country.

Bill gave me a lot of interesting family information. Then my Father drew close. He said he went to his grave *unfulfilled*. He apologized for not knowing me, but *Camilla*, he said, was very controlling—he was weak and easily persuaded. He is not happy with the decisions he made, and there were many things he wanted to tell me but was unable to. Now, in Spirit, he knows all there is to know about me. He had no idea how I suffered over the years and wished he could have been there for me, but he's proud to see how well I coped in making sure my family were cared for.

He sees me when I cry and listens when I talk of my scars—but I fail to display my wounds. Bill said my Dad was with me at Craig's funeral (*alas, I never knew*). He went on to say there is hatred deep within me, and the completion of my book will put an end to the past, and I will sleep easier.

Forty minutes later, I was delighted when my Son came through. Bill said he was different now—*meaning the deformity from surgery was no longer with him*. Craig said I was a good Mother, he is proud of me and loves me dearly. He recalls the lovely cuddles when he was young. Apparently, when you return to Spirit, you remember everything from the moment you are born—*so that was music to my ears*.

Then he apologized for not speaking. I am unsure if he meant not speaking over the years or towards the end when he was ill. Spirit said he was a man of few words (*he says what he means and means what he says*), which made sense because Johnny was the same.

Bill went on to say Craig heard my gentle words before he passed and *he wasn't scared—that must have been when I tried to reassure him*. He may have been ill, but he was aware of everything that was going on, which is why *one* should be careful what they say when visiting. That leaves me wondering what else he heard in the six days he spent in the hospice—apparently, your hearing is the last thing to go.

What Bill said next surprised me: although my Son had already passed, he *watched* as I held his hand and heard my sharp intake of breath. Craig said it was Nan who came for him, and there was *glitter* as she reached to take his hand... *how beautiful*.

I would like to thank Bill for my reading—it gave me hope and brought me peace when I was low and grieving.

As my reading came to an end, Bill said… *"Do you know what your Son has just said to me?"*

- *I'M HOME* -

Printed in Great Britain
by Amazon

62781119R00198